How To Grow
HEALTHY HOUSE PLANTS
by Rob Herwig

Editor-in-Chief: Carl Shipman; Senior Editor: Jonathan Latimer;
Art Director: Don burton; Book Design: Amber Snyder;
Typography: Cindy Coatsworth, Connie Brown, Kris Spitler.

Published by HPBooks®, P.O. Box 5367, Tucson, AZ 85703   602/888-2150
ISBN: Softcover, 0-89586-026-0
Library of Congress Catalog Card Number: 79-84701
© 1975, 1979 Zomer & Keuning Boeken B.V., Wageningen.
This text © 1979 Fisher Publishing, Inc.
Printed in U.S.A.

Cover photo: George deGennaro Studios

House Plant Handbook

Selecting Your House Plants

The first step in selecting a plant is to consider your location in terms of temperature, light and humidity. The information in this book will help, but it is always a good idea to talk with your nurseryman. He can advise you on local conditions and suggest plants that do particularly well in your area. The information in the next few pages can be used as a guide to the plant descriptions following page 10, which give details on plant requirements for light, temperature, water, humidity and soil.

BEFORE YOU BUY

Examine the plant carefully. It should have good color, a full shape and the leaves should look healthy. Leaf size should be roughly equal on all parts of the plant, and new growth should be visible. Check carefully for pests. Check to see if roots are growing through the drainage hole in the pot. This indicates it is potbound and you should select another plant. Beware of bargain plants. Incidentally, you will get longer enjoyment from a flowering plant if you purchase it with buds rather than blossoms.

Take care to protect your plant when you bring it home. Many plants need time to adjust to their new surroundings.

When you get the plant home, water it thoroughly. You can also spray or dip your plant in a weak tea solution to remove insects and prevent disease. Let the plant dry, out of the sun, and keep it isolated for a week or so. If it isn't healthy, you don't want it to infect your other plants. Then begin normal care.

HARDY CHOICES

There are a number of varieties that are easy to maintain and stand up well under most conditions. Hardy plants grown for their foliage include *Cissus, Ficus, Monstera* and *Sansevieria, Dracaena* and many species of *Philodendron*. Relatively hardy flowering house plants include *Azaleas*, some *Pelargoniums* and many *Saintpaulias*. You should also consider the many succulents and cacti available.

Caring for Your House Plants

◉ LIGHT

Plants use light to manufacture food and to grow. Aside from cacti, few house plants can withstand direct sunlight all the time. Generally, blooming plants and plants that bear fruit require more light than foliage plants. When considering the amount of light required by various plants, I distinguish between *full sun, light shade, shade* and *deep shade. Full sun* means that a plant prefers an unscreened south-facing window. *Light shade* may be created in the same window—for instance, by half-closing a venetian blind—but an east-facing window, which receives full sun only until about 10 am, may also come under the heading light shade. When I speak of *shade,* I might mean a north-

---

A Place For Your Plant

This chart lists a number of plants that do well under the conditions of temperature and light in most homes. Individual plant descriptions, which follow page 10, provide additional information about each plant. The temperatures given are for summer nights, but most plants prefer cooler conditions in winter. Most plants adjust to slightly warmer or cooler or lighter or darker conditions if given proper care.

Night Temperature	Full Sun	Light Shade	Shade or Deep Shade
Cool 37° to 50°F (3° to 10°C)	Acacia Lilium Narcissus Pittosporum Sempervivum Solanum	Azalea Camillia Campanula Crocus Primula Skimmia	Aucuba Fatshedera Fatsia Hedera Phyllitis Rhoicissus
Moderate 50° to 60°F (10° to 16°C)	Agapanthus Aloe Citrus Echeveria Lantana Laurus Rosa Sedum Yucca	Begonia Chrysanthemum Clivia Fuchsia Hydrangea Impatiens Pilea Saxifraga Tulipa	Asparagus Aspidistra Cissus Howeia Pellaea Pteris Schefflera Selaginella Tetrastigma
Warm 60° to 68°F (16° to 20°C)	Ananas Bougainvillea Canna Cereus Coleus Haemanthus Nerium Opuntia	Begonia Crassula Dieffenbachia Dracaena Gardenia Pilea Saintpaulia Stephanotis	Adiantum Bertolonia Chlorophytum Ficus Monstera Sansevieria Siderasis Syngonium

facing window not darkened by trees, but the term applies equally to a position about 6 feet (2m) from a south-facing window. *Deep shade* refers to positions that receive very little daylight. Only the very strongest plants can survive with so little light.

You can easily determine the strength of light in a room or corner. On a cloudless day in May or July use a photographic light meter or, if necessary, a camera with a built-in light meter. Adjust to ASA 50 or 18 DIN and read at 1/125 of a second. Hold the light meter or camera about 8 inches (20cm) away from a white card. The aperture or *f*-number reading will give you the strength of light as follows:

Full sun: *f*-16 to *f*-22, approximately 170,000 to 360,000 lux.
Light shade: *f*-8 to *f*-11, 40,000 to 80,000 lux.
Shade: *f*-4 to *f*-5.6, 10,000 to 20,000 lux.
Deep shade: *f*-2.8, 5,000 lux.

5,000 lux at midday is about the minimum amount of light most plants need to survive. If you want to place a plant in a less favorable position, you will probably have to use artificial lights. Spotlights help to some extent, but two 40-watt "daylight" fluorescent tubes, placed 15 to 20 inches (40 to 60cm) above

Orient the white card so it catches the sunlight and measure the intensity with your camera or light meter.

the plants, are better.

The amount of time a plant spends in the light each day also affects its health. Plants require at least 6 hours of darkness in every 24 hours. With artificial light the on- and off-periods can easily be controlled with a time switch. If you dislike the bleak light provided by fluorescent tubes, you can set the clock to switch on during the night, from 2 or 3 a.m. until 8 a.m. for example.

In natural surroundings, the length of day is increased or shortened with the change of the seasons. Some plants, such as *Fuchsias,* will only bloom when the daylight exceeds a certain number of hours per day, as would happen in spring and summer. For most plants, the shorter days of fall and winter signal them to begin their period of dormancy. But some plants, notably Christmas cactus, *Chrysanthemums* and poinsettias, begin their period of bloom as the days shorten. They can be forced to bloom in any season by artificially decreasing their period of light to less than 12 hours a day. If you try this, be sure you create a regular schedule. Even a few minutes of light at the wrong time can delay blooming for weeks.

Most plants will lean toward the source of light whether it is a fluorescent lamp, a window or the sun. Turning your plants occasionally, especially rapidly growing seedlings, will keep them erect.

TEMPERATURE

In this book I always indicate the **minimum night temperature** in summer. Between 61° and 68°F (16° and 20°C) is considered *warm,* 50° to 61°F (10° to 16°C) *moderate,* and 37° to 50°F (3° to 10°C) *cool.* Night temperatures have been chosen because daytime temperature may vary enormously with the intensity of sunlight. Near a closed window a reading of 90°F (41°C) may easily occur, which would be fatal to many plants.

In winter many plants enjoy a resting period when the temperature, light, and consequently their moisture requirements are lower.

Many cacti and other succulents must be kept dry at 40° to 50°F (5° to 8°C). When a plant does require a resting period, the minimum winter temperature is indicated.

WATER

More plants are killed by overwatering than by any other problem, but you must use common sense. Plants in small pots easily become too dry, especially when the pots are made of clay. The danger of overwatering can be lessened if the pot has good drainage with holes in the bottom. But in ornamental containers without drainage holes, overwatering can be disastrous.

How Do You Tell—Water requirements vary considerably from plant to plant. By the time your plant droops from lack of water, it may be too late. Plunge the plant or water it thoroughly and it should come back in a short time. Few plants can stand to have this happen more than once. One of the best methods for telling when your plant needs water is to feel the soil. If it feels dry, stick your finger about 1/2 inch (1cm) below the surface. If it still feels dry, water. If it feels moist, wait a day or two and check again.

There are several types of moisture meters available. Some work by electricity and some by a chemical reaction to moisture.

When I suggest keeping a plant *dry,* it is sufficient to trickle a few drops of water just inside the rim of the pot from time to time. The soil should remain crumbly and feel fairly dry. *Moderately moist* means that the soil is allowed to dry out almost entirely before watering again. *Constantly moist* indicates that you should always be able to feel moisture. *Wet* means that water will appear when you press the soil with your finger.

Basically there are three methods of watering.

Top-Watering—The easiest way to water your plants is to pour water on top of the soil. Stop when you see water flowing out of the drain hole in the pot. Water in the morning to allow time for the water to soak in. Soil left wet overnight can

A well-designed watering can has a long spout and a capacity of five pints (3 liters) or more.

Plunging your plant occasionally will assure a thorough watering.

become a breeding ground for plant diseases. Water close to the base of the plant and try to avoid wetting the foliage or disturbing the soil. You can add liquid fertilizer with your normal watering. Also, any salts accumulated on the surface of the soil will be flushed away.

Bottom-Watering—Plants with tender roots, such as *Saintpaulia,* the African violet, can be watered by placing the pot in a saucer and filling the saucer with water. The water is drawn into the soil through the hole in the bottom of the pot. Stop when you see damp spots on the surface of the soil. Remove excess water from the saucer. Feeding with this method is a problem because the salts accumulate on top of the soil. This chalky white matter can injure your plants, but it is easily flushed away by top-watering.

Plunging—A third method of watering is to *plunge* or *submerge* the pot in water. This is often done with shrubby plants in well-draining pots which easily shed excess water, or as emergency care for plants that have dried out. Plunging removes air from the soil as can be seen from the little bubbles that will appear in the water. Leave the pot submerged until the bubbles stop. Then allow it to drain so that the soil absorbs fresh air. A small amount of fertilizer may be added to the bath, which should be kept fairly warm, 68° to 86°F (20° to 30°C).

Hard Water—In the case of sensitive plants, such as *Azalea,* soft water should be used. Tapwater is unsuitable if the hardness exceeds 150ppm (parts per million), and it should not be used for acid-loving plants. Check with your local water department. Rainwater is best, provided it has been brought to the correct temperature. The only other solution is to soften the tapwater. Ordinary water softeners which use coarse salt are unsuitable because they merely exchange the *hard* calcium and magnesium for the sodium ions in the salt. The *carbonate hardness,* damaging to sensitive plants, is not reduced. In fact, it is slightly increased. Tapwater should be softened by total or partial *demineralization.* Demineralizing filters which attach directly to your tap are available. The filter is filled with minute plastic grains that trap everything except the water. After a time the plastic discolors and must be replaced. Distilled water can be bought from supermarkets and drug stores, but it is cheaper over the long run to buy your own filter. Room-temperature water is always better than cold water.

HUMIDITY

Atmospheric humidity affects the extent to which a plant *transpires* or loses water to the atmosphere. This is separate from the moisture needed at a plant's roots and is indicated separately in the plant descriptions.

Transpiration also depends on the pores on the plant's surface. Plants with shiny, leathery leaves, such as many *Ficus* varieties, transpire very slowly and therefore tolerate dry air. Most succulents are even more adaptable because they can close their pores entirely.

Heated houses are usually very dry because increasing the air temperature lowers its relative humidity. There are a number of ways you can help maintain proper humidity for your plant.

Grouping—Placing plants together in groups can help prevent drying out. As plants transpire, they increase the humidity around them. Plants grouped together create microclimates for each other. It is best to group plants with similar watering needs, both for convenience and for the health of the plants.

Misting—Frequent misting or spraying, preferably with mineral-free water to avoid the formation of a white deposit on the foliage, may increase the atmospheric humidity to some extent. Remember, you are trying to increase the humidity, not dampen the foliage. Plastic or metal misters are available.

Stone and Tray Method—One of the best ways to maintain high humidity for indoor plants is to place them on a tray filled with stones or

When using a mister, stand back. You are trying to increase the humidity, not dampen the foliage.

pebbles that are kept constantly wet. Use a plastic or rust-proof tray and fill it with a layer of stones 1 to 2 inches (3 to 5cm) thick. Fill the tray with water up to the level of the stones. Set your plants on top of the stones, but not touching the water. Evaporation will keep the humidity high.

Humidifiers—By far the best solution is to purchase an electric humidifier or evaporator. A humidifier disperses water in minute particles with an electric fan. An evaporator is the modern equivalent of a boiling kettle, but the water does not actually boil. It is thermostatically maintained at a temperature of 203°F (95°C). This apparatus is noiseless and consumes approximately 300 Watts and about 3/4 of a pint of water every hour. Mineral deposits from the water may be removed from time to time with a descaler.

Washing Foliage—One of the best things you can do for a plant with shiny or smooth foliage is to wash its leaves. This slightly raises the humidity, clears the pores of dust, and helps control pests. Use clear, lukewarm water and either spray the leaves or wash them gently with a soft sponge. If you have problems with pests, wash the leaves with a weak solution of one tablespoon of soap to one quart of water. Rinse the leaves with clear water after this bath and let the plant dry out of the sun. It is best to do this in the morning. Leaf polish, oils or waxes can harm your plants and are not recommended.

A word of caution: Plants with hairy leaves should not be washed. Instead, remove the dust from the leaves with a small artist's brush. Pests on these plants, and on cacti, can be removed with cotton swabs dipped in alcohol.

▼ SOIL

The soil mix preferred by each plant is included in the plant description later in this book.

The standard potting mix available in nurseries is suitable for most, but not all plants. Some plants like an acid soil, rich in humus. You can make such soil yourself by mixing standard potting mix with wet peat moss or sphagnum moss. Other plants may prefer alkaline, porous soil. In this case the standard potting mix should be mixed with sharp sand or perlite. The acidity or alkalinity is usually given a pH rating, meaning the percent of hydrogen in the soil. A pH of 7 is neutral. Below 7 is acid, above is alkaline. Test kits are available at most nurseries.

Special mixtures are available for cacti and for orchids or bromeliads. Cactus mix contains sharp sand or perlite which drains well and helps aeration. Orchid or bromeliad mix, usually called the *growing medium,* contains chopped fern roots or osmunda fiber and sphagnum moss. Both special mixes are easy to buy.

When you buy standard potting mix, make sure it is *sterile,* which means it is free of disease or weeds. You can sterilize garden soil by placing it in an oven at 200°F (95°C) for an hour. Baking soil creates a strong odor, but it does not last.

Soil-less mixes are available. They tend to wash out of the pot easily because they are lightweight. They have few natural nutrients and plants may require extra feeding.

A good standard potting mix you can make contains one part garden

Shown here, clockwise from top left, are peat fiber, coarse or sharp sand, standard potting mix and sphagnum moss.

top soil, one part humus or compost, and one part clean sharp sand or perlite. Add a small amount of charcoal to absorb salts and gases.

FEEDING

With the instructions for soil in each plant description, I have included directions for feeding or fertilizing your plants. Most plants absorb the necessary nutrients from the soil to keep them alive. Even if a plant is given fresh, nutritious soil every year, it may need feeding after a few months. The more rapidly a plant grows, the more nutrients it needs.

Fertilizers provide three basic nutrients for plants. These are usually listed on the label in numbers representing the proportion of each in the mix. A *5-10-5* mix means it contains 5 percent nitrogen, 10 percent phosphorus and 5 percent potassium. The other 80 percent is filler. A *5-10-5* mix is a good formula for house plants.

Nitrogen encourages leaf growth and makes the foliage green. Phosphorus is used by the plant in growing healthy roots and stems. Potassium, or potash, is used in producing blossoms and in warding off disease. Most mixes also contain other trace elements, such as calcium, copper, iron, sulfur or zinc. These are listed on the label.

Fertilizers come in many forms. Granules or sticks of slow-dissolving fertilizers can take two or three months to release their nutrients. Water-soluble types in powder or liquid form begin to work almost immediately.

As a rule, either a liquid or powdered *chemical* fertilizer is used, but *organic* fertilizers, such as dried cow manure, blood meal or bone meal are equally suitable. Their major drawbacks are their odor and the long time it takes for them to work. Some plants, such as *Azaleas* or *Gardenias,* require a special *acid mix* which is available at nurseries.

It is important never to exceed the quantities indicated by the manufacturer. It is better to give repeated doses of a weak solution than infrequent doses of a strong solution. Make sure the label specifically states the product is suitable for house plants.

During the dormant season when the plant develops few, if any leaves or flowers, feeding is usually unnecessary. One good rule of thumb is to feed whenever a new leaf appears. Top-water occasionally with plain water to wash away any salts built up in the soil.

In many cases repeated repotting gives better results than endless feeding. The potting soil eventually turns into a kind of trash heap for everything the plant is unable to digest. A good rule to follow is: The more you have to water and feed, the more often a plant should be repotted. If you are worried about overfeeding your plant, don't feed it.

POTTING AND REPOTTING

At one time all house plants were grown in unglazed red clay pots. They were thought to be best because of their porosity, but we now know that roots can absorb the necessary air through the surface of the soil, provided it is kept porous. A great deal of water is evaporated from clay pots, making the soil inside 2° to 4°F (1° to 2°C) cooler than in other types of pots. This is a big advantage for plants that like cool roots, such as ferns. In sunshine the moisture evaporates quickly and after a time the pot begins to look unsightly because of the salt deposits that collect on the surface. Placing clay pots inside other pots is one remedy.

When they were first introduced, plastic pots presented problems for many growers because no water evaporates through the pot wall. This cuts water requirements considerably. A medium-sized plant needs only about 1/3 of the water it would require in a clay pot. Also, plastic is light and plants can tip over easily.

Plastic plant cylinders and ceramic pots are non-porous and need drainage holes. Stoneware, porcelain or glass containers have the same problem. If you wish to grow plants in these attractive containers, water

with the greatest care. Without a drainage hole, water soon collects in the bottom of the container and this is extremely harmful to roots. Metal containers should not be used because the metal can poison your plant.

Repotting is necessary when the root system fills the pot, when the pot breaks and when the plant shows symptoms of disease. In the case of young plants, repot at least once a year at the beginning of the growing season to allow room for new growth. If your plant wilts between normal waterings, has roots growing through the drainage hole, or if its lower leaves are turning yellow, it is probably time to repot.

The new pot should be 1-inch (2cm) larger for plants in 10-inch (25cm) or smaller pots, 2-inches (5cm) larger for plants in pots larger than 10 inches (5cm). Wash the pot with soap and hot water to destroy any bacteria. Rinse thoroughly with water. If the pot is made of porous material, let it soak for an hour or so in water before potting, then let it dry for a few minutes. Completely dry porous pots steal water from the root-ball.

It is best to water the soil thoroughly before removing the plant from its old pot. This should loosen the soil and make the root-ball easier to remove. With pots less than 8 inches (20cm) in diameter, place one hand over the soil with your fingers on both sides of the stalk, and tip the pot upside down. If the plant does not drop into your hand, strike the rim against the edge of a table or workbench. It should drop. Do not disturb the old soil that clings to the roots. In the case of ferns, the roots may have attached themselves to the inside of the pot and you may have to work them loose with a sharp, thin blade.

Plants in larger than 8-inch (20cm) pots require a different method. Wrap the rim of the pot with a cloth pad or several layers of folded newspaper. Then lay the pot on its side and tap against the protected rim with a wooden or rubber mallet, turning the pot a few degrees

To assure good drainage, place a layer of gravel or pieces of broken pottery in the bottom of pots.

after each tap. The plant should fall loose after a few taps.

Roots which have grown through the drainage hole should not be cut off; it is better to break the pot. If you leave the root-ball intact, repotting can be done at any time of the year. If a section of the root system is damaged, remove part of the foliage to compensate.

For pots larger than 6 inches (15cm), place a 1/2- to 1-inch (1 to 3cm) layer of rocks or broken pottery on the bottom for drainage. Put a thin layer of fresh soil over the rocks and place the root-ball on top. The top of the root-ball should be at the same level as it was in the old pot. Press the soil down well so the plant does not settle when watered. Surround the root-ball with fresh soil, pressing down well. Tap the pot to make sure the soil is packed firmly around the root-ball. Use a stick to press if you need to. The new soil *must be firm* around the roots.

Water thoroughly once, but do not water heavily for the next month. This will allow the roots to grow into the new soil, a process that requires air as well as water in the soil.

PINCHING AND PRUNING

Pinching and pruning are used to keep the house plants compact and full, to promote flowering, and to train growth. To pinch back a plant, all you do during the growing season is pinch off the growing tip with your forefinger and thumb. Pinch the tip off near the leaf joint below it. Most plants have buds where a leaf joins the stem. When the tip of the stem is removed, these usually start to grow. Pinching back these tips will cause even more buds to develop and give a much fuller shape. Because flowers are produced at the ends of the tips, the more tips, the more flowers. Proper pinching can often eliminate the need for pruning, but plants with single growing stems such as *Dracaena*, should not be pinched.

Pruning is more drastic and done much less frequently. It is usually only necessary when a plant has completely overgrown its location or to compensate for damage from disease or to the root-ball during repotting. Some plants can be cut back severely after the growing period and will come back vigorously. Others cannot stand having all their leaves removed. The descriptions of individual plants contain specific information. Be sure to use a *sharp* knife or shears. Pruning should always be done *above* but close to a leaf joint or *eye*. The eye will develop into a new shoot; its position will dictate the direction of the shoot, especially in shrubby plants. Remove crossing branches;

Prune just above the leaf joint. Use a sharp knife or shears.

keep the shape open so that all shoots will receive adequate light. If the plant bleeds after pruning, the wound should be closed with charcoal, ash or plant seal available at nurseries.

Root pruning is used to control the growth of the plant. It must be done carefully or the plant will die. During its growth period, usually in spring, remove the plant from its pot. With a sharp knife, cut away an equal amount of roots from all sides of the root-ball. Do not hack or saw. When you replace the plant in its pot, there should be about one inch (3cm) of space on all sides. Fill the space with fresh soil and water the plant. Pruning foliage will help the plant recover. This technique is not recommended for plants with fleshy roots, such as ferns.

Propagating Your Plants

There are a number of ways you can add to your collection of house plants, but propagation is one of the easiest and most fun. Here are some general instructions.

CUTTINGS

Cuttings will often root in water, but better results are achieved in a mixture of equal parts of coarse sand and fine peat which should be discarded after one use to avoid diseases. Powdered rooting hormone will insure success if applied before putting the cutting in the soil. Keep the rooting medium moist but not soggy. Cuttings may be taken in various ways:

Tip Cuttings—The most common method is to take tip-shoots, about 2-1/2 to 3 inches (6 to 8cm) in length, and cut them just *below* a leaf joint. The lower leaves are gently removed and the cutting is inserted in the growing medium. Leaves left on the cuttings must not be allowed to let too much moisture evaporate for there are no roots to make up for the loss. Leaves that end up below the surface of the soil will rot.

Eye Cuttings—Plants, such as *Ficus,* can be propagated from a section of

stem with one leaf. The leaf is rolled up and tied in order to reduce evaporation. The new plant will grow from an almost invisible eye in the joint where the leaf meets the stem.

Leaf Cuttings—The leaves of foliage begonias, *Sansevieria, Saintpaulia* and other plants may be cut into sections from which roots will develop. In the case of other species, such as *Dracaena,* the cuttings may consist of sections of the stem. About 1 inch (3cm) of the leaf or leaf stem is inserted in the rooting medium. When new leaves have formed and reached about 1/3 the size of the original leaf, the cutting should be planted in the proper soil.

Succulents and cacti can be propagated with leaf cuttings, but they should be allowed to dry out before planting in a moist mix of equal parts sharp sand and peat. Cuttings from succulents can be taken from early spring to late summer; cacti from late spring to August.

A propagator which provides bottom heat is very useful for cuttings, but you can accomplish much the same effect by placing the pot with the cutting inside a plastic bag. Use sticks or wire to keep the bag from touching the cutting. Place it in a bright spot, but not direct sunlight, where the temperature is 60°F (15°C) or more. Remove the cutting when growth appears and plant in the soil specified in the plant description.

AIR-LAYERING

A very special method of propagation is air-layering. Here the cutting is induced to form roots before it is severed from the mother plant. This is done particularly in the case of single-stemmed plants such as *Ficus, Monstera, Philodendron* or *Syngonium.* A leaf is removed from a node and an incision is made in the stem just below the node. A wooden match is inserted in the cut to keep it open, and rooting hormone is dusted on the cut with a fine brush. The whole thing is wrapped in damp sphagnum and covered with plastic. Continue normal care for the plant. Roots will develop in a few weeks, then the new plant can be cut free and set in the soil mix for that species.

CROWN OR ROOT DIVISION

An easy way to propagate plants with more than one stalk is to cut the root-ball into two or more sections and pot each separately. Foliage plants, such as *Nephrolepis*, or Boston Fern, should be divided in early spring. Flowering plants, such as *Saintpaulia*, should be divided when they are not in flower. Foliage plants should be pruned back first to avoid each division being lopsided.

Each division must have a share of the old plant's roots. Most plants should be placed in pots 2 inches (5cm) larger than the diameter of their root-ball. Fast growing plants, such as *Asparagus*, need a pot 4 inches (10cm) larger. Water thoroughly once after they are potted and then sparingly until new growth appears.

SEED

As a rule, seeds are sown in early spring when days get longer. The seedbed may consist of standard potting mix thinned with an equal amount of coarse sand. Special seed compost is also available. Many seeds require extra heat in order to germinate, and in such cases a heated propagator is best. If you don't have a propagator, use a plastic pot. Wash it with soap and water to remove bacteria. A plastic bag placed over the pot will hold heat and moisture

Sprinkle the seeds over the soil and cover with a thin layer of finely shredded sphagnum moss. Then set the pot in a bowl of warm water until the surface appears moist. Let the pot drain, cover with a plastic bag and set in a bright location out of direct sunlight.

First, two seed leaves appear followed by a pair of true leaves. Now the seedlings must be given more room to develop. Lift them by their leaves, not their stems, and plant them in the soil mix suggested in their plant description.

SPORES

Ferns do not develop seeds or flowers. Instead, during spring and summer they develop *spores* on the underside of their fronds. The visible black spots on the fronds are actually spore cases. You can obtain spores by taking a frond from the plant when the cases have turned black, and storing it in a paper bag. After a week the cases will have dried and released the spores. If you pour the contents of the bag onto a white piece of paper, the small gray spots that look like dust are spores. They are so light your breath can blow them away.

Spores should be sprinkled over a mix of equal parts peat and standard potting mix in a plastic pot. Set the pot on a saucer filled with water and cover with a plastic bag. Keep the saucer filled. When a green slime appears on the soil, it means you are having success. There are both male and female spores and they must mate to produce new plants. This slime is the ideal environment.

When the ferns are about 1-inch (3cm) tall, remove the plastic bag and gently lift 1/2-inch (1cm) squares of ferns and soil and place in other pots. You can divide them again, if you wish, when they get to be about 2-inches (5cm) tall.

OFFSETS AND SUCKERS

A number of plants are propagated by separating offsets from the mother plant. Most bromeliads reproduce this way. Wait until the young plant has developed its own roots, then cut it from the old one. Plant the new one in the soil mix suggested for the species.

Some plants, *Nephrolepis* or Spider Plant for one, send out new plants at the end of long suckers or runners. If you provide a place for this young plant to root, it will soon take off on its own. When you see that it has rooted, the sucker can be cut off and thrown away.

Pests and Diseases

The listing here is not exhaustive, but it does present the pests and diseases you are most likely to encounter with house plants. Most problems with plants are the result of improper care, so check the chart on page 9 for common symptoms and causes.

PESTS

Aphids—These small gray or green insects are visible on the undersides of leaves and on stems. They suck out plant juices and cause curled and yellowed leaves. They spread very fast and require immediate control. Rinse the plant in soapy water or spray with insecticide containing pryethrum or rotenone.

Mealybugs—Hidden under leaves, these sucking insects look like bits of cotton. They cause pale foliage, leaf or bud drop, and stunted growth. Treat with a cotton swab dipped in alcohol and wash the plant with soapy water. Heavy attacks can be treated by spraying with malathion. **CAUTION: Malathion is very toxic to humans, pets and some plants.**

Mites—These are too small to see, but you can see their effects. Curling leaves, withered buds or tips, and webs on the undersides of leaves are sure signs. Cut away infected parts and spray with dicofol. In many cases, particularly in the case of the *cyclamen mite,* all you can do is discard the plant.

Nematodes—These invisible round worms eat the roots of the plant. Repot with sterilized soil or treat soil with Vapam.

Red Spiders—Large numbers leave webs that make the foliage look dusty. Leaves become yellowed or bronze, and fall. Badly infected plants can be dipped in a solution of 2 teaspoons malathion to each gallon of water. Some plants may have to be discarded. These pests are especially fond of ivy, but do not like high humidity.

Scale—This term covers several parasites that look like hard-shelled lumps on stems or the backs of leaves. They suck juices and stunt plant growth. The first sign may be light colored spots on leaves. Scrub infected parts with a brush and soapy water. Heavy infections can be treated with pyrethrum or rotenone sprays or dipped in a malathion solution as with red spiders.

Slugs and Snails—Both feed on leaves at night and leave a trail of silver slime. Keep your plants clean and pick these pests off by hand if you see them. A saucer of beer or grape juice set next to the plant will attract and kill them.

Sowbugs—These grayish black crawling pests eat young stems and roots. Pick them off by hand or spray the soil with malathion.

Thrips—These tiny insects cause a white mottling on leaves. New growth is distorted. Spray with malathion.

Whiteflies—Pale or yellowing leaves that eventually drop are signs of whitefly larvae. Mature whiteflies rise like a cloud when the plant is disturbed. Spray with rotenone or malathion several times over a period of weeks. Whiteflies are difficult to eradicate.

DISEASES

Before you decide your plant is diseased, make sure it is getting proper care. Here are some of the most common diseases.

Bottrytis Blight—This fungus thrives on wet foliage. Gray, brown or yellow blotches on leaves or a gray mold are sure signs. Infected parts should be discarded and the plant can be sprayed with zineb or captan. Give the plant better air circulation and avoid overcrowding, overwatering or overfeeding.

Crown or Root Rot—Plants that turn brown and suddenly wilt may be suffering from rot. The problem is usually related to poor drainage. Repotting can help, and the soil can be sprayed with benomyl.

Fungus Leaf Rot—Blotches on leaves

that wither and die may indicate this fungus. Cut off infected leaves and keep other leaves dry. Give the plant better air circulation and lower humidity. Spray with zineb or benomyl. If the infection is too bad, discard plant.

Mildew—A white or gray powder on leaves, stems or flower buds indicates mildew. Leaves may also curl. The usual cause is too much water. Cut down on watering and, if necessary, spray with sulfur, zineb or benomyl.

Common Problems With House Plants

The problems listed here are generally due to mistakes made in caring for the plant. If your problem is not found here, check the plant description and the discussion of Pests and Diseases. If you still do not find an answer, take the plant to your nurseryman for an opinion. Do not treat your plant until you know what the problem is. Wrong treatment can be as injurious to your plant as the disease!

Problem	Frequent Cause
No Growth	Usually means insufficient light. Move to brighter location.
Unbalanced Growth	Turn plant when watering for even exposure to light.
Leggy Plant	Insufficient light. Move to brighter location. Too much nitrogen can also be a cause. Reduce feeding.
Small Flowers or No Bloom	Overfeeding promotes foliage but not blossoms. Withhold fertilizer. Insufficient light can also be a cause. Move to brighter location.
New Leaves are Small	Plant may need feeding or a new location. In some species, such as *Philodendron*, the cause may be too much light. In others, such as *Saintpaulia*, it may be too little light.
Curled Leaves	Too much light or heat. Try moving plant. Check for aphids.
Brown Leaf Tips or Spots	Drafts, too much sun and too low humidity can all cause brown spots. Try moving plant. Salt build-up in the soil also may be cause. Repot plant.
Spots on Leaves	Cold water on leaves or overwatering can be causes. Aerate soil and try bottom watering.
Pale Leaves with Green Veins	Too little light, poor drainage or an iron shortage are possible causes. Move plant and treat with chelated iron.
Yellow Leaves	Low humidity, too much light or too much heat can all be causes. Plant may be potbound or underfed. Move and repot if necessary.
Leaf Drop	Changes in location, temperature, or light conditions can cause foliage to drop. Try to minimize these changes and let the plant adjust to its location. Drafts should be avoided. Insufficient water or fertilizer can also be a cause.
Dull or Crackling Leaves	Low humidity is probable cause. Mist more frequently or try the stone and tray method.
Wilt	Dry soil, too little or too much light, too high temperatures or lack of moisture in air. Move plant to cooler location. Mist more frequently or use stone and tray method. Check for potbound condition.
Plant Dries Out Too Quickly	Soil is too porous or plant is potbound. Repot.
White or Green Stain on Sides of Pot, White Scum on Soil	Salts accumulated from fertilizer. Flush soil with water several times. Repot if desired. Wash pot carefully.

Terms You'll Need

BROMELIAD

The 2,000 species of this plant family are related to *Ananas,* the pineapple. Most are stemless. Clusters of leaves form a *vase* or cup that should be kept full of water. They are prized both for their beautiful foliage and their striking flowers. Most indoor varieties are epiphytes, or air-plants. Flowering can be encouraged by placing a bromeliad in a plastic bag with a ripe apple. The apple releases ethylene gas which will encourage blossoming. Many bromeliads die after flowering, but produce new plants as offsets around their base. Examples include *Aechmea, Guzmania, Tillandsia* and *Vriesea.* For further information, write the Bromeliad Society, 1811 Edgecliff Drive, Los Angeles, CA 90026.

CACTUS

This family of succulent plants is usually noted for their spines. These plants are specially adapted to arid conditions and usually leafless. Their stems have evolved into cylinders or pads that store water. Most have thick skins to reduce evaporation and many produce large and beautiful flowers. Almost all are native to the Americas. There are jungle varieties that are epiphytic. Propagation is by offsets or seed, but most kinds can be grown from cuttings. Let the cutting dry until the cut end is covered with a cork-like surface. Then insert it in sand. When handling cactus, wrap it carefully in an old piece of carpet or several thicknesses of newspaper. This will protect it from injury and you from its spines. Varieties include *Cephalocereus, Echinocereus, Gymnocalycium, Opuntia, Rebutia* and *Zygocactus.* Write The Cactus and Succulent Society of America, Inc., Box 167, Reseda, CA 91335 for information.

EPIPHYTE

Epiphytes or air-plants grow naturally without soil. They support themselves on trees or rocks, but they are not parasites. They live on the rainwater that runs off their hosts and the organic material that gathers around their roots. There are epiphytic plants in many families including some bromeliads, cacti, ferns and orchids. Most epiphytic house plants are native to the tropics.

FERN

Grown primarily for their foliage, a wide variety of these perennials is available for both indoor and outdoor cultivation. They have no flowers and are propagated by division or from *spores* which are usually formed on the underside of their leaves, called *fronds.* Most like high humidity, filtered sunlight and cool, but not damp, roots. Incidentally, osmunda fiber is made from the fibrous roots of the Osmunda fern. Others include *Asparagus, Nephrolepis* and *Pellaea.* Additional information can be obtained from The American Fern Society, c/o Biological Sciences Group, University of Connecticut, Storrs, CT 06268.

GESNERIAD

This family of plants generally has hairy leaves. Many kinds are grown as house plants. Propagation is usually by stem or leaf cuttings. Examples are *Achimenes, Saintpaulia* and *Sinningia.* Both the American Gesneria Society, 11983 Darlington Avenue, Los Angeles, CA 90049, and the American Gloxinia and Gesneriad Society, Inc., Eastford, CT 06242 can be contacted for additional information.

ORCHID

Known for their beautiful blossoms, orchids comprise one of the largest plant families, and many can be grown successfully indoors. All require high humidity and bright light, though not direct sun. Some require warm temperatures and others prefer cool. Most are susceptible to very subtle changes in culture, and slight variations can make the difference between success and failure. One way to insure success is to buy a mature plant *in sheath.* This means the flower buds are almost ready to open. Some varieties can be obtained for as little as ten dollars. Species include *Cattleya, Lycaste* and *Paphiopedilum.* For further information write The American Orchid Society, Inc., Botanical Museum of Harvard University, Cambridge, MA 02138.

SUCCULENT

Succulent is a descriptive term, rather than a family name. For example, most cacti are succulents, but many succulents are not cacti. Succulents have thick, fleshy parts that are used to store water during dry seasons in their natural habitats. Many, such as *Lithops,* are notable for their strange appearance. Most are slow-growing and some produce magnificent flowers. Most need dryness, well-draining soil and require little attention, but not all like full sun. Examples are *Aloe, Sansevieria, Sedum* and *Sempervivum.* Write The Cactus and Succulent Society of America, Inc., Box 167, Reseda, CA 91335 for information.

Plant Names

Most plants have two kinds of names: a *common name* and a *scientific name.* Different plants can have the same common name, as with *Tradescantia* and *Zebrina* which are both known as Wandering Jew, or the same plant can have different common names, as with *Maranta,* The Prayer Plant, also known as Arrowroot or Ten Commandments.

The great Swedish scientist Linnaeus invented the scientific system in the eighteenth century. Each plant has a two-word name. The first word is its *genus,* and the second is its *species* within that genus. In some cases this is further refined by naming each variety within a species. This is signified by enclosing the variety in single quotes as in *Ficus elastica* 'Variegata' which is a mottled form of the Indian Rubber Tree.

Scientific names have the disadvantage of being in Latin, but they do tend to stay the same throughout the world. Because of this I have chosen to list the plants in this book by their Latin names, and to include the common names in the index. If you know *Philodendron* or *Begonia,* you are already using some Latin names. Knowing the correct scientific name will insure that you get the plant you want when you go to a nursery. The best current authority is *Hortus Third,* published by MacMillan.

There is one further fact you should know. In the United States new varieties can be *patented.* New varieties of roses and African violets are often patented. A royalty is paid to the originator for each plant of that variety raised and sold commercially.

Abutilon

The *Abutilon* is a shrubby plant from South America with attractive, bell-shaped flowers and leaves shaped like those of a Maple tree. *Abutilon* is extremely vigorous and I grow specimens up to 16 feet (5m) within about two years. If you wish to achieve similar results bear in mind that the plant should be repotted frequently. Start in early spring with a cutting in a 4-1/2-inch (12cm) pot. In late May it should be transferred to an 8-inch (20cm) pot and by early August you will need a small tub. In September growth will gradually cease and during the winter the plant can remain in the tub. A cool location is preferable in winter, approximately 50° to 60°F (10° to 16°C), but if you don't mind the leaves dropping, it can stay in the living room. Repot in March into a larger tub. Within two months you may have to consider a tub with a diameter of 2 to 3 feet (60 to 80cm). By late July the tallest shoots may have reached 16 feet (5m). Naturally such a large plant needs plenty of water: about 10 quarts (10 liters) on a sunny day. Support is essential because the long shoots are limp. In the third year the plant will become too large for the house, so take a cutting and grow a new one.

If you choose to keep *Abutilon* small, pinching back new shoots when they are a few inches high will induce branching and extend its bloom. It can be trained to hang or grow upright.

The upper photograph shows *Abutilon megapotamicum*, nick-named Weeping Chinese Lantern or Belgian Flag because of its red and yellow flowers which are shaped like small rockets. A green-leaved variety is also available.

The large specimens described above are grown primarily with the beautifully marked *Abutilon striatum* 'Thompsonii,' shown in the foreground of the lower photograph. It is the finest variety available and produces orange flowers. The green-leaved *Abutilon hybridum* behind it, with pink, red or yellow flowers, may be grown from seed. Both bloom intermittently throughout the year.

Abutilon will develop yellow leaves. Remove them and new growth will replace them quickly. Watch for mealybugs, mites, scale and whiteflies.

- Full sun is essential for flowering.
- Moderate: 50° to 60°F (10° to 16°C) at night. Minimum temperature in winter 55°F (12°C).
- Give plenty of water in summer: water moderately in winter. Mist often.
- Reasonably tolerant of dry atmosphere in winter.
- Standard potting mix. Feed regularly with low nitrogen fertilizer.

Acacia

Kangaroo Thorn

Acacia armata, illustrated here, bears a close resemblance to *Mimosa* but it loves coolness. It bears clusters of fuzzy yellow flowers in late winter. Care is extremely simple but a cool location in winter is absolutely essential. Pinching back new growth will help maintain a compact shape and encourage flowering. Older plants may need staking. In summer the pots, which should not be too large, are best placed in a sheltered sunny outdoor position. *Acacia armata* does not grow taller than 60 inches (150cm). A true *Acacia* would soon outgrow a greenhouse. Propagation is best achieved from cuttings. Seed has to be prepared because it does not easily germinate. Insect pests include mealybugs, scale and whiteflies.

- Always a well-lit position.
- Cold: 40° to 50°F (3° to 10°C) at night; cool location in winter is essential.
- Water moderately; soil must not dry out. Needs good drainage.
- No special requirement. Mist occasionally.
- Standard potting mix with some sharp sand added.

Acalypha

Chenille Plant
Red-Hot Cattail

These fine plants originate in Australia. They are particularly attractive in appearance: one species has long red tails and the other produces beautiful variegated foliage. Their popularity as house plants is undoubtedly due entirely to their appearance because they require high humidity and their cultivation presents problems. It is usually impossible to keep the *Acalypha* through a cold winter.

If you want to keep these fine plants on a permanent basis, you should grow your plants from cuttings, which is not too easy. If you decide to try, spring is the only possible time to start. Root the cuttings in a sandy potting mix. Adequate bottom heat is essential.

The photograph shows *Acalypha hispida*, the Red-Hot Cat's Tail or Chennile Plant. The tails may grow as long as 20 inches (50cm). Usually they are red, but there is a white form called 'Alba.' Both have hairy leaves and need pinching and pruning to control growth. They bloom year round, but most profusely in fall and winter. Dead flowers should be removed. Pruning severely in spring will encourage a summer bloom.

The other photograph shows a detail of the Chenille Plant's sister species, *Acalypha wilkesiana.* Here the flowers are far less conspicuous but the

Acalypha (continued)

leaves are much more beautiful. 'Musaica' shows a mosaic pattern in red and orange. 'Marginata' has orange-brown, pink-edged leaves. In 'Obovata' the foliage is olive-green with an orange margin which eventually fades. 'Godseffiana' develops spotted leaves with a creamy margin.

In my experience these plants may be kept indoors provided they are sprayed regularly and have partial shade in summer. Do not spray flowers. In a greenhouse they present no problems. Watch out for mealybugs, red spiders and scale. If plants become straggly, prune them back to 4 to 8 inches (10 to 20cm) and they will come back strong.

- Plenty of light is necessary for fine coloring; direct sun is harmful.
- Moderately warm: 50° to 60°F (10° to 16°C) at night. Minimum of 50° to 65°F (17°C) in winter.
- Keep moderately moist but not soggy.
- Requires high to very high humidity throughout the year. Spray regularly.
- Standard potting mix; adding a small amount of peat moss can help. Feed monthly from March to September with mild liquid fertilizer.

Achimenes
Monkey-Faced Pansy
Orchid Pansy

This plant is grown from scaly root-stock called a *rhizome*. Plant them in April in moist peat moss, 1/2 to 1 inch (2 to 3cm) deep. Keep moist during the growing season. An indoor propagator is practically indispensable for this purpose. During the flowering period, which lasts from June to October, the plant should be generously watered and fed. Flowering hybrids are often available from nurseries at this time. Toward autumn the plant is gradually allowed to die back by withholding water. The dead stems are removed and the rhizomes are kept throughout the winter in dry peat moss at the minimum temperature indicated below. *Achimenes* are particularly suited to hanging baskets. Pinch back to maintain shape.

- A fair amount of light but out of direct sunlight. Does well in artificial light.
- Warm: 60° to 70°F (16° to 20°C) at night; minimum of 55°F (14°C) in winter.
- Water moderately. Keep roots moist. Requires good drainage.
- Likes a humid atmosphere. Mist regularly.
- Requires acid, porous soil. A mix of 1 part standard potting mix, 2 parts peat and 1 part sand works well. Feed every 2 weeks during growing season with mild liquid fertilizer.

Acorus
Sweet-Flag

The ordinary Sweet-Flag is a waterplant used in garden ponds. *Acorus gramineus*, the grass-like Sweet-Flag in the photograph, is a native of Japan and has a strong lemon scent. It is not winter-hardy. Indoors the soil should be kept constantly moist. It is best to put the pot in a large saucer filled with water. The most beautiful form is the variegated 'Variegatus' shown here. Propagation is by division of existing plants. Mature plants prefer to be potbound. If the temperature is kept moderate, the care of these plants presents no problems. This plant grows well under artificial light.

- Tolerates a fair amount of shade but a position near a south-facing window is acceptable.
- Cold to moderate: 40° to 50°F (5° to 10°C) at night. 75°F (25°C) in day with adequate ventilation.
- Water frequently; does not mind wet feet.
- Normal room atmosphere provides adequate humidity. Spray frequently.
- Equal parts peat moss, perlite, sand and standard potting mix. Feed with mild liquid fertilizer once every six months. Do not feed new plants for 6 months.

Adiantum
Maidenhair Fern

The Maidenhair Fern is a difficult plant to grow because it will not tolerate dry air. It requires good drainage but do not allow its roots to dry. In winter the fronds die back and should be removed. Watch for aphids, mealybugs, red spiders or thrips. Wash the fronds with a weak solution of soap and water to control these pests. Do not use pesticides. This plant does well when potbound, but does need occasional repotting. The best time is February or March. It is best to use clay pots. The roots tend to stick to the insides of the pot and care is needed to work them loose. *Adiantum tenerum* on the left in the photograph, has leaf-stems that are deep black. *Adiantum cuneatum* on the right, also called *A. raddianum*, is much more freely branching.

- Prefers shade. Needs coolness at the roots.
- Warm: 60° to 70°F (16° to 20°C) at night, minimum 60°F (16°C) in winter.
- Water often with tepid soft water; plunge if necessary. The soil-ball must not dry out. Water less in cool weather.
- Does not tolerate dry air; likes frequent spraying.
- 1 part vermiculite, 2 parts peat moss and 2 parts standard potting mix. Feed every 3 months with very weak solution of liquid fertilizer.

Aechmea

Aechmea is a member of the large Bromeliad family, a group of plants with leaves growing in a vase or rosette shape, usually with fine clusters of flowers. The rosettes of all bromeliads die after flowering. They are therefore disposable plants which may be placed in any position because while they are flowering the foliage is already dying. Mature plants reach 18 to 24 inches (45 to 60cm).

During flowering one or more baby rosettes develop at the foot of the plant. As soon as the old foliage is obviously deteriorating, and this may take a fairly long time, the young rosettes may be removed and grown separately. With luck the new plants will flower by the third year. During the growing season it is advisable to keep water in the funnel at the center of the rosette all the time. Water when the soil is dry to the touch. If the plant is growing well but does not flower, try wrapping it in a plastic bag with some ripe apples for a few days. The ethylene gas released by the apples should induce flowering.

By far the best known species is *Aechmea fasciata*, shown above. It has green and white marbled foliage. The flower cluster blossoms consist of pink bracts and small blue blossoms which later fade into pink. The entire rosette may grow to a diameter of 24 inches (60cm) and may last as long as 5 months. The lower photograph shows *Aechmea fulgens*, another popular species with dark green leaves. Its flower cluster consists of oblong stalks of coral-red buds from which berrylike flowers appear.

Less well known species are *Aechmea chantinii*, with conspicuous horizontally striped leaves and small red flowers in yellow bracts; *Aechmea miniata* with narrow green leaves and a red stalk in which only the small petals are blue; and *Aechmea weilbachii*, which has green rosettes of narrow leaves, while the stalk is coral-red with blue sepals.

Pests to watch for include scale and thrips. Yellow leaves may mean either too much direct sun or too cool temperatures.

☀ Likes a well-lit position, not hot sun. Tolerates diffused sunlight.

🌡 Warm: 60° to 70°F (16° to 20°C) at night.

💧 Keep the soil barely moist. Water directly into vase.

♨ Preferably fairly humid, but will tolerate a dry atmosphere. Spray often.

▼ Orchid potting mix or a porous mixture such as equal parts bark chips, humus, peat moss and sand. Feed in spring and summer by spraying leaves with a weak fish emulsion or put 2 or 3 drops into the vase each month.

Aeonium

These plants develop particularly fine rosettes, unusually placed at the top of succulent stems. This is because the lower leaves are continually dropped, creating the effect of a Bonsai tree. When detached, rosettes root fairly easily.

The species illustrated is *Aeonium balsamiferum*. A form more frequently encountered is *Aeonium arboreum*, which grows wild along the Mediterranean. *Aeonium domesticum* is a low-growing species. *Aeonium swartzkopf* has black leaves. In summer these plants prefer to stand outdoors but the pot should be buried in the soil. In winter treat as succulents. Repot in spring, but only if necessary. Use clay pots rather than plastic.

- A very well-lit position is excellent: only the midday sun should be avoided.
- Moderate: 50° to 60°F (10° to 16°C) at night.
- Requires little water: the pot-soil should dry out in between waterings.
- Likes a dry atmosphere.
- Standard potting mix.

Aeschynanthus

**Basket Vine
Lipstick Plant**

Aeschynanthus is gaining in popularity, which is undoubtedly due to its striking tubular flowers. *Aeschynanthus* needs a humid atmosphere. The dry air of a living room will certainly create problems. Frequent spraying helps to some extent but the use of a humidifier is even better. A sunny kitchen or bathroom can be ideal for these plants.

On this page you see the species *Aeschynanthus lobbianus* or Lipstick Vine. The good thing about this plant is that the empty dark-colored pods in the foreground will later produce flowers. These start as small round balls at the bottom of the pods. If you buy this plant covered with pods you can be sure that it will flower for several months, provided you maintain a sufficiently high temperature. This plant is often confused with *Columnea*.

A different species *Aeschynanthus pulcher,* has drooping stems and brilliant red flowers in summer.

A third fine species is *Aeschynanthus speciosus,* shown in the upper photograph on the following page. The small-flowered species with marbled foliage, *Aeschynanthus marmoratus* or Zebra Basket Vine, is now rarely grown.

These plants were originally epiphytes living in

Aeschynanthus (continued)

damp forests. The pot-soil should therefore be mixed with sphagnum and kept moist but not soggy. These plants prefer warmth, humidity and good light. They do not mind being potbound. If the plants are grown in hanging pots do not forget to water regularly. These are thirsty plants. In winter they may be kept cooler and drier, which will encourage flowering. Propagation in spring is from cuttings, which will root only under glass or plastic and with extra bottom heat.

After flowering, prune stems back to a height of 6 inches (15cm) or so to encourage new growth. Drafts or improper watering may cause the lower leaves to drop. If the plant looks straggly, prune the longest stems back as far as 2 inches (3cm). If new growth does not appear, reduce water and withhold fertilizer.

- Slight shade is best. Does well in artificial light.
- Warm: 60° to 70°F (16° to 20°C) at night; during resting period 65° to 70°F (18° to 20°C); to encourage bud formation 55° to 60°F (12° to 15°C).
- Keep soil moist using tepid water.
- High humidity is desirable. Mist regularly.
- Use African violet potting mix. Adding small amounts of crushed charcoal helps. Feed monthly with mild acid fertilizer.

Agapanthus

African Lily
Lily-of-the-Nile

This African lily is easy to grow indoors but prefers a sunny balcony or garden. Flowers appear from July to September on stalks up to 30 inches (75cm) long. In winter the plant should not be cooler than 40°F (5°C). In spring the fleshy roots can be divided or gently repotted, but keep them potbound for a good bloom. In late fall the plant becomes dormant. Water monthly and stop fertilizing until growth begins. Remove dead stems. Watch for mealybugs, thrips and scale. *Agapanthus africanus*, shown here, has blue or white flowers. Dwarf varieties are *Agapanthus 'Peter Pan'* with blue flowers on 12- to 18-inch (30 to 45cm) stalks and *Agapanthus 'Dwarf White'* with white flowers on 18- to 23-inch (45 to 60cm) stalks.

- Requires plenty of sunshine.
- Moderate: 50° to 60°F (10° to 16°C) at night. The cooler the plant is kept in winter, provided it is frost free, the better it will flower.
- Keep moderately but constantly moist.
- Normal living room atmosphere is sufficiently humid. Spray daily from March to November.
- Mix 1 part peat and 2 parts standard potting mix. Feed every 2 weeks from March to November with mild liquid fertilizer.

Agave

There are many *Agave* species and the larger forms are found growing wild in all southern countries. It may take as long as 60 years for an *Agave* to flower. Therefore, species with interesting foliage are most in demand. The most popular is the so-called Century Plant, *Agave americana*. The upper photograph shows the variegated form 'Marginata'. In 'Medio-picta' and 'Striata' the stripe runs down the center of the leaf instead of along the margin. If the plant *should* ever produce a flower at the top of a tall stem, its death is approaching.

The smaller species are more suitable for indoors. They develop beautiful rosettes of variously colored leaves. The lower photograph shows *Agave filifera*, or Thread Agave, which develops thin hairs along its leaves. *Agave ferox* has much wider, vigorous, fleshy leaves ending in sharp points; they are a beautiful steel-blue in color. Another exceptionally fine form is the fairly small *Agave victoriae reginae*. This plant develops a very regularly shaped, spherical rosette of dull green leaves 4 to 5 inches (10 to 15 cm) long with a narrow white margin. Many other species will be found in the catalogs of cactus and succulent growers.

All species may be placed outdoors from late May on, but this is not essential. A cool and very dry location in winter is highly desirable. They are normally potbound, but can be repotted in spring before new growth appears. When repotting, a layer of rocks or broken pottery should be placed in the bottom of the pot and the potting soil should be mixed with sharp sand. This is the best way to guarantee adequate drainage. Be careful with water because these plants rot easily. Brown spots on the leaves may indicate excessive heat, lack of sunlight or too high humidity. Watch out for mealybugs and scale.

Agave are easily grown from seed. It is also possible to take runners, if they develop, and plant them in sandy soil after letting them dry out. Or, new plants that appear near the base of an older plant can be divided and planted.

☼ Full sun. They may be put outside in summer.

🌡 Moderate: 50° to 60°F (10° to 16°C) at night. Minimum in winter, 40° to 45°F (4° to 6°C).

💧 Requires little water. Let soil dry completely between waterings. Needs good drainage.

🔅 Prefers dry air.

🪴 Equal parts standard potting mix and sharp sand. Feed once a year with a half-strength solution of mild liquid fertilizer.

Ageratum

Floss Flowers

In some countries the *Ageratum* is best known as a garden or balcony plant but it can be grown indoors as well. Young plants are bought in spring, planted in standard potting mix and placed near a sunny window, preferably in a well-ventilated location. It is possible to keep them through the winter, to be grown into large plants in the following season. In spring cuttings may be taken. These are best grown in an indoor propagator. Plants may also be raised from seed sown in heated soil from February on.

- ☀ A sunny position.
- 🌡 Moderate: 50° to 60°F (10° to 16°C) at night.
- 💧 Soil must be kept constantly moist. Water moderately.
- ☷ Likes a moderately humid atmosphere.
- 🪴 Standard potting mix.

Aglaonema

Chinese Evergreen
Spotted Evergreen

Aglaonema costatum has a spreading habit and dark green white-blotched leaves. It resembles *Dieffenbachia*, but is not as hardy. 'Silver Queen' is shown here. It does best in wide shallow pots filled with coarse soil and does not mind being pot-bound. Older plants may shed lower leaves. They can be propagated from stem or tip cuttings set in a heated indoor propagator. The Chinese Evergreen, *Aglaonema modestum*, has shiny dark green leaves which should be sponged every two to three weeks with room-temperature water. Do not use leaf shiners. Liquid exuded from the leaf tips can spot wood finishes. Watch for aphids, mealybugs, red spiders, scale or thrips.

- ☀ Tolerates a great deal of shade as well as diffused sunlight.
- 🌡 Warm: 60° to 70°F (16° to 20°C) at night. In winter the temperature may fall to 60° to 65°F (16° to 18°C).
- 💧 Water generously during the growing period, using tepid water. Keep somewhat drier in winter.
- ☷ Moderate humidity. Mist frequently.
- 🪴 Standard potting mix or water with charcoal chips. Feed every two weeks with mild liquid fertilizer.

Allamanda

Allamanda is a tropical climber which will thrive only in warmth and high humidity. It is best grown in a heated greenhouse. Nevertheless, there are people who, by means of frequent spraying, succeed in keeping the plant in good condition and even in bringing it through the winter. A humidifier in the house can be a great advantage. In the spring and summer, support the long shoots with wires or train up a wall. Cut them back drastically in winter in order to reduce evaporation. Repot young plants in spring. Older plants should be kept potbound to encourage blooming. Propagation is from cuttings grown in heated soil. The photograph shows *Allamanda cathartica*. Watch for mealybugs, red spiders and scale. **NOTE: Flowers of this plant are poisonous. Keep out of reach of children or pets.**

Light to medium shade.

Warm: 60° to 70°F (16° to 20°C) at night.

Water moderately during the dormant season; generously in the growing period. Needs good drainage.

High humidity is essential. It can be kept in the livingroom only if frequently sprayed.

1 part vermiculite, 1 part peat moss and 2 parts standard potting mix. Feed weekly from April to November with mild liquid fertilizer.

Alocasia

Magnificent foliage plants from tropical Asia, related to *Anthurium*, these should be cared for approximately as is *Caladium*. This means a great deal of moisture both in the atmosphere and in the soil, and a fairly high temperature. They should be kept moderately dry in winter but should not be allowed to dry out as much as *Caladium*. Naturally, a heated greenhouse is the best solution, but the plants can be kept for some months in the livingroom—especially *Alocasia sanderiana*, shown here. Propagation is from shoots or from division of the root-stock. Sowing is also possible.

Slight shade preferred.

Warm: 65° to 70°F (8° to 20°C) at night. In winter, the temperature should not fall below 65°F (18°C).

Soil should be kept fairly moist.

Humid atmosphere. Spray regularly.

Equal parts leafmold, peat moss and sphagnum. Feed weekly with mild liquid fish fertilizer from April to September.

Aloe

First-Aid Plant

This genus of succulents embraces a large number of species, most of which are easy to grow. It should not be confused with the *Agave*, which belongs to the Amaryllis family. The Aloe is a member of the Lily family and it flowers much more easily than the *Agave*. Aloe leaves contain a sticky fluid that gives relief for pain from small cuts or burns. It was used by the Romans for first aid.

In the photograph I have assembled a few well-known species, two of which are in flower. Above right is *Aloe variegata*, the Tiger Aloe, one of the forms most suitable for the windowsill. Its leaves are beautifully marked and the flowers range in color from pink to red. Above left is a small specimen of *Aloe arborescens*, a tree-shaped aloe which may grow as tall as 10 feet (3m). New side shoots are constantly produced. This species also flowers readily. Below right is *Aloe humilis*, which remains small and has a prickly leaf rosette. The small plants below left are called *Aloe bakeri* and *Aloe stans* or *Aloe nobilis* which has orange-red flowers.

It is not difficult to keep an *Aloe* in good condition for many years, particularly if you keep their pots well-drained and make the soil mixture extra porous by adding coarse sand or perlite. Standing water is fatal, especially at low temperatures. You should also avoid spilling water on the foliage for this will remain in the hollows at the base of the leaves and cause decay. Watch for mealybugs or scale. Older plants often lose their lower leaves, but are still healthy.

If you want your plant to flower, it is best to keep it about 45°F (8°C) in winter and practically cease to water it. Flowers usually appear between December and February. On sunny days in summer, water generously. The plant can be propagated by rooting side shoots or by dividing plants into clumps. *Aloes* can also be grown from seed which germinates readily: this is the simplest method to obtain rare species.

 Full sun if possible.

Moderate: 50° to 60°F (10° to 16°C) at night. Keep cold in winter.

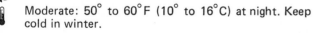 Water moderately in summer, hardly at all in winter. Soak thoroughly but let soil dry between waterings. Needs good drainage.

Very tolerant of dry atmosphere.

Mix 1 part standard potting mix and 2 parts sharp sand. Feed monthly from April to August with a mild liquid fertilizer.

Ampelopsis

You really should try this *Ampelopsis brevipedunculata maximowiczii* 'Elegans,' if only because of its imposing botanical name! It is as easy to grow as its name is difficult to pronounce, provided you place the plant outdoors from time to time and keep it cool, especially in winter. In the cold season most of the foliage will probably drop, but after repotting in spring new leaves will soon appear. This should be done each year. The plant feels most at home in a cool hall. If you have a patio, it can be planted outside. It will survive winter cold if given light protection. Propagation is from cuttings.

 Semi-shade.

Moderate: 50° to 60°F (10° to 16°C) at night to cool 35° to 50°F (3° to 10°C). Requires a cool location in winter.

Water moderately.

Fairly tolerant of dry living room atmosphere.

Standard potting mix.

Ananas   Pineapple

This ornamental form of the edible pineapple produces small fruits topped by a shock of leaves as shown in the photograph of *Ananas comosus* 'Variegatus.' The plants are fairly expensive but they are incredibly strong and will give you pleasure for months even in a shady room. As in all bromeliads, the old rosette will then die but it is easy to grow a new one from the shock of leaves at the top of the fruit. This should be cut off, together with a thin slice of the flesh. Let it dry for a few days, then plant it in sandy soil or even in plain water. Keep it moderately warm and let the roots develop. Transplant to standard potting mix. The same method can sometimes produce a new plant from the leaves of a commercially grown pineapple.

Plenty of light and sun.

Warm: 60° to 70°F (16° to 20°C) at night. Temperature in winter: 60° to 65°F (15° to 18°C).

Keep the soil fairly moist. Water more in the growing period.

Fairly high humidity required. Spray frequently.

Standard potting mix. Fertilize monthly with mild fish fertilizer.

Anthurium

Flamingo Flower
Painter's Palette

Since World War II *Anthurium*, or the Flamingo Plant, has become very popular as a house plant and for cutting. Cut flowers keep two to three weeks in water.

Anthurium is a tropical plant, requiring warmth and humidity. Some varieties can reach a height of 3 feet (1m). The modern *Anthurium scherzerianum* hybrids, above left in the photograph, are reasonably tolerant of the dry atmosphere in a living room, but low temperatures can do irreparable damage. The best known color is scarlet but pink, mottled and white forms are available.

Anthurium andraeanum hybrids are the forms usually grown for cutting but they may serve as house plants as well, as shown on the right in the photograph. The species illustrated in the foreground is *Anthurium crystallinum*, which derives its decorative value chiefly from the fine foliage. This species can be successfully grown only in a greenhouse because it needs high humidity.

It is essential to repot *Anthurium* every year, mainly to get rid of the harmful unabsorbed minerals retained in the old soil. Water generously when the plant is in flower and feed every two weeks with diluted liquid fertilizer. Spray the leaves frequently with tepid water, but do not use tapwater which is usually far too hard. Methods for softening water are given in the introduction.

When repotting, the plant can be propagated by division of larger specimens. When a Flamingo Plant has become unsightly, the stem may be cut up and the sections rooted in osmunda fiber in a heated indoor propagator.

These plants like being potbound but occasionally roots of older plants may appear on top of the soil. These roots are very sensitive and should be covered with a sphagnum moss. Moisten the moss with warm water daily. Watch for mealybugs, mites, red spiders, scale and whiteflies. Insecticide sprays will damage flowers. Fertilizer can burn roots.

Well-lit position out of sun. Does poorly in artificial light.

Warm: 60° to 70°F (6° to 20°C) at night. Minimum of 60°F (6°C) in winter. Grows best at 80° to 90°F (20° to 30°C).

During flowering water liberally using tepid, lime-free water. Water less at other times but keep soil moist. Needs good drainage.

High humidity. Mist twice a day if possible.

Equal parts standard potting mix and fir bark. Feed every 2 weeks from February to August with mild liquid fertilizer.

Aphelandra

Aphelandra squarrosa, shown here, has beautiful foliage, but is difficult to grow in a dry living room. If you have forced-heating or a humidifier, you will probably be more successful.

After flowering in spring and summer, the plant should be kept drier and cooler. It can be kept through the winter; in the second year it may grow to 3 feet (1m) tall. Repotting should be done in March. Pruning can control size and will encourage new shoots. Prune back half of previous season's growth when repotting. Do not remove aerial roots. Propagation from young shoots will succeed only in an indoor propagator. Watch for scale and whiteflies. Leaves will dry and drop if the temperature is too low, but they drop normally after flowering. Too little humidity will cause rolled leaf edges and brown spots.

☼ Well-lit position out of the sun.

🌡 Warm: 60° to 70°F (6° to 20°C) at night.

🪣 Water freely, especially in the flowering season. The soil-ball should never dry out.

〰 Fairly high humidity; spray frequently. Keep a little drier in winter.

▼ 1 part standard potting mix, 1 part perlite, 2 parts peat moss. Feed every 2 weeks with mild liquid fertilizer from March to September.

Aporocactus

This is one of those old-fashioned hobby plants rarely for sale in a nursery. Fortunately it grows readily and you might be able to obtain a cutting from a friend. Cuttings should be allowed to dry out for a few days before being set in very sandy soil. Later they should be transferred to a cactus mixture.

The plant is best grown in a hanging pot. In summer it should be watered freely but in winter it must be kept much drier and cooler to encourage flowering.

The species illustrated is *Aporocactus flagelliformis*. In a less well-known species, *Aporocactus flagriformis*, the stems are ribbed.

☼ Very light and sunny.

🌡 Moderate: 50° to 60°F (10° to 16°C) at night. Keep cool in winter to encourage flowering.

🪣 Water freely in the growing season, far less in winter, but do not allow to dry out completely.

〰 Normal living room atmosphere is sufficiently humid.

▼ Special cactus mixture.

Araucaria

Norfolk Island Pine

Araucaria is often sold at Christmas and makes a very good specimen plant. Overwatering in the dormant season, inadequate humidity, direct sun or drying of the soil-ball may cause loss of the lower branches. This can create a decorative effect, but if you dislike a bare stem you might purchase two or three *Araucarias* of varying heights and plant them together in a tub, but don't overcrowd. Repot as necessary but only in next larger size pot.

Araucaria is slow growing but it can become 6 feet (2m) tall. It can be kept for years. Pruning can ruin this plant and the foliage should not be handled. Pests to watch for are aphids, leaf miners, mealybugs, mites and scale. Propagation is from tip cuttings but is very difficult. The photograph shows *Araucaria heterophylla.*

- Good light out of sun. Needs good air circulation.
- Moderate: 50° to 60°F (10° to 16°C) at night. Minimum temperature in winter 35° to 40°F (3° to 5°C).
- Keep moderately moist using tepid water. Needs good drainage.
- Moderate to high humidity. Spray frequently but not directly on foliage.
- 1 part perlite, 2 parts peat moss and 3 parts standard potting mix. Feed with mild liquid fertilizer every month from April to September.

Ardisia

Coral Berry
Spear Flower

The *Ardisia crenata,* also known as *Ardisia crispa,* shown here is gaining in popularity. The graceful, long lasting red berries are this plant's main attraction. If you wish to keep the plant through the winter, it should not be placed in too warm a location and it should be sprayed regularly. In spring prune down to 2 inches (5cm) and keep soil dry until new shoots appear. Select three strongest shoots and cut away others. Repot if necessary. Feeding should begin about a month after repotting. In summer the plant will produce pinkish-white flowers. Pinch back shoots to prevent a straggly form. This shrub can reach 3 feet (1m) tall.

Ripe berries may be sown in December but this should be done in a greenhouse. Do not confuse this plant with *Skimma japonica.*

- Well-lit to sunny location, well-ventilated in flowering period.
- Moderately warm: 50° to 60°F (10° to 16°C) at night. In winter, 55° to 60°F (12° to 15°C).
- Keep the soil fairly moist with tepid water.
- Moderate humidity. Mist regularly with tepid water but not directly on flowers. Keep drier during flowering period.
- Standard potting mix. Feed weekly with small amounts of liquid fertilizer, except during dormancy.

Asparagus

Ornamental asparagus is a strong plant and will survive some ill-treatment. It is not a true fern but grows fast and looks similar.

A great deal of *Asparagus setaceus*, better known by its former name *Asparagus plumosus*, upper photograph on right, is used in formal flower sprays. It is not exactly a fascinating house plant but it will keep very well, especially in a dark corner. Larger plants develop tendrils.

Asparagus densiflorus 'Sprengeri,' usually called Sprenger Asparagus, is an attractive house plant. It is very strong and will thrive at a distance of several feet from a window. It can also be placed outdoors in summer. It is shown on the left in the upper photograph. Its chief characteristics are small white flowers, small red berries, prickly tendrils and a drooping form which makes it suitable as a hanging plant.

An attractive wide-leaved asparagus is *Asparagus falcatus*, upper photograph in the center. It is very useful in plant combinations. *Asparagus meyerii* or foxtail asparagus fern has upright arching stems that resemble the tail of a fox. They can reach 2 feet (60cm) in length.

The lower photograph shows a very old-fashioned ornamental asparagus, *Asparagus asparagoides*. Among older nurserymen it is probably better known as *Medeola.* It is a good hanging plant for the living room.

All ornamental asparagus plants should be fed monthly, expecially in summer. Direct summer sun can cause yellowing, as can too little nitrogen. They will stand being potbound but should be repotted every spring; a good-sized rock or piece of broken pottery should be placed over the hole in the pot to prevent roots from growing through. Pinch off tips to maintain shape. Mature plants may reach 2 feet long (60cm) or more. Turn them to keep them well-shaped. Older plants will benefit from hard pruning. They should be divided when white roots appear on top of the soil. These are a sign of overcrowding and depletion of the soil. Propagation is also from seed.

Will thrive in a well-lit place. Does well in artificial light.

Moderate: 50° to 60°F (10° to 16°C) at night, summer and winter.

Water frequently in summer, a little less in winter. From time to time plunge the entire pot in water. Needs good drainage.

Moderate humidity. Mist frequently.

Equal parts standard potting mix, peat moss and perlite. Feed every 2 months with mild liquid fertilizer.

Aspidistra

Cast-Iron Fern

Although sometimes considered old-fashioned, an *Aspidistra* grown in a beautiful plastic cylinder is a fine sight. It is exceptionally strong and will thrive well away from a window. It tolerates the dry atmosphere of a living room even where the temperature is very high, but avoid stagnant water in the pot and direct sun. Repot in early spring before new growth begins. Leaves should be washed occasionally. Major pest to watch for is scale. The species shown here is *Aspidistra eliator* which grows to 3 feet (1m) high. There is a variegated from 'Variegata,' but this is a less hardy plant. Propagate by root division but do it very gently. Roots are likely to break during division, so plant several pieces together.

 Shady position is acceptable. Does well in artificial light.

Moderate to cool: 45° to 55°F (8° to 13°C) at night.

Maintain constant moisture.

Moderately high; dry air is tolerated reasonably well. Mist frequently.

Standard potting mix. Fertilize every two weeks from March to October with a mild liquid fertilizer.

Asplenium

Bird's-Nest Fern
Spleenwort

Several members of this genus are protected by law, so make sure you obtain yours from a respectable source. These ferns need a humid atmosphere and do well in terrariums. They thrive when pot-bound and prefer clay pots. Be careful when repotting because roots stick to the inside of the pot. Wash foliage every two weeks and remove wilted fronds. Watch for aphids, mealybugs, red spiders and thrips. Use soap and water to control pests. Insecticides will kill your plant. *Asplenium nidus* or Bird's-Nest Fern, at the rear, is grown from spores and may reach 3 feet (1m) tall. In the foreground is *Asplenium daucifolium*, also called *Asplenium viviparum*. It develops small plantlets on its fronds which may be grown separately.

Requires little light. Avoid drafts.

Moderate: 50° to 60°F (10° to 16°C) at night. *Asplenium nidus* prefers it a little warmer: not below 55°F (13°C) in winter.

Soil must never dry out. Plunge in water from time to time. Water frequently with tepid water in the growing season, less at cooler temperatures.

Fairly high humidity; spray often. In winter plants may turn brown from too much humidity. Mist often.

1 part sharp sand and 3 parts standard potting mix. Feed April to August with mild liquid fertilizer.

Astrophytum

Natives of Mexico, this genus embraces particularly fine cacti. The photograph shows a flowering *Astrophytum myriostigma* or Bishop's Cap. The body of the plant is covered with innumerable small white flakes. The other species illustrated is *Astrophytum ornatum* or Star Cactus, with spiralled ribbing also covered with white spots. There is also *Astrophytum asterias*, the Sea Urchin, which has the shape of a flat sphere. This species has woolly white aereoles instead of spines. *Astrophytum capricorne*, or Goat's Horn is a green sphere with silver markings. It produces a yellow flower with a red throat.

All species must be kept cool in winter or they will not flower. Propagation is from seed.

☀ Well-lit sunny location. Strains without spines require partial shade.

🌡 Warm: 60° to 70°F (16° to 20°C) at night. Cool: 40° to 50°F (5° to 10°C) in winter.

💧 Water sparingly in summer, none in winter. Allow soil to dry completely between waterings.

〰 Very low humidity.

🪴 Special cactus mixture.

Aucuba

This is an excellent shrub for a room which remains unheated in winter. If you water it from time to time this plant will stand up to frost, for the common *Aucuba japonica* 'Variegata' grows wild where temperatures drop to 10°F (-10°C) in winter. It should be repotted in March, but only to the next size pot. Wash the foliage every few weeks to control pests such as aphids, leaf miners, mealybugs, mites and scale. The yellow-spotted ornamental form 'Crotonifolia' will tolerate slightly higher temperatures. Propagate from cuttings in moderate bottom heat. Mature plants reach up to 15 feet (4.5m). Prune in late winter to control size and encourage new growth.

☀ Satisfied with little light.

🌡 Cold: 35° to 50°F (3° to 10°C) at night. Ornamental strains must be kept frost free in winter.

💧 Keep moderately moist in summer. Water sparingly in winter. Mist frequently.

〰 Fairly tolerant of dry atmosphere; spray occasionally in winter.

🪴 1 part sharp sand and 3 parts standard potting mix. Feed with mild liquid fertilizer from April to September.

Azalea

Rhododendron

The correct names of indoor azaleas are *Rhododendron indicum*, shown in the upper photograph, and *Rhododendrum obtusum*, below. Most plant lovers still call them by their old name *Azalea* so that is where they are placed in this book. *Rhododentrum obtusum* also grows in gardens, where it is known as the Japanese Azalea. The greatest attraction of growing azaleas is of course to induce them to flower in subsequent years. After flowering in early spring, the plant should be placed in a frost-free location but kept as cool as possible. It will develop a number of new shoots which must be removed after a few weeks. Shoots appearing after mid-April may be left. Toward the end of May the *Azalea* should be placed in the garden or on a balcony, where it will continue to grow. A shady, not too dark spot is best.

If the pot is too small, the plant should be repotted in acid soil after blooming. It is best to use plastic pots to prevent the soil-ball from drying out. Azaleas may also be planted without pots in prepared soil. By late September buds will have formed and the plant may be brought indoors. Stop feeding and cut back on water, but keep soil moist. Do not immediately place your plant in a warm living room because it will drop its buds. It may be brought into a heated room only when flowering starts. Then it should be placed as close to the window as possible because it will be slightly cooler there. Spray as often as possible, even twice a day. Remove faded flowers. Lack of water or light may cause leaves to drop. Too much calcium will cause yellowing. Pests include aphids, mealybugs, red spiders, scale, thrips and whiteflies.

Japanese Azaleas may be treated in the same way and may also be left in the garden. They should be given some protection during their first winter.

Always water azaleas with rainwater or softened tapwater and occasionally plunge the pots in a bath. Propagation from cuttings is difficult and usually requires a greenhouse.

☼ Well-lit position but does not tolerate full sun.

🌡 Moderate to cool: 40° to 60°F (5° to 16°C) at night.

💧 Water liberally in the flowering season. Keep soil moist.

〰 Moderate humidity. Spray frequently.

🪴 Acid potting soil mix. Feed every 2 months with acid fertilizer from time flowers fade to the appearance of buds in fall.

Begonia

Begonias are among the most widely grown and diversified house plants. Species discussed here are grown for both their blossoms and their beautiful foliage. In each group there are three basic types. *Fibrous-rooted* begonias form masses of fibrous roots. *Tuberous-rooted* begonias are grown from tubers and are ideal for hanging baskets on a porch or patio that is protected from direct sun. *Rhizomatous-rooted* begonias form a rhizome, a thick stem which is used in the wild to store water for use during dry seasons. Nearly all species are extremely easy to propagate, especially from tip or nodal cuttings.

On this page are two specimens which can be grown indoors or out. If you want to grow them indoors, the first requirement is to keep them cool, particularly the tuberous varieties. If you can keep them below 70°F (20°C) in summer, they will thrive. The upper photograph shows a *Begonia semperflorens* or Wax Begonia, a fibrous type that only grows to about 6 inches (15cm) high. These plants are often grown from seed, especially for use as bedding plants. The F1 hybrids are the most vigorous though not necessarily the most beautiful. The most common colors are white, pink and red, and there are single and double-blossom forms. The foliage is green or bronze-colored. After one or two years the plants clearly deteriorate, but it is easy to take cuttings. These will root in water.

In the lower photograph you see a number of large-flowered tuberous begonias. In winter the tubers should be kept dry at 50°F (10°C). About mid-March they can be brought into growth in damp peat in a moderate temperature and then divided. Press the tuber into the soil with its concave side up until it is just visible on the surface. After the growing season, either indoors or out, water should be gradually withheld until finally, about the end of September, the stems are cut off and the tubers removed from the soil. Let them dry before storing them in dry peat moss.

 Moderate daylight; diffused sunlight if necessary but never full sun. Does well in artificial light.

Cool: 40° to 60°F (5° to 15°C) at night. Minimum of 50°F (10°C) in winter.

Keep constantly moist. Needs good drainage.

Any atmosphere is acceptable in the flowering season. Misting can help but do not spray directly on flowers.

Standard potting mix with peat moss added.

Begonia (continued)

WINTER-FLOWERING BEGONIAS

An important commercial group consists of the so-called winter-flowering begonias. Even though other begonias may also flower in winter and winter-flowering forms may flower in other seasons, this particular group is called winter-flowering because at one time it was considered unusual that these hybrids flowered in winter.

The small-flowered type is known as the *Lorraine begonia* and is shown in the upper photograph. It is available in numerous colors and has a very long flowering season. The plants require feeding and a great deal of light. After flowering, the stems should be pruned and the plants must be allowed to rest. They are then repotted before being brought into growth once more.

The large-flowered winter-flowering begonias are called *Eliator* hybrids. They are tuberous-rooted and their flowers are usually single, although occasionally double or semi-double forms are available. These plants are even more sensitive to mildew than the small-flowered forms. This sensitivity explains the success of the *Rieger begonias*—the lower photograph shows 'Schwabenland'—a vigorous strain with medium-sized flowers. These are not as susceptible to mildew as the large-flowered strains. Many colors are now available.

To encourage begonias to flower in winter, switch on a 60-watt bulb placed 20 to 30 inches (50 to 80cm) above the plant at dusk. Leave the light on until bedtime. The artificial lengthening of the day will induce flowering throughout most of the winter. A summer bloom can be forced by keeping the plant in darkness a few hours each day. After flowering, reduce water and use a sharp knife or razor blade to cut the stems down to about 3 inches from the soil. Repot in the next size pot and withhold water and fertilizer until new stems appear. You'll have new blossoms in three or four months.

Experts grow these begonias from seed but where small quantities are concerned it is easier to grow cuttings. Both side shoots and tip cuttings are suitable for this purpose.

Plenty of light but not full sun.

Normal room temperature. A few degrees lower will help the plant last longer.

Keep constantly moist.

Ensure moderate humidity.

Standard potting mix with the addition of a little extra peat moss.

Begonia (continued)

FOLIAGE BEGONIAS

Among the many species of foliage begonias, the Rhizomatous-rooted *Begonia rex* hybrids shown in the upper photograph, are the best known. The leaves have a metallic sheen and occur in the most magnificent colors. In a fairly cool environment, 60° to 65°F (15° to 18°C) that is not too dry, these plants can be kept in good condition throughout the winter, even at some distance from a window. Propagation is extremely simple. A leaf is cut into 1/5-inch-square (0.5cm) sections and these are pressed on the growing medium. This should be done in a heated indoor propagator.

 Requires a fair amount of light, possibly diffused sunlight, but never full sun.

 Warm: 60° to 70°F (16° to 20°C) at night.

Keep moderately but constantly moist, using soft water (pH 4.5 to 5). Needs good drainage.

Fairly high humidity is preferred.

Standard potting mix with peat or leaf mold added. Feed monthly from February to October with half-strength solution of mild liquid fertilizer.

SHRUB-LIKE BEGONIAS

Of the numerous botanical begonias occasionally available, a tall shrubby example is shown in the lower photograph. It is easily grown from cuttings and is equally simple to care for. It requires generous feeding and, if it is repotted when necessary, a shrub may grow to a height of 6 feet (2m).

GENERAL COMMENTS

None of the begonias enjoy long life. After thriving for several months to a year they suddenly deteriorate and are frequently attacked by mildew. If you take a cutting, which may be done at any time of the year, it will have a chance to grow into a healthy plant and begin the cycle again. Pinch back straggly growth to encourage the bloom and maintain a compact form. Wash the foliage every few weeks with room-temperature water to clear pores. Remove dead blossoms because they can be a source of infection.

It is best to use plastic pots for begonias. This keeps the soil-ball from drying out, something no begonia can tolerate. On the other hand be careful not to drown these plants. Standing water will cause root or tuber rot. Provide adequate drainage and use a porous, nutritious soil mixed with leaf mold. Pests to watch for include mealybugs, scale, slugs or snails, and whiteflies. Further information about your plant can be obtained by writing The American Begonia Society, 1431 Coronado Terraces, Los Angeles, CA 90026. They publish a monthly journal entitled *The Begonia*.

Beloperone

Shrimp Plant

Beloperone guttata is sometimes sold as *Justicia brandegeana.* It has attractive flowers with brown bracts that look like shrimp and give it its common name, Shrimp Plant. It is among the very few house plants which do not need protection from midday sun. In summer it may be put on the balcony or in the garden. After the dormant season, which lasts from about October to February, the plant should be pruned a little, repotted and brought into growth again. Pinch it back for full growth and to encourage blooming. Cuttings can be taken throughout the year. Watch for aphids and whiteflies. Leaf drop indicates too little water. Too much shade will make top leaves lose color.

- A sunny location
- Moderate: 50° to 60°F (10° to 16°C) at night. In winter keep at 55° to 60° (12° to 16°C).
- After it starts into growth, until August, water freely; then reduce watering but make sure the soil-ball does not dry out.
- Tolerant of dry living room air. Spray frequently.
- Standard potting mix. Feed with mild liquid fertilizer every two weeks from February through September.

Bertolonia

Though these are exceptionally fine plants for the hothouse, *Bertolonias* cannot be equally recommended for the living room. Nevertheless they are sold regularly and therefore included here. The most successful method of growing the plants indoors is in a container in combination with other plants; this will provide some degree of humidity. In a closed plant window or plant case there is no problem. *Bertolonia* also does well in artificial light.

Propagate from seed in an indoor propagator in January or February. Young plants are the finest and it is therefore advisable to sow new specimens every year.

The species illustrated is *Bertolonia marmorata.*

- Grows best in a shady spot. Good in artificial light.
- Warm: 60° to 70°F (16° to 20°C) at night. In summer, during the daytime, 70° to 75°F (20° to 22°C). Try to maintain a constant temperature.
- Water moderately freely.
- Humid atmosphere essential.
- Fir chips or coarse soil mixed with peat moss.

Billbergia

Queen's Tears

Billbergia windii, illustrated here is one of the few bromeliads that are easy to care for. New shoots develop even while the main rosette is in flower. The following year several of the rosettes may flower simultaneously. This plant is a fast grower and has more developed roots than most bromeliads. It will do well in almost any location. Keep the funnel at the center of the leaf rosette filled with water, but soil may also be watered. Propagate by division of offshoots.

Queen's Tears, *Billbergia nutans,* has long, grass-like leaves and delicate blossoms with green, blue and red markings. Usually several plants are clustered together and it is sometimes difficult to find the funnels for watering.

- A well-lit spot preferred but will accept a fair amount of shade. Keep out of drafts.
- Moderate: 50° to 60°F (10° to 16°C) at night. During the day the temperature must not fall below 55°F (12°C).
- Freely in summer, sparingly in winter depending on the room temperature.
- Reasonably tolerant of dryness.
- Standard orchid or bromeliad potting mix. Feed every three weeks with mild liquid fertilizer when not in flower.

Blechnum

Deer Fern

The *Blechnum gibbum* fern is rarely seen. Nevertheless it is one of the finest indoor species. Its ideal environment is in a moderately warm greenhouse where the fronds may reach a length of 3 feet (1m). After some years the plant develops a small trunk and resembles a palm.

Ensure constant humidity and do not allow the temperature to rise too high. The soil-ball should always be kept moist. Feed during the growing season with very mild fertilizer. Too strong a mix will burn this plant. Wash leaves occasionally and watch for mealybugs, red spiders, scale and thrips. Propagation is from spores in a heated seed-bed.

- Well-ventilated location; give plenty of room. No direct sun. Does well in artificial light.
- Warm: 60° to 70°F (16° to 20°C) at night. Maximum temperature in winter 60° to 65°F (16° to 18°C).
- Water freely from March to July, then moderately. The soil-ball must not dry out.
- Moderately high humidity.
- Mix 1 part peat moss, 1 part vermiculite and 2 parts standard potting mix. Feed with very weak liquid fertilizer from March to November.

Bougainvillea

The sight of these plants creates nostalgia for the southern areas where enormous *Bougainvillea spectabilis* specimens tumble over walls and balconies. The form usually found at a nursery is the *Bougainvillea buttiana,* shown here, which is a less vigorously branching strain. It may be difficult to bring the plant into flower a second time. To do this, a dormant period at a low temperature is essential in winter. The plant will drop most of its leaves and you should stop fertilizing. From March on it must be given a well-lit, warm position. Late in May it is best placed outdoors. If pruning is required this should be done immediately after flowering. Pinching the tips of new growth will encourage branching. Propagate in spring from cuttings using high bottom temperature. Mealybugs and scale are sometimes a problem. Soil should be neither too acid nor too alkaline.

- Well-lit and sunny location.
- Warm: 60° to 70°F (16° to 20°C) at night. 4° to 5°F (6° to 8°C) in winter.
- Soil-ball must never dry out. Water freely in summer, sparingly in winter. Needs good drainage.
- Moderate humidity. Spray frequently.
- Standard potting mix. Feed weekly from March to November with mild liquid fertilizer.

Browallia   Saphire Flower

Browallia speciosa shown here is a little-known annual house plant marketed from June on. It can give you a lot of pleasure until the end of the flowering period, especially if you give it a position where the temperature does not rise too high. Feed regularly. In February these plants may be sown in a heated propagator. Pick out a few for each pot and pinch out their tips to encourage fullness. Repot when they are growing well. All this is much more easily done in a heated greenhouse. New plants may also be grown from cuttings in August. Watch for aphids, leaf miners, mites and whiteflies. Pinch back stems to maintain shape and encourage blooming. This plant likes being potbound.

- Intolerant of direct sunlight but likes a very well-lit spot.
- Moderate: 50° to 60°F (10° to 16°C) at night. Not very sensitive to temperature.
- Keep the soil-ball moderately damp.
- Reasonably tolerant of dry atmosphere. Mist frequently, especially during hot weather.
- Standard potting mix. Feed monthly from November to March with diluted mild liquid fertilizer. Otherwise, feed weekly.

Brunfelsia

Yesterday, Today, and Tomorrow
Chameleon Plant

The full name of the plant in this photograph is *Brunfelsia pauciflora* var. *calycina* also known as *Brunfelsia calycina* or *Francisea calycina*. While some people think it is difficult to grow, others find it easy. Important factors are a moderate but constant temperature and attention to the two dormant seasons. The first of these falls in winter. Temperature should be kept between 55° to 60°F (12° to 14°C) and little water should be applied. The second dormant period occurs after flowering, about May or June, when the plant should again be kept fairly dry. Pinch back tips to maintain shape and encourage blooming. Prune only very lightly. Propagation from cuttings will be successful only in a heated tray, which can also be used to grow plants from seed.

- Semi-shade, definitely no direct sunlight.
- Moderate: 50° to 60°F (10° to 16°C) at night. Very sensitive to fluctuating temperature.
- Water moderately, a little less in the dormant seasons. Needs good drainage.
- Requires fairly high humidity. Mist twice a day.
- Mix 1 part vermiculite and 2 parts standard potting mix. Soil should be aerated monthly. Feed weekly with mild liquid fertilizer from March through September.

Caladium

Mother-In-Law Plant
Elephant's Ear

This tuberous plant has translucent leaves colored red, pink, green silver or white. Sometimes one plant will have several colors on a single leaf. It is potted in March and brought into growth at about 75°F (25°C) in high humidity. Start feeding when leaves first appear. Once the leaves are growing well, the plant may keep for months, even in a cool living room or hall. From the end of September on, gradually decrease the water supply until all the foliage has died. Remove dead foliage as it withers. The tuber may spend the winter either in or out of the pot at a temperature of 50° to 60°F (10° to 16°C). The variety illustrated is *Caladium bicolor* 'Candidum.' Tuber clumps may be split when repotting in spring. Watch for aphids, mealybugs, red spiders, scale and thrips.

- Somewhat shady position.
- Warm: 60° to 70°F (16° to 20°C) at night.
- Water freely in spring and summer, then gradually decrease. Needs good drainage.
- Fairly high humidity. Mist frequently with tepid water.
- 1 part sand, 1 part standard potting mix and 2 parts peat moss. Feed weekly from April to September with mild liquid fertilizer.

Calathea

Peacock Plant
Rattlesnake Plant

The three best known of the approximately 150 *Calathea* species are illustrated here. *Calathea ornata*, above, has striped leaves. The stripes turn ivory in more mature plants. In the center is *Calathea makoyana*, sometimes called the Peacock Plant because of the feathery design of the olive-green stripes and ovals on a paler green background. The lancet-shaped leaves of *Calathea lancifolia*, below left, are regularly marked with alternate large and small dark green blotches. In many of these plants the underside of the leaves are in various shades of red. The other common varieties not shown are *Calathea insignis*, called the Rattle-snake Plant which has long yellow-green leaves with olive-green stripes, and *Calathea zebrina*, or Zebra Plant, which has alternating bars of olive-green and pale yellow.

Calathea does best in shallow pots or deep pots partly filled with rocks. The best soil to use is a coarse and porous mixture high in humus. Good drainage is essential. Wash leaves monthly with room-temperature water to clear pores. Do not use oils. Remove withered leaves.

The high humidity required for a healthy plant creates a problem. Daily spraying with tepid water helps a little but it is not enough. The pot may also be placed above a bowl filled with water to create a damp environment, but it should not stand in water. A more expensive solution is the purchase of a humidifier. As the soil is exhausted fairly rapidly, it is advisable to repot once a year in June or July. For the same reason the plant should be fed every two weeks with a mild liquid fertilizer.

Late June is the best time for propagation. This may be done in two ways: by division or from tip cuttings. To encourage rooting, the temperature is best kept at about 65°F (17°C). Like the pot-soil, the growing medium must be coarse and porous. Pests to watch for include aphids, mealy-bugs, red spider, scale and thrips.

Requires a fair amount of shade. No direct sun. Does well in artificial light.

Warm: 60° to 70°F (16° to 20°C) at night. Not below 60° to 65°F (16° to 18°C) in winter.

Water moderately, using tepid, soft water. The soil-ball must not dry out but should not be soggy.

High humidity, especially when the leaves appear. Mist often with tepid, soft water.

1 part peat moss, 1 part perlite and 2 parts standard potting mix. Feed every 2 weeks from March to October with mild liquid fertilizer.

Calceolaria

Pocket Plant
Slipper Flower

The *Calceolaria* hybrid most generally available is *Calceolaria herbeohybrida* 'Multiflora Nana.' Because of its attractive coloring and unusual pouch-shaped flowers, it is a popular house plant. Nevertheless it is somewhat demanding. It should never be put in too warm an environment or in a draft, for this will invite aphids. It requires a slightly humid atmosphere, but the soil must not be too damp and it must be kept out of the sun. Pinch back to maintain shape and encourage blooming. If all these demands are met the plant will give pleasure for a long time but it should be regarded as an annual. Propagation is from seed in July to August, which requires a cool greenhouse, or from cuttings. Watch for aphids, red spiders, slugs or snails, and whiteflies. Treat by spraying with pyrethrum or rotenone. Gray mold can also be a problem Water on the leaves may cause crown rot.

☀ Well-lit position, out of the sun.

🌡 Cold: 35° to 50°F (3° to 10°C) at night.

💧 Reasonably moist soil. Water regularly and do not let the soil-ball dry out.

☷ Fairly high humidity required. Mist often but not directly on blossoms.

▼ Standard potting mix. Feed monthly with mild liquid fertilizer except during blooming.

Callistemon

Bottle Brush

Callistemon citrinus, formerly called *Callistemon lanceolatus*, is one of the few species whose unusual blossom occurs at an early stage in its development. The red color is provided by the stamens. Because it is so easy to care for it is rather surprising that *Callistemon* is rarely grown in the living room. In areas with moderate climates it is grown outside as a large bush or even a hedge.

It is best to repot this plant in early March. For successful flowering it requires fresh air and light. Prune drastically in spring to encourage a bushy form. Afterward give a lime-free feed every two weeks until August. Occasional doses of iron will help keep the plant healthy.

☀ Well-lit location; place outdoors in summer.

🌡 Moderate: 50° to 60°F (10° to 16°C) at night. Keep cool in winter 40° to 45°F (5° to 8°C).

💧 Water moderately using soft water.

☷ Tolerates dry air.

▼ Standard potting mix with peat moss. Soil must be lime-free. Feed every 2 weeks from March to August with mild liquid fertilizer.

Camellia

Japonica

This plant dislikes changes in temperature, irregular watering or being moved. Even a change in humidity can cause it to drop its buds. Until the buds open, keep at a maximum temperature of 45°F (12°C); then it may be kept a little warmer. After flowering keep about 45° to 50°F (6° to 10°C). The photograph shows *Camellia japonica* 'Chandleri Elegans,' the strongest variety. Buds appear in clusters. Removing all but one will increase the size of the flower. Propagation is from stem cuttings in January or February. Use a hormone rooting powder. Camellias last many years and can be grown as a shrub or small tree. Repot if necessary after flowering. Watch for aphids, mealybugs, mites and scale. Yellow leaves with green veins mean too little acidity in the soil.

- Light shade; in summer in the garden or on the balcony.
- Cold: 40° to 50°F (5° to 10°C) at night. This plant is very sensitive to temperature variations.
- Water fairly freely using tepid water. Needs good drainage.
- Average humidity. Mist often with tepid water.
- Acid mixture with pH 4.5 to 5.5. Equal parts standard potting mix, peat moss and humus. Feed monthly in spring and summer with special acid fertilizer.

Campanula

Bell Flower
Falling Stars

This is an old-fashioned house plant. It is particularly appropriate for adding color to a rock garden or for a hanging pot or basket. The varieties most generally available are the white *Campanula isophylla* 'Alba' and the blue 'Mayi.'

Its cultivation is relatively simple. In sunny weather, water frequently to avoid yellowing of the leaves. Remove faded flowers. In winter, place in a cool room after removing the foliage. Water very sparingly. Water more freely and feed the plant in spring when it starts into growth. Insufficiently rich soil leads to yellowing foliage. 'Mayi' is more difficult to raise than 'Alba,' and requires more warmth.

Propagating from cuttings is child's play. Use 2 to 4-inch (5 to 10cm) long tip shoots. Watch for mealybugs, scale, slugs or snails, and whiteflies.

- Well-lit spot, keep out of the sun.
- Cool to moderate: 40° to 55°F (5° to 12°C) at night. Very sensitive to frost.
- Maintain constant moisture; soil-ball must not dry out. Needs good drainage.
- Moderate humidity. Mist occasionally.
- 1 part standard potting mix, 1 part sand and 2 parts peat moss. Feed weekly with mild liquid fertilizer.

Canna

Originally *Canna* was a garden plant. It grew fairly tall, especially in southern regions, and was consequently unsuitable for indoors. Dwarf forms of *Canna indica* have now been developed, such as 'Lucifer,' on the left in the photograph. 'Perkeo' is all red and 'Puck', on the right, is yellow. They will reach a height of 4 feet (120cm). An added advantage is the fact that they need not be screened from even the brightest sun. However, the large surface area of the foliage means that a great deal of moisture is evaporated in direct sunlight and generous watering is essential. Repot in spring in fresh soil. Propagation is from offsets of the rootstock—a job for a knowledgeable amateur—or from seed.

- Requires plenty of light and sun.
- Warm: 60° to 70°F (16° to 20° at night. Keep in a moderately warm room in winter.
- Water moderately; liberally in hot weather.
- Tolerant of normal room conditions. Enjoys fresh air from time to time.
- Standard potting mix. Feed weekly with mild liquid fertilizer.

Capsicum

Christmas Pepper
Ornamental Pepper

This plant is usually sold with the fruit already formed and ready to ripen, which means it is in the last stage of its one-year life. After it drops its fruit, which is edible but very hot, it will not reproduce again indoors. If you want to see the *Capsicum annuum*, shown here, in all its phases, sow it under glass in February or March. Be sure to maintain an adequate temperature. After a month the little plants may be placed in their own pots where they will eventually reach a height of 12 inches (18cm). A sunny position with a temperature of about 60°F (15°C) and moderately moist soil will ensure early flowering. White flowers are followed by red fruit. Sunshine is needed to ripen the fruit, but too much heat will cause it to drop. Wash leaves occasionally. Watch for whiteflies.

- If possible in a sunny spot, but preferably no sun between 10 a.m. and 5 p.m.
- Moderate: 50° to 60°F (10° to 16°C) at night. In summer the plants may be placed outdoors.
- Requires fairly moist soil, water regularly.
- Reasonably tolerant of dry air.
- Standard potting mix. Feed monthly with mild liquid fertilizer. Cease when fruit appears.

Catharanthus

Madagascar Periwinkle
Vinca Rosea

The *Catharanthus* genus occurs wild from Java to Brazil. Of the five species, only *Catharanthus roseus*, a native of Madagascar, is available for use as a house plant. The oval leaves have central white veins. The 'Alba' variety illustrated here produces red-centered, white flowers. Another species has rose-red flowers. If you study the photograph carefully, you will notice the plant's resemblance to the well-known garden plant *Vinca minor* or Periwinkle. It is for that reason that the *Catharanthus* was formerly called *Vinca rosea*. This shrubby plant is usually grown from seed as an annual but it may also be grown successfully from cuttings.

- Requires a well-lit, sunny position.
- Moderate: 50° to 60°F (10° to 16°C) at night. In order to be able to take cuttings, keep at 50° to 70°F (10° to 20°C) in winter.
- Keep the soil moderately damp. Water regularly to ensure that the soil-ball does not dry out.
- Tolerant of normal living room conditions.
- Standard potting mix.

Cattleya

Easter Orchid
Christmas Orchid

This Brazilian epiphitic orchid is commonly used in corsages. Some hybrids bloom three times a year. *Cattleya* develops a zig-zag rhizome along the surface of the soil. Roots develop on the lower side and stems from the top. The swollen lower part of the stem is called a *pseudobulb*. After flowers fade the plant rests. Do not feed or overwater. Begin normal feeding and watering when growth resumes. When the rhizome has grown across the pot, it should be divided, each piece containing at least four pseudobulbs. Plant them on the surface of the growing medium with the oldest pseudobulb next to the edge of the pot. The pot should be 1/3 full of rocks and broken pottery to insure proper drainage. These plants need support. *Cattleya labiata*, *C. trianae*, the Christmas orchid, or *C. gastrelliana*, the Easter orchid, are all good choices for indoors.

- Needs bright light, but not direct sun.
- Moderate: 50° to 60°F (10° to 16°C) at night.
- Keep growing medium moist during growing period. Needs good drainage.
- Prefers high humidity.
- Commercial orchid mix. Feed monthly during growing season with special orchid fertilizer.

Cephalocereus

Old Man Cactus

Even the smallest seedlings of *Cephalocereus senilis*, or Old Man Cactus, are white-haired. To keep the hair clean, place some pebbles on the soil. If the hair becomes matted, wash it gently with a weak solution of soap and water, and comb it out. Be sure to rinse thoroughly.

The Old Man grows very slowly. Inadequate humidity in summer frequently leads to an attack by mealybugs and red spiders. The Old Man will flower only in its native habitat, for the pink flowers will not appear until the cactus reaches a height of 20 feet (6m) or more. It can be grown from seed, thinly covered in finely sifted sandy soil.

- Requires plenty of sun.
- Warm: 60° to 70°F (16° to 20°C) at night. In winter the temperature must not drop below 60°F (16°C).
- Water moderately in summer; keep dry in winter.
- Requires somewhat humid atmosphere. In summer occasional misting advisable, but do not spray the plant itself.
- Cactus potting mix. Use special cactus fertilizer every two weeks.

Cereus

Hedge Cactus

The best known species, *Cereus peruvianus* shown in the center of this photo, comes from the southeastern regions of South America and is extremely vigorous. To the right you see the 'Monstrosus' variety. Its strange shape is caused by a disturbance in the growing point which leads to the constant production of new tips. The cactus shown on the left is *Cereus neotetragonus*.

Most *Cereus* species flower at an advanced age but in *Cereus chalybaeus* flowers may be produced by relatively young plants whey they are about 20 inches (50cm) tall.

Propagation is from cuttings which should be dried before planting, or from seed.

- A well-lit, sunny position to induce growth.
- Warm: 60° to 70°F (16° to 20°C) at night. Minimum of 40°F (3°C) in winter.
- Water sparingly. Spray the plant occasionally to remove dust and clear pores.
- Low humidity is acceptable.
- Cactus potting mix.

Ceropegia

Rosary Vine
String of Hearts

This small succulent is an ideal house plant. It grows fast and is excellent for a hanging basket. *Ceropegia woodii*, shown here, has tiny purple flowers.

In thriving plants, small bulb-like swellings called *corms* or *bulbils* develop in the angle between the stems and the marbled fleshy leaves. These may be used to grow new plants. Ordinary cuttings will also root readily if the cut surface is first allowed to dry. Plants may be grown from seed as well.

In winter this plant will sometimes become dormant and look wilted. Don't worry. Withhold water until new growth appears and the plant will continue to thrive. Pinch back stems to near the soil level to encourage new growth. Prune straggly stems. Watch for mites.

- Tolerates both sun and semi-shade.
- Moderate: 60° to 70°F (10° to 16°C) at night; keep cool in winter, although it may be left in the living room.
- Water sparingly when soil is dry. Needs good drainage.
- Very tolerant of dry air.
- Equal parts standard potting mix and coarse sand. Fertilize every two weeks with mild liquid fertilizer.

Chamaecereus

Peanut Cactus

This dwarf cactus is cultivated on a large scale. Properly cared for, it will flower profusely in spring or summer. For up to a week the scarlet flowers of *Chamaecereus silverstrii*, shown here, will close at night and reopen in the morning.

To propagate this plant break off a section and allow the wound to dry. Then set the cutting in a sandy soil mixture. It will root fairly easily. Growing from seed also presents few problems.

Repotting is particularly difficult because the runners are very fragile.

- Good light but not too much sun.
- Moderate: 60° to 70°F (10° to 16°C) at night. Keep cool in winter. It will even tolerate frost.
- Water regularly, but sparingly in summer. Keep dry in winter.
- Low humidity.
- Cactus potting mix.

Chamaedorea
Parlor Palm

The popularity of *Chamaedorea elegans* or Parlor Palm, shown here, is due in part to its interesting arrangement of leaves. It also produces small yellow berries. The 'Bella' strain is the smallest, growing to 3 to 4 feet (1m). Another species, *Chamaedorea costaricana*, has lacy leaves and grows in a clump to 6 feet (2m). Propagation is by division, but rooting may present problems. Germinating seeds takes a long time because the seeds are very hard. For the first two years keep the seedlings in a shady, humid and warm environment. The foliage should be rinsed regularly with soft water. Trim brown tips from fronds. Watch for mealybugs, mites, red spiders, scale and thrips.

☀ No direct sun but good light. No drafts.

🌡 Moderate: 60° to 70°F (10° to 16°C) at night. Maximum night temperature in winter: 60°F (15°C).

💧 Water liberally in summer; plunge once a week. In winter water sparingly. Needs good drainage.

💦 Moderate humidity. Spray occasionally, frequently in warm weather.

🪴 1 part peat, 1 part vermiculite and 2 parts standard potting mix. Feed monthly from March to September with a weak solution of mild liquid fertilizer.

Chamaerops
Fan Palm
European Fan Palm

This is the only palm which grows wild in Europe. *Chamaerops humilis*, shown here, may grow slowly to 16 feet (5m). In a tub in the living room it will rarely exceed 3 feet (1m) but will have a spreading form. It is not difficult to grow from seed. Young plants are potted in a loamy mixture rich in humus and kept out of direct sunlight. Soil should be pressed down, but not compacted. Within two years you will have a fine plant.

This is a hardy plant. In winter it may be placed in a relatively dark position. Be careful of its sharp spines, however. Wash the leaves monthly to clean pores. Watch for mealybugs, red spiders, scale and thrips.

☀ May be placed in a well-lit spot in summer but out of direct sun. Provide ventilation but no drafts.

🌡 Moderate: 50° to 60°F (10° to 16°C) at night. Keep cool but frost free in winter.

💧 Water freely in summer. In winter keep moderately moist. Needs good drainage.

💦 Normal humidity. In summer it may be outdoors.

🪴 1 part peat moss, 1 part vermiculite and 2 parts standard potting mix. Feed weekly from March to September with weak solution of liquid fertilizer.

Chlorophytum

Airplane Plant
Spider Plant

The variegated form *Chlorophytum comosum* 'Variegatum' shown here has an all-green relative *Chlorophytum capense*. Both are excellent for hanging baskets.

To prevent the loss of color, make sure your plant receives adequate light and not too much water or fertilizer. Your plant will not run short. Its tubers store reserve food. Cut off yellowed foliage and brown tips which will occur unless conditions are perfect. Current evidence suggests that brown tips result from chemicals in tap water. Turn the plant occasionally to obtain a more symmetrical growth. Watch for scale.

Propagation is easy. Small white flowers appear at the end of long stems. These develop into small plantlets which can be detached and potted separately. Or the plants can be divided.

- Tolerates sun as well as shade. Does well with artificial light.
- Moderate: 50° to 60°F (10° to 16°C) or warm: 60° to 70°F (16° to 20°C) at night.
- In summer, water freely; a little less in winter.
- Reasonably tolerant of dry air but enjoys being sprayed occasionally.
- Standard potting mix. Feed every 2 weeks with mild liquid fertilizer.

Chrysanthemum

Marguerite
Mum

Chrysanthemum indicum hybrids flower in fall when the days grow shorter. By adjusting artificial light, they can be made to flower at any time of the year. Also, growth is inhibited by artificial means in order to produce compact and free-flowering plants. It is best to buy compact plants with buds rather than blossoms. They will last longer. Check carefully for aphids before you buy. After flowering your mum may be planted in the garden, but there will be a period of adjusting to new conditions. Large flowered mums form a single bud at the top of their stem which must be removed to encourage side shoots which will also produce flowers. Pinch back straggly stems to encourage bloom and maintain shape. Prune after blooming and reduce water. Yellow leaves indicate too cold a location, damp soil or too cold water. Watch for aphids, thrips and whiteflies.

- Partial shade. Full sun in winter.
- Moderate: 50° to 60°F (10° to 16°C) at night. It can survive the winter at 40° to 45°F (4° to 6°C).
- Water moderately freely. Make sure the soil-ball does not dry out. Needs good drainage.
- Reasonably tolerant of dry air.
- Standard potting mix.

Cissus

There are not a great number of truly indestructible house plants. In addition to the universally known *Ficus,* the *Monstera* or Swiss Cheese Plant, and the *Sansevieria,* two such plants are illustrated here. *Cissus rhombifolia* on the right, more often referred to as *Rhoicissus* or Grape Ivy, is the stronger of the two.

Whenever I encounter a dark green foliage plant in a dark room desperately reaching for the light it is almost certain to be a *Cissus rhombifolia.* This does not mean that you should immediately transfer yours to the windowsill. No need to overdo it. It enjoys moderate temperatures, but it will adapt. This species may even flower, though rather inconspicuously. Pinch it back to maintain its shape.

The common *Cissus antarctica* in the center is slightly less hardy. It produces large, undivided foliage instead of the triple leaves of the former species. This plant is less tolerant of dry air and occasionally presents problems in cultivation. For the sake of completeness I've shown *Cissus discolor* on the left, a magnificent foliage plant which is difficult to maintain.

Somewhat easier to grow is *Cissus striata,* a hanging plant with small five-pointed leaves sometimes called Miniature or Dwarf Grape Ivy. This plant should not be kept in too warm a location.

All *Cissus* species belong to the grape family and consequently prefer porous soil. They may be pruned in early spring and repotted whenever they seem too crowded. Cuttings root easily, especially with some bottom heat. Wash the leaves occasionally and watch for mealybugs, mites, scale and whiteflies. Brown spots are usually caused by too much light or water.

Other members of the family are described under *Ampelopsis, Rhoicissus* and *Tetrastigma.*

☀ Thrives in well-lit or in dark places, depending on the species.

🌡 Moderate 50° to 60°F (10° to 16°C) at night. Minimum temperature in winter, 45°F (7°C).

💧 Water moderately; keep moist. Needs good drainage.

〰 Humidity depends on species. Mist frequently.

▼ Standard potting mix. Feed every two months with mild liquid fertilizer.

Citrus

Grapefruit, Lemon, Lime, Orange

The ornamental orange shown here is called *Citrus microcarpa.* If it is bearing fruit when you buy it, place it in a well-lit but not too warm spot. A low temperature in winter will encourage flowering. Place outdoors in late May to encourage natural pollenation. Bring inside in September. Pinch to control shape and improve bloom. Watch for mealybugs, red spiders and scale. The fragrant flowers develop into fruit, but it make take a year before they attain the correct color. Propagation in spring is from tip cuttings set in bottom heat. Lemons, *Citrus limon,* limes, *Citrus aurontifolia,* and grapefruit, *Citrus paradisi,* can also be grown indoors. If space is a problem, consider dwarf varieties. *Citrofortunella mitus,* the Calamondin orange, prefers acid soil.

- ☀ Sun or light shade. In summer put plant outdoors as much as possible, either in the garden or on a balcony.

- 🌡 Moderate: 50° to 60°F (10° to 16°C) at night. Cool in winter.

- 💧 Water freely in summer. In winter the soil-ball should be kept moist. Needs good drainage.

- 💦 Moderate humidity. Mist frequently.

- 🪴 1 part humus and 2 parts standard potting mix. Crushed charcoal can help. Feed every 2 months from March to August with mild liquid fertilizer.

Cleistocactus

This is a large genus of tall, often white-haired cacti that look similar to the Old Man cactus, *Cephalocereus senilis.* This fast growing cactus may bear narrow, elongated flowers at the top. Before they do, the plant must grow to 20 to 40 inches (50 to 100cm) in height, depending on the species. Unlike most other cacti, *Cleistacactus* species do not have to be kept absolutely dry in winter. Nor do they need a temperature below 60°F (15°C). A humid atmosphere in spring and summer is more appreciated.

The plants are best grown from seed, but cuttings may be taken as well. This is a good cactus for beginning a collection. The form illustrated is *Cleistocactus strausii jujuvensis,* or Silver Torch.

- ☀ Well-lit sunny position throughout the year.

- 🌡 Warm: 60° to 70°F (16° to 20°C) at night. Keep cool in winter.

- 💧 In summer water moderately but adequately. Do not let it dry out completely in winter.

- 💦 Dislikes dry air.

- 🪴 Cactus potting mix.

Clerodendrum

Bleeding Heart
Glory Bower

Clerodendrum thomsoniae, shown here, called *Clerodendron*, is a climber best suited to a moderately warm greenhouse where the stems may grow to 13 feet (4m). By timely pruning and by pinching off the tips it may be grown into a compact house plant. If generously sprayed it will keep for a long time, especially in summer. In early December the plant is best placed in a cool position and watered very sparingly. Toward the end of February it should be drastically cut back and repotted. Blossoms only occur on new growth, so don't be afraid to prune severely. It is a very fast grower. Once the plant starts into growth it should be moved to a warmer spot. The long shoots need support and can be trained. Watch for mealybugs and red spiders.

Propagation is from stem cuttings in spring.

- A well-lit location but not in the sun.

- Moderate: 55° to 60°F (12° to 16°C) at night. In winter keep at 50° to 55°F (10° to 12°C).

- Keep constantly moist. Less water is needed in winter. Needs good drainage.

- Fairly high humidity. Spray frequently.

- Equal parts peat moss, perlite and standard potting mix. Feed every 2 weeks from March to September with mild liquid fertilizer.

Cleyera

Cleyera japonica, shown here, is sometimes called *Eurya japonica*. The green-leaved specie has white flowers and red fruits. The 'Tricolor' strain is grown for its fine foliage. It rarely flowers.

To maintain a well-shaped plant, you should occasionally remove the tips, but only after flowering. A young plant may not bloom until its third year. A change in location or incorrect temperature or watering may cause its buds to drop. Repotting is best done in spring, but this plant will bloom better if potbound. Do not forget to press the soil down well. Tall plants may need staking. Watch for aphids, mealybugs, mites and scale. *Cleyera* may be propagated from tip cuttings, which require bottom heat to root successfully.

- Keep out of sun but in good light. May be placed outdoors in summer. Place out of drafts.

- Moderate: 50° to 60°F (10° to 16°C) at night. Keep cool in winter at about 50°F (10°C).

- Water moderately using soft water. Do not let the soil-ball dry out. Needs good drainage.

- Moderate. Spray occasionally with tepid water.

- Likes some acidity. Mix 1 part perlite, 1 part standard potting mix and 2 parts peat moss. Feed every 2 weeks from January to August with mild acid fertilizer.

Clivia

Kafir Lily

The *Clivia miniata*, shown here, grows to 3 feet (1m) high and puts out clear signals when it needs care. Yellow spots on the leaves indicate either too much water or water in the heart of the plant. If the leaves split vertically it needs more sun. Mature plants bloom from December to April. Flowers are followed by red berries. If no flower stem appears, it means that you have watered too freely from October on. The soil should be kept just moist until the flower stalk reaches 6 inches (15cm); then water normally. The plant may also be moved to a slightly warmer position. *Clivia* does well with crowded roots, but it should be repotted carefully every two or three years. Propagation is by division of small plants that form at the base of the older plant or by seed. Pests to watch for are mites and scale.

- Semi-shade, may be placed outdoors, in summer.
- Moderate: 50° to 60°F (10° to 16°C) at night.
- Water fairly freely in summer but avoid stagnant water in pot. In winter keep dry.
- Moderate humidity but day air is tolerated.
- Standard potting mix with bone meal added. Feed weekly from March to September with mild liquid fertilizer.

Codiaeum

Croton
Joseph's Coat

The foliage of *Codiaeum variegatum pictum* varies from yellow or pale green to red or almost black. The plant is a native of Eastern Asia and grows to about 15 inches (30cm). It does not like to be potbound and should be repotted in March. Do not use too large a pot, however. To maintain its fine coloring it should be given adequate light and air. A sudden change in temperature or air may cause the leaves to drop or lead to mildew, red spiders, and thrips. Aphids, leaf miners, mealybugs and mites can also be problems. Regular spraying and placing the pot in a water-filled dish will help.

Propagation is from mature shoots which need a high bottom temperature to root. Rooting powder should be applied first. Root under glass or plastic at a temperature of 75° to 85°F (25° to 30°C).

- Sun or light shade. Needs good air circulation.
- Warm: 60° to 70°F (16° to 20°C) at night. 60° to 45°F (16° to 18°C) in winter.
- Keep fairly moist in spring and summer. Less in winter. The soil-ball must not be allowed to dry out, but must not be soggy.
- Beware of dry air; spray regularly.
- Standard potting mix. Feed every 2 months from March to July with mild liquid fertilizer.

49

Coelogyne

Among the 200 *Coelogyne* species, an epiphytic evergreen orchid, *Coelogyne cristata* is well suited for indoors. Other species which may be grown indoors are *Coelogyne dayana, C. massangeana* and *C. pandurata*. All these orchids have a dormant season in winter lasting six to eight weeks during which the night temperature should not drop below 55°F (14°C). In *Coelogyne cristata*, shown here, the flowers appear from January to April. After flowering, the plants may be repotted either in special orchid baskets or in pots filled to a third of their depth with rocks or pieces of broken pottery. Watch for aphids, mealybugs, scale, slugs and snails, and thrips. Orange dust on the leaves is rust. Treat with a fungicide. Gray mold on leaves is caused by drops of water.

- Semi-shade or filtered light.
- Warm: 60° to 70°F (16° to 20°C) at night. In winter 55° to 60°F (14° to 16°C) is adequate.
- Water fairly freely, using demineralized soft water. Water sparingly in winter dormancy.
- High humidity. Spraying can stain flowers.
- Special orchid mixture of fir bark. Fertilize every 2 weeks during the growing season with mild liquid fertilizer.

Coleus

Flame Nettle
Painted Leaf Plant

Native to tropical Africa, *Coleus* grows rapidly and has few requirements. The multicolored Blumei hybrids shown here have an upright form and larger leaves than *Coleus pumilus* with its hanging stems. *Coleus* loses color in winter and may drop its leaves. Propagate in spring from tip shoots rooted in water in a dark bottle, in moist vermiculite or from seed in February or March. Prune to control size and increase branching. Flowers should be removed in fall. *Coleus* may be attacked by mealybugs, scale, slugs or snails, and whiteflies. Rinse leaves with tepid water to control pests and clear pores. If pests get out of control, the whole plant can be plunged in a weak solution of insecticide. Older plants often develop root gall through no failure in care. It is best to replace the plant.

- Needs balanced light. Either too much sun or shade will cause fading. Does well in artificial light.
- Moderately warm: 55° to 65°F (14° to 18°C) at night.
- In summer water freely using soft water, pH 4 to 4.5. Keep moist. Needs good drainage.
- Reasonably high humidity. Spray frequently, particularly when the temperature is high.
- 1 part peat moss, 1 part perlite and 2 parts standard potting mix. Feed every 2 weeks with mild liquid fertilizer.

Columnea

Both *Columnea microphylla,* the variegated form shown in the lower photograph, and *Columnea hirta,* upper photo, are epiphytes from Costa Rica and are good hanging-basket plants. They prefer a coarse soil, such as African Violet mix or a mixture of two parts standard potting mix and one part sphagnum moss with a few pieces of charcoal. In the flowering season be generous with organic liquid fertilizer. Flowering will be more profuse if you keep the plant in a cool environment and water more sparingly in winter. Plants sometimes reach a length of 3 feet (1m). They do not mind being potbound.

After flowering the plant must be pruned because *Columnea* only flowers on new shoots. The shape of the plant and the distribution of the flowers will also benefit and, as an extra bonus, cuttings may be planted. This is best done from March to May. The cuttings should be about 4 inches (10cm) in length. Place them in a mixture of equal parts peat and sand and keep them at a minimum temperature of 70°F (20°C) until they are well rooted. This takes two to three weeks. Transfer in groups of three or four to fairly shallow pots. Once the little plants are growing well, pinch out the tips to encourage bushy growth. Ensure high humidity by using the stone and tray method or a humidifier. These plants are prone to root or crown rot from overwatering. Brown spots on the leaves are caused by misting directly on them. Pests include leaf miners, mealybugs and mites.

Among the 200 *Columnea* species, which are clearly related to *Aeschynanthus,* the following are most suited to living room cultivation. *Columnea banksii* has scarlet, two-lipped flowers and drooping or creeping stems with small oval leaves. It flowers in spring. *Columnea gloriosa* has trailing stems with rounded oval hairy leaves ranging from green to reddish-brown, and orange-red flowers with a yellow throat. *Columnea kewensis* is semierect in form but the stems will droop at a later stage. *Columnea microphylla* is a smaller species and *Columnea schiedeana* is a climber.

- Hang or place in slight shade out of any drafts. Does well in artificial light.

- Warm: 60° to 70°F (16° to 20°C) at night. In autumn keep at 50° to 60°F (10° to 15°C). In winter at 60° to 65°F (15° to 18°C).

- Keep the soil moist, using tepid soft water.

- Constant, fairly high humidity. Spray often but not directly on leaves.

- Coarse mixture of 2 parts standard potting mix and 1 part sphagnum moss. Feed every two weeks with mild liquid fertilizer from January to October.

Cordyline

This plant with its magnificent foliage must be kept warm and moist. Dropping foliage and yellowing leaf-tips indicate too low humidity. The *Cordyline terminalis,* shown here, is among the most delicate species. Cordyline likes being potbound but can be repotted every second or third year in April or May. When a *Cordyline* loses its lower leaves it may be air-layered. New plants may be grown from tip cuttings or stem sections with at least three eyes. These sections, called *Ti logs,* are often imported from Hawaii. Dip in rooting powder and keep the bottom temperature at 80° to 85°F (26° to 30°C). It can also be grown from seed sown in February. Do not spray leaves because they will spot. Oiling leaves should also be avoided. Watch for aphids, mealybugs, scale and thrips.

- Fairly good light but will tolerate shade. Likes artificial light.
- Warm: 60° to 70°F (16° to 20°C) at night. Temperature in winter 40° to 45°F (4° to 7°C).
- Soil-ball must be neither too dry nor too wet. Less water is needed in winter. Needs good drainage.
- Constant, high humidity essential.
- Standard potting mix. Feed every two months with mild liquid fertilizer.

Cotyledon

This genus of succulents embraces about 50 species and can be divided into evergreen and deciduous groups. Among the latter are *Cotyledon paniculata* and *Cotyledon reticulata,* which must be kept dry until the first small leaves appear in late fall. Of the other group *Cotyledon orbiculata* and *Cotyledon undulata,* shown here, are the best known species. Both have clustered leaves and orange-red flowers, but *Cotyledon orbiculata* grows much larger.

A good soil mixture may be obtained by combining equal parts of sand, loam and leaf mold. Propagation is from cuttings in summer or from seed.

- Sunny position.
- Warm: 60° to 70°F (16° to 20°C) at night. Temperature in winter about 50°F (10°C).
- Water sparingly. The leaves must not get wet. Deciduous species must be kept dry when the leaves have dropped.
- Low humidity is sufficient.
- Equal parts sand, loam and leaf mold.

Crassula

Chinese Rubber Plant
Jade Plant

This genus comprises 300 succulents, most of which originate in the Cape Province of South Africa. Like most other succulents, they require a sunny position, low humidity, little water and a loamy, porous soil mixture. A low temperature in winter prevents lanky growth, attacks by aphids and loss of foliage. Also watch for mealybugs, red spiders, scale and thrips. Do not treat with malathion as it will injure or even kill this plant. Wash the leaves with a mild soapy solution instead.

Propagation is from tip or leaf cuttings. Always allow the cutting to dry a little in the shade before rooting it in a mixture of equal parts of sand and peat. New plants may also be grown from seed which will usually germinate in two weeks. Repot in March when the plant puts out new shoots. Standard potting mix is good but special cactus mixture is suitable as well. Crussula likes being pot-bound. Foliage should be wiped with a sponge about once a month but be careful because water will spot leaves. Do not use oils or leaf shiners. Remove any dried leaves.

The upper photograph shows *Crassula portulacea* on the left, which has stumpy, shiny green leaves, branches freely and may grow to a height of 3 feet (1m). It rarely flowers. *Crassula lycopodioides*, which grows to about 10 inches (25cm) and has small white flowers, is in the middle. *Crassula crenulata* on the right is similar. Its red flowers form clusters.

On the left in the lower photograph you see *Crassula perforata* with gray-green triangular opposite-growing leaves joined at the bottom. The flowers are yellow, 1 to 2-1/2 inches (3 to 6cm) in length. In the background on the right is *Crassula rotundifolia* which, as the name indicates, has circular leaves. They are gray-green in color, often merging into pink along the margin. The flowers are yellow. In the foreground on the right is *Crassula marginalis rubra.* It is very suitable for hanging because of its drooping stems. This species has small, heart-shaped leaves, slightly reddish in color. The small white flowers provide added decoration.

- ☼ Needs full sun; in late May it may be placed outside. Likes artificial light.

- 🌡 Warm: 50° to 60°F (10° to 16°C) at night. A temperature of 45° to 55°F (6° to 12°C) in winter encourages flowering.

- 🪣 Water sparingly throughout the year, in winter keep practically dry but do not let the plant shrink. Needs good drainage.

- 〰 Low humidity.

- 🪴 Standard potting mix. Feed every 2 weeks with mild liquid fertilizer from February to October.

Crocus

Although they are widely grown in gardens, it is not difficult to bring crocuses into flower indoors. Suitable bulbs are potted in October and, if possible, buried in a spot in the garden which will not be too frozen in January. Protect the pots with dead leaves or straw. A cool cellar will do equally well, provided the bulbs are kept in total darkness. During this period water sparingly. As soon as the buds can be felt, the containers may be brought into the light. Be sure not to place them in too warm a place and keep the atmosphere moist by spraying or by half-covering the emerging plants with a plastic bag. Buds may not open if soil dries out. Too high a temperature will shorten flowering period. After the bloom, old bulbs can be discarded or planted outdoors. This process is called *forcing* and the bulbs will probably not produce additional flowers for several years.

- Semi-shade.
- Cool: 35° to 50°F (3° to 10°C) at night. Higher temperatures shorten bloom.
- Water moderately. Too much water may cause root rot but do not let soil dry out.
- Moderate humidity. Mist from time to time but not directly on blossoms.
- Mix of 1 part perlite and 2 parts standard potting mix.

Crossandra   Firecracker Plant

This evergreen native of India grows up to 18 inches (45cm) tall in a 5-inch pot. Without adequate humidity, this is a difficult plant to grow. In combination with other plants in a large container, it presents few problems. Too much sun will cause the leaves to roll up. Overwatering will cause yellow leaves and water that is too cold may cause brown spots on the lower leaves. In spring, prune to shape the plant. It should be placed in a slightly cooler spot and given less water in the winter dormant season. It is best to root cuttings in spring with bottom heat. Place a few together in one pot. Repot when they become potbound. Watch for mealybugs, mites, red spiders, scale and whiteflies. Shown here is *Crossandra infundibuliformis*, which means funnel-shaped.

- Semi-shade in summer. Good light in winter, but not in full sun. Avoid drafts.
- Warm: 60° to 70°F (16° to 20°C) at night. In winter the temperature must not drop below 55°F (12°C).
- Water freely in the growing season, using soft room-temperature water.
- High humidity is essential. Mist frequently.
- Equal parts sand, peat moss and standard potting mix. Feed every 2 weeks with mild liquid fertilizer.

Cryptanthus

Earth Star

The compact multi-colored plants illustrated on this page are all bromeliads, rosette-shaped plants which die after flowering. In these plants the flowers are inconspicuous. As a rule, numerous new rosettes develop next to the old one so that it is hardly noticeable when the plant is dying.

A heated greenhouse is almost essential to keep these plants in good condition for several years. But if they are kept out of the sun, they will keep successfully in the living room for quite a long time, especially in summer when the heating is off. It is advisable to combine several plants in a shallow pottery bowl.

The upper photograph shows *Cryptanthus acaulis* on the left and the very striking *Cryptanthus bromelioides* 'Tricolor' on the right. Kept in good light, some varieties will produce pink foliage. *Cryptanthus bivittatus* is shown on the left in the lower photo. On the right is *Cryptanthus zonatus* 'Zebrinus' with its unusual markings. When buying one of the latter, search until you find a good specimen. Sometimes the markings will be blurred as a result of inadequate light.

Although most bromeliads are found growing on the branches of trees in the wild, *Cryptanthus* may be found at ground level as well. Because of this, normal potting mix may be added to the special bromeliad or orchid mix. It does not mind too much if it is temporarily kept dry. In winter it may be watered even more sparingly than in summer and from time to time put a little foliage fertilizer in the spray, but do not feed directly to roots.

Propagation is by removing young rosettes together with some roots and planting them in the soil mix below.

🌣 Slightly shady position.

🌡 Warm: 60° to 70°F (16° to 20°C) at night. High temeparture in winter, 70° to 75°F (20° to 22°C).

💧 Water very sparingly in funnel. Do not allow the soil-ball to dry out.

💦 High humidity is required. Mist frequently.

🪴 Porous mixture, rich in humus. Orchid or bromeliad potting mix, or fir bark mixture work well.

Ctenanthe

This cheerful foliage plant has proved to be fairly hardy and has therefore become more in demand in recent years. It is particularly suitable for plant containers in a warm room because the other plants keep the air somewhat more humid. Plenty of light is desirable to maintain the foliage marking, though less light will be tolerated. *Ctenanthe,* usually pronounced 'Stenanthe' develops a spreading root system and therefore does best in shallow containers or in a garden. It is propagated from stem cuttings. The species illustrated is *Ctenanthe lubbersiana. Ctenanthe oppenheimiana* 'Variagata' has more pointed leaves and very clear markings.

- Semi-shade.
- Warm: 60° to 70°F (16° to 20°C) at night. In winter a daytime temperature of 65° to 70°F (18° to 20°C) is sufficient.
- Keep moderately moist, using soft water, pH 4.5.
- Spray regularly to keep the air humid.
- Leaf mold mixed with peat. Fertilize regularly.

Cuphea
Cigar Plant

Cuphea ignea, a plant with long-lasting, bright red tubular flowers with black tips, is usually grown from seed and brought to market in full flower. It may be placed outside in the sun in summer. It makes a neat shrub even in a small pot.

If you want to keep a plant through the winter, it must be kept cool and watered very sparingly. It should be repotted in spring. In February or March cuttings may be rooted in bottom heat and these will soon develop into mature plants. Place a few together in a pot. As a rule the mother plant will not flower as well as the new plants. Pinch back to encourage blooming and a compact shape. Watch for mealybugs, mites and scale.

- Well-lit, sunny spot. This plant enjoys fresh air.
- Moderate: 50° to 60°F (10° to 16°C) at night. Keep cool but frost free in winter.
- Maintain constant moisture. Mist frequently.
- Normal living room atmosphere is sufficiently humid.
- Standard potting mix. Feed monthly with mild liquid fertilizer.

Cyclamen

Cyclamen is a common gift plant from September to April. It should always be kept in a cool environment. If it is suddenly transferred to a warm room the leaves will quickly droop. No amount of watering will counteract this. In fact, excess moisture may cause the bud to rot and kill the plant.

The secret is to keep the temperature at 50° to 60°F (10° to 16°C) and to pour tepid water into the saucer beneath the pot every other day, removing the excess after 15 minutes. If your house has single-glazed windows, the temperature near a north-facing window will be approximately right in November, provided you keep the plant out of the draft from central heating. Faded blossoms should be removed. If the foliage droops, either because of the temperature or through lack of water, plunge the plant immediately. When you water regularly, add water at the edge of the pot. Do not pour directly on the plant.

It is perfectly possible to keep a cyclamen from year to year. After flowering, which is usually finished by late spring, decrease the water supply until all the leaves have faded. Leave in the pot for about a month and then repot the bud in a slightly larger pot with fresh potting mix; adding a little clay helps. Water sparingly to bring the bud into growth and be sure to keep cool. Occasionally give your plant some fertilizer.

In summer the cyclamen may be grown in a sheltered, shady spot in the garden, but beware of night frost. Watch for aphids, mealybugs, and whiteflies. There is also a mite known as the Cyclamen mite to beware of. If they appear, discard the plant.

The upper photograph shows pink and red forms of *Cyclamen persicum*. Both are commonly available. Some strains have fringed flower petals. Below you see a small-flowered, fragrant cyclamen with a very natural appearance.

Cyclamens may be grown from seed under glass, at a temperature of 60° to 70°F (15° to 20°C). It will take almost 15 months before flowers appear.

Some shade is required. Bright sunlight makes them droop quickly. Keep away from drafts.

Cold: 35° to 50°F (3° to 10°C) at night.

During the flowering season water fairly freely using soft, tepid water. Needs good drainage.

Fairly high humidity. Leaves should be sprayed frequently.

Mix 1 part perlite and 2 parts standard potting mix. Feed weekly with mild liquid fertilizer from October to April.

Cyperus

Umbrella Plant

Fine large specimens of the umbrella plant are greatly in demand because the plant is very hardy as well as decorative. Most species are not very demanding in regard to light and temperature. As far as watering is concerned, the rule is always to keep the roots soaking wet. Other plants would suffer, but the *Cyperus* thrives in water. The best known species is *Cyperus alternifolius* which grows to 3 to 5 feet (1 to 1.5m). Its shape resembles narrow-leaved 'umbrellas' on tall stems. It rarely flowers. *Cyperus alternifolius gracilis*, shown on the left, is very similar but smaller; it rarely exceeds 16 inches (40cm) in height.

The plant shown on the right in the photograph is *Cyperus diffusus*, a low-growing species with fairly wide leaves. It flowers readily. The most decorative species, which is also the most difficult to grow, is the Paper Reed, *Cyperus papyrus*, from which the ancient Egyptians made their famous papyrus. This is actually a hot-house plant, found in every botanical garden. It is occasionally grown successfully indoors; the stems may then grow to 6 feet (2m). The leaves are very narrow; and it has drooping, radiating blossoms. It is best placed in a very large plant community, but it must have its own container which should be constantly filled with water.

All umbrella plants dislike excessively dry air. They should never be placed above a radiator. After planting, cover the soil with a layer of pebbles or wood chips to reduce evaporation.

Cyperus is very easily propagated. It may be divided when being repotted or cuttings may be taken. When dividing, the smaller, outer divisions will produce more vigorous plants than the older center. In fact, you can discard the center if you wish. When taking cuttings use the young tip-shoots with about 2 inches (5cm) of the stem. Cut the leaves back to half their size and root in damp sand. Old plants can be pruned down to their base and will recover vigorously. Withered roots should be removed. Watch for mealybugs, scale, slugs and snails, and whiteflies.

Slight shade. Does well in artificial light. Needs air circulation.

Moderate: 50° to 60°F (10° to 16°C) at night. In winter preferably 50° to 55°F (10° to 12°C), but may be kept in a heated room.

Permanent footbath required. Use lime-free water.

Fairly high humidity desirable. Spray often.

Mix 1 part peat moss, 1 part perlite and 2 parts standard potting mix. Feed every 2 weeks from February to October. Feed monthly in winter. Use mild liquid fertilizer.

Cyrtomium

Holly Fern

Crytomium or Holly Fern is very suitable for cool locations. In a lower temperature the air will automatically be more humid, which is what this fern needs. It can also survive with little light. The species photographed is *Crytomium falcatum*. It likes being rootbound, but when you repot do not completely cover the root ball. This is best done in February or March. Use clay pots and cut back to encourage new growth. Remove aerial roots and withered fronds if they appear. Wash fronds about once each month. Treat pests, which include aphids, mealybugs, red spiders and thrips, with soap and water. Do not use insecticides.

- Satisfied with little light.
- Moderate: 50° to 60°F (10° to 16°C) at night.
- Water freely in the growing season. In winter keep moderately moist. Lower temperatures mean less water required.
- Requires high humidity. Spray often with room temperature water.
- Mix 1 part vermiculite with 2 parts peat moss and 2 parts standard potting mix. Feed with very weak solution of liquid fertilizer.

Cytisus

Broom

Where heating engineers gained ground, the good old broom lost it, for the most favorable temperatures for this plant are between 55° to 65°F (12° to 18°C). If you have a room which always remains reasonably cool, this shrub may be kept through the winter without problems. Decrease the water supply in proportion to the lowering temperature. Flowers appear fairly early in spring. Broom may be transferred to the warm living room, but it will need frequent spraying. After flowering it can be cut back to avoid becoming straggly. It should also be repotted at that time. Propagation is from cuttings.

The plant illustrated is *Cytisus racemosus*.

- In summer a sunny spot outdoors is acceptable; in winter, a little shade.
- Cool: 40° to 50°F (3° to 10°C) at night. Must be kept cool in winter, 40° to 45°F (4° to 8°C).
- When in flower water normally. Water sparingly in winter.
- Moderate humidity.
- Standard potting mix.

Dendrobium

Some species of this fine old orchid, like *Dendrobium nobile*, may be cultivated in a living room. Most dendrobes flower in spring and require a complete rest in winter without water at about 50°F (10°C). *Dendrobium thyrsiflorum* requires a slightly higher temperature and can be watered sparingly once each month in the dormant season. There are evergreen *Dendrobes*, which keep their leaves for two or three years, and deciduous types, which shed their leaves just before flowering. Most dendrobes are remarkably free of insect problems but may develop fungus or mold. Wash leaves with water regularly. Too much light will turn leaves yellow; too little will inhibit blossoming. The form illustrated is the greenhouse plant *Dendrobium zeno ceylon* 'Glory.' For further details, consult a book on orchids.

- ☀ Requires a very well-lit position.
- 🌡 Warm: 60° to 70°F (16° to 20°C) at night. Cool in winter or warm throughout the year, depending on the species.
- 💧 Water moderately with tepid soft water.
- ⛆ Higher or lower humidity depending on the species.
- 🪴 Orchid potting mix or mix 1 part sphagnum with 2 parts fern roots or shredded fir bark.

Didymochlaena

This fern with its difficult name is fairly common. The photograph shows *Didymochlaena trunculata*, which has feathery brownish leaves and does very well in plant boxes placed in a not too warm location during winter. Be sure that the soil-ball never dries out entirely. This will cause the foliage to drop. Repot at the end of winter. Cut back a little and place the plant in a warmer spot to bring it into growth. Use plastic pots. Feed fairly generously during the growing season. Propagation is by division or from spores which appear on the underside of the fronds.

- ☀ Will thrive in a shady position.
- 🌡 Warm: 60° to 70°F (16° to 20°C) at night. Keep cool in winter 55° to 60°F (14° to 16°C).
- 💧 In the growing season water freely using soft water, pH 5.
- ⛆ In summer, spray several times a day. Do not spray in winter.
- 🪴 Standard potting mix. Feed regularly during growing season with very mild liquid fertilizer.

Dieffenbachia

Dumb Cane
Mother-In-Law Plant

These striking evergreen foliage plants originate in tropical regions of the Americas, but have adapted to the dry atmosphere of centrally heated houses. Even so, the best results are achieved by frequently spraying the foliage or raising the humidity by some other means such as a humidifier. *Dieffenbachia* does not really enjoy the warmth of our living rooms and offices.

Some confusion exists in the naming of the various species. The best known is called *Dieffenbachia seguine.* Its leaves are an elongated oval shape, 8 to 16 inches (20 to 40cm) in length, 4 to 8 inches (10 to 20 cm) wide. They are always shiny with variegated marking. Various forms are available. 'Rudolph Roehrs' is very pale yellow-green with dark margins and central veins. A hybrid called 'Arvida' or 'Exotica' has green foliage with very irregular white mottling. It is shown in the upper photograph. The biggest and thickest leaves are produced by *Dieffenbachia amoena*, shown in the lower photograph. The leaves grow up to 30 inches (80cm) in length and the plants grow to 40 inches (1m). There is also *Dieffenbachia bowmannii,* which is also green but with larger leaves. *Dieffenbachia exotica* produces green leaves with white spots and tends to stay smaller than other varieties.

NOTE: The juice of *Dieffenbachia* contains strychnine and is poisonous. Few people eat their house plants, but there are known instances of children biting into a *Dieffenbachia* and suffering severe poisoning. The sap will burn the mouth and can even paralyze the vocal cords.

These plants do well when potbound. Overwatering can cause rotting. Leaves should be washed with water once a month, and withered leaves should be removed. Do not use oil on leaves to shine them. Watch for aphids, mealybugs, red spiders, scale and thrips.

Propagation is from tip shoots rooted under glass. Bare plants may be cut back drastically or air-layered. Usually they will then put forth new shoots.

- Semi-shade, never direct sunlight.
- Warm: 60° to 70°F (16° to 20°C) at night. In winter the temperature must not drop below 60° to 65°F (15° to 18°C).
- In summer water fairly freely using soft, tepid water. Allow soil to dry out between waterings. Needs good drainage.
- Fairly humid atmosphere required throughout the year. Mist frequently.
- Standard potting mix. Feed every 2 weeks from February to October with a mild liquid fertilizer.

Dionaea

Venus Flytrap

In recent years this plant has become widely available. It is an amusing insectivore, native to North Carolina, but it is not easy to keep in good condition. *Dionaea muscipula* is actually a greenhouse plant and requires a very humid atmosphere. It is therefore best grown in a glass case, an indoor greenhouse or under a glass dome. But do not pick too dark a spot. Probably the greatest problem is that the plant must be kept cool. Although it may grow well in a warm environment, it will usually not survive for long.

The plant can be propagated by division, from leaf cuttings or from seed.

- ☀ Well-lit, sunny position. On very hot days provide some shade.
- 🌡 Cool: 40° to 50°F (3° to 10°C) at night. In winter keep cool but frost free.
- 💧 Water fairly freely. Make sure the soil-ball does not dry out.
- ≈ High humidity required.
- 🪴 Mix of sphagnum, sand and peat moss.

Dipladenia

Diplandenia is by nature a greenhouse plant and has a difficult time in the dry atmosphere of a living room. Nevertheless, a plant kept in my neighbor's living room had 20 flowers at one time, so it is worth trying. It is a vine and needs support. The most difficult problem is to provide the correct winter temperature. Spray the foliage frequently, cut back a little in spring and repot, and it may flower again. Propagate from cuttings in bottom heat and under glass.

The plant illustrated is *Diplandenia sanderi* 'Rosea,' the strongest of the hybrids. It is sometimes sold under the name *Mandevilla*.

- ☀ Requires a fair amount of light but will not tolerate direct sunlight.
- 🌡 Warm: 60° to 70°F (16° to 20°C) at night. In January and February keep a little cooler 55° to 60°F (12° to 15°C); otherwise 65°F (18°C).
- 💧 Water normally in summer, a little less in the dormant season.
- ≈ High humidity required.
- 🪴 Standard potting mix. Feed every 3 weeks during growing season with mild liquid fertilizer.

Dipteracanthus

Trailing Velvet Plant

There are innumerable small, tropical, multi-colored foliage plants which cannot live on the windowsill but are very suitable for planting in a glass case, bottle garden or window greenhouse. One of these is the *Dipteracanthus devosianus*, illustrated here. A humid atmosphere is a pre-requisite. Grow the plant in a warm environment throughout the year. In the growing season provide some nutrition and take cuttings when the plant becomes too straggly. These will root under glass in bottom heat. It is best to repot after flowering. Use a shallow pot. Pinch back stems in spring to maintain shape and improve bloom. Too much sun or too little humidity will cause the leaves to roll. Watch for red spiders and thrips. This plant is frequently sold under the name *Ruellia*. *Fittonia* is one of its well known relatives.

- Semi-shade or diffused sunlight.
- Warm: 60° to 70°F (16° to 20°C) at night.
- Water regularly: soil should be constantly moist. Needs good drainage.
- High humidity. Mist frequently.
- 1 part sharp sand, 1 part standard potting mix and 2 parts peat moss. Feed from March to September with mild liquid fertilizer.

Dizygotheca

False Aralia
Threadleaf

The photograph shows *Dizygotheca elegantissima*, with its narrow leaves, and the relatively rare *Dizygotheca veitchii*, which has wider and shorter leaves of a deeper green. Both species like bright light and some warmth. Because they require a fairly humid atmosphere, they are not likely to do well if placed on a windowsill. You might try one in an entrance hall or a corridor. Properly cared for they reach a height 3 to 5 feet (1 to 1.5m) and can last for years. Wash the foliage once a month with water. Too much or too little water will cause leaf drop, but old plants drop their lower leaves naturally. These plants like being potbound. Watch for aphids, mealybugs, red spiders, scale and thrips.

Propagation is from seed or stem cuttings.

- Well-lit, but out of direct sunlight. Does well with artificial light.
- Moderate: 50° to 60°F (10° to 16°C) at night for older plants. Slightly warmer for younger specimens. Not below 60°F (15°C) in winter.
- Water moderately, allow the soil to dry out between waterings. Needs good drainage.
- Requires a fairly humid atmosphere. Mist frequently.
- Standard potting mix. Feed every two weeks from February to October with mild liquid fertilizer.

Dracaena

Dragon Tree

The *Dracaena* species is increasingly popular because they are decorative and possess amazing powers of resistance. They are almost impossible to kill and are satisfied with little light. Larger specimens are capable of creating a very agreeable atmosphere in offices and living rooms. They may be left undisturbed for years on end.

There are numerous species, most of which have been used as house plants for nearly a century. *Dracaena deremensis,* shown in the upper photo on this page, originated in tropical Africa, where it must surely grow like a weed. Even in a dry living room it can reach 15 feet (4.5m) in height. Like most *Dracaena* species, this plant develops a strong trunk ending in a shock of leaves. In the variety 'Bausei' a broad white strip runs down the gray-green leaf. 'Janet Craig' has long, narrow green leaves and does well with little light. 'Warnecker,' the variety in the upper photo, has narrow white lines along the margins of its leaves.

Dracaena draco is also known as the Dragon Tree. Specimens a thousand years old have been found in Tenerife and other places. It will do well in the living room, but is difficult to obtain. It grows to a height of about 4 feet (1.2m) and the leaf rosettes are dark green without marking. It is easily grown from seed but grows slowly. In winter it may be kept in a cool spot, 50°F (10°C).

Dracaena fragrans shown on this page in the lower photograph, was already a popular house plant in our grandparents' day. It is sometimes called the Corn Plant. The leaves are broader and more rounded than in *Dracaena deremensis.* This species, too, is extremely hardy. 'Massangeana,' illustrated here, has a golden central stripe on a grass-green background. It can grow 6 feet (2m) tall. 'Lindenii' has golden margins on its leaves.

The plant in the lower photograph is a so-called Ti-plant. In some parts of the world these *Dracaenas* are grown on a large scale. After a few years the trunks, by then quite large, are cut down and their foliage removed. Then they are exported dry to the United States and Europe. If after several months the dry trunks, either whole or cut in sections, are planted in damp soil, they will put forth new growth. Roots develop at the bottom and within a short time, a plant several feet in height is obtained. A florist can combine two or three trunks in a good looking tub or cylinder and will be able to charge a hefty price for the arrangement. The plants are worth the expense.

Dracaena (continued)

Dracaena godseffinana, or Gold Dust Plant, shown on this page in the upper photograph, bears no resemblance to the other species. The leaves are small and mottled and do not form rosettes. This species is less well-known and is not quite as hardy. It grows to 3 feet (1m). 'Florida Beauty' is a variety that has leaves that are mostly white or yellow.

Dracaena marginata, this page, lower photograph, is a modest, narrow-leaved species and is probably the hardiest of them all. It will grow in the most unlikely dark corners, but it needs bright light to keep its color. Two or three specimens of varying height can be planted in one pot. It is sometimes called Spanish Dagger or Red-Margined Dracaena. Full-grown species can be 8 feet (2.5m) tall.

Another very strong species is *Dracaena hookeriana,* a native of South Africa; it has narrow green leaves up to 30 inches (80cm) in length. There are also variegated strains, including among others, 'Latifolia' and 'Variegata.' *Dracaena reflexa* readily develops several trunks or branches; the white-variegated strain 'Song of India' is particularly well-known.

Dracaena sanderiana was at one time very popular, but is now seen less often. The fairly small, pointed leaves grow in rosettes and are usually bright green with a pure white margin. These plants have a much more compact form than, for instance, *Dracaena deremensis* and are thus easily recognized.

Dracaena species can really be killed only by drowning or by too cold an environment. The danger of drowning is particularly great where the plant is set in a plastic pot. In some cases it is sufficient to water once every two weeks or so.

Dracaenas do not mind being potbound, but they can be repotted in spring. Wash leaves monthly with soft room-temperature water and remove withered leaves. Do not use leaf shiners. Watch for aphids, mealybugs, red spiders, scale and thrips. Cuttings can be taken from tip shoots, preferably in spring. Root them under glass, removing some or all of the leaves.

☼ Well-lit spot but no direct sun. Does well in artificial light.

🌡 Warm: 60° to 70°F (16° to 20°C) most species like to spend the winter at 60° to 65°F (16° to 18°C).

💧 The soil-ball must not dry out but it should not be too wet. Needs good drainage.

░ Moderate humidity is adequate. Mist frequently.

▼ Standard potting mix. Feed monthly from February to October with mild liquid fertilizer.

Duchesnea

Indian Strawberry

It is evident from the photograph that *Duchesnea indica* is related to the domestic strawberry, *Fragaria ananassa.* However the house plant produces yellow instead of white flowers from June on and makes an attractive hanging plant. The attractive red berries which follow are of decorative value only. The runners of this plant are reasonably winter-hardy. Given some protection, they will stand up to some frost and may be kept outdoors in winter. The mother plant rarely survives.

Propagation is from runners or seed. Sow in April in a moderately warm seedbed. Germination will follow in three to four weeks.

☀ In summer hang in good light either indoors or out. In winter move indoors.

🌡 Moderate: 50° to 60°F (10° to 16°C) at night. Prefers to be kept cool in winter 50° to 55°F (10° to 12°C) but may remain in the living room.

💧 Freely in summer, sparingly in winter.

〰 Moderate humidity.

▽ Standard potting mix.

Echeveria

Mexican Firecracker
Plush Plant

In this genus of succulents the sappy leaves usually grow in rosettes. They vary greatly in color and shape, but are nearly always beautiful. They are undemanding plants and it is therefore not surprising that they are popular.

The photograph on this page shows a flowering *Echeveria agavoides* at the rear, which is widely grown. On the left is a so-called cristate or crest-forming variety called *Echeveria agavoides* 'Cristata.' To the right you see the blue-green rosette of *Echeveria elegans*, or Mexican Snowball. Most species are easily brought into flower, provided they are kept cool in winter.

In summer *Echeveria* species may safely be placed outdoors. The color of the rosette will improve in the sun. Water reasonably freely in dry weather, but be careful with watering when the skies are cloudy. The same applies in the winter season when you should give only enough water to prevent the leaves from shriveling up. Excess moisture will rapidly cause root rot. Watch for mealybugs and scale.

The plush plant, *Echeveria pulvinata,* is one of the sturdiest varieties. Its leaf rosettes are densely covered with white hairs and their edges become reddish in cool weather. It can reach 18 inches tall

Echeveria (continued)

(45cm) and sometimes has a branching form. It produces red flowers in winter.

The photograph shows the hairy rosette of *Echeveria setosa* on the left, which flowers in May-June, and on the right, the slightly larger *Echeveria secunda* 'Pumila.'

Because of its numerous runners, the species *Echeveria carnicolor* is sometimes used as a hanging plant. Trunk-forming species which may grow to 28 inches (70cm) include *Echeveria coccinea* and *E. gibbiflora.* Propagation is by rooting young rosettes.

☀ A well-lit or sunny position throughout the year. In summer place the pot outdoors. Does well in artificial light.

🌡 Moderate: 50° to 60°F (10° to 16°C) at night. 45° to 50°F (6° to 10°C) in winter.

💧 Water sparingly. Needs good drainage.

▥ Low humidity.

▼ Cactus mixture or 1 part standard potting mix and 2 parts sharp sand. Feed monthly from April to August with mild liquid fertilizer.

Echinocactus

Barrel Cactus
Golden Ball

Echinocactus grusonii or Golden Barrel, shown here, is a native of Mexico. After several years of careful cultivation *Echinocactus grusonii* may reach 3 feet (1m) tall. To achieve this it is essential to keep the cactus fairly cool in winter; otherwise rotting may occur. In some climates it will not flower and its decorative value is then due entirely to its beautiful sharp spines. Large specimens are expensive. Propagation is from seed. Be particularly careful with young seedlings. Repot yearly to replenish soil nutrients.

☀ May be put in direct sun except in spring.

🌡 Warm: 60° to 70°F (16° to 20°C) at night. Cool in winter 45° to 50°F (8° to 10°C).

💧 Keep completely dry during the winter dormant season, but do not let plant shrivel. Water sparingly at other times. Needs good drainage.

▥ Dry living room atmosphere is excellent.

▼ Cactus mixture or 1 part standard potting mix and 2 parts sharp sand. Fertilize monthly in spring with high potassium, low nitrogen fertilizer.

Echinocereus

Rainbow Cactus

This group of small branching cacti rarely grows more than 12 inches (30cm) tall. Specimens more than two years old will produce flowers, but most of the year it is the shape and the spines that give these plants character. *Echinocereus gentryi,* shown here, has a branching form with round, columnar stems. There are also thornless and spined forms. *Echinocereus dasyacanthus,* or Rainbow Cactus, is covered with soft spines and produces yellow flowers. *E. echrenbergii* has purple-red flowers.

All-green species prefer a sunny outdoor location in summer. Hairy specimens do best kept in a greenhouse or on a windowsill. A low temperature in winter will encourage flowering. Propagation is from detached columns or from seed.

 Plenty of light and sun throughout the year; green forms outdoors in summer.

Warm: 60° to 70°F (16° to 20°C) at night. Keep cool in winter.

Keep fairly dry, expecially in winter. Use slightly alkaline water (pH 7-7.5).

Moderate humidity.

Cactus mixture or 1 part standard potting mix and 2 parts sharp sand.

Echinopsis

Easter Lily Cactus
Sea Urchin Cactus

These cacti are always globular in shape. Their flowers appear enormous in proportion to the small body of the cactus. Many hybrids are available in addition to the original botanical species. *Echinopsis mamillosa,* illustrated here, is a hybrid. The red, white or pale lilac flowers are often fragrant and usually appear at night during summer. With normal care these plants will present few problems. Good light will encourage the bloom. Make sure your plant is kept cool in winter. Propagation is from seed.

 A sunny spot preferred.

Warm: 60° to 70°F (16° to 20°C). Keep cool in winter.

Keep fairly dry throughout the year. Withhold water in winter.

Low humidity; thrives in dry air.

Cactus mixture or 1 part standard potting mix and 2 parts sharp sand. Fertilize monthly with mild liquid fertilizer.

Epiphyllum

Leaf Cactus
Orchid Cactus

These cacti have flat leaves that are scalloped and have no spines. They are not very attractive, but they produce magnificent flowers in all shades of red, purple, pink and white. They are relatively easy to grow from cuttings or seed. The roots are used mainly for holding onto trees rather than for drawing nourishment. It therefore does not require a very large pot. Staking is usually required to encourage upright growth or they can be placed in hanging containers. From late May on it is advisable to place the plants outdoors in a shady spot. Bring them indoors toward the end of September. Keep very dry from December to February. Gradually increase the watering when the first buds appear. Flowering usually occurs between February and June. Place in a cool place as soon as flowering is completed. Repot if potbound.

- Keep out of the sun but give plenty of light. In summer keep in a sheltered outdoor position.

- Moderate: 50° to 60°F (10° to 16°C) at night. Keep cool in winter at 45° to 50°F (8° to 10°C).

- Water freely using tepid water with pH 4.5 to 5. Water very little in winter. Needs good drainage.

- Average to high humidity.

- African violet mix. Feed every 2 weeks from March to September with low-nitrogen fertilizer.

Episcia

Flame Violet
Peacock Plant

These foliage plants are native to Brazil and Columbia. Their trailing form makes them excellent for hanging pots. After flowering, pruning the runners will give larger leaves and a better bloom. Overwatering is a major danger. Leaf spot disease and root rot may occur. Watch for leaf miners, mealybugs, mites and nematodes. Blackening of the leaves indicates too low a temperature. The plant should not be moved during winter dormant period. *Episcia dianthiflora,* shown here, is a good hanging plant. Some species have bronze leaves. *Episcia cupreata* has copper-colored leaves and orange-red flowers. Propagation is from runners rooted at a bottom temperature of at least 70°F (20°C) under glass or plastic.

- A shady spot but not too dark. Does well with artificial light.

- Warm: 60° to 70°F (16° to 20°C) at night. Below 55°F (12°C) will kill the plant.

- Keep the soil moist with tepid water.

- High humidity is required, especially at high temperatures. Do not spray directly on leaves.

- Mix 1 part standard potting mix, 1 part sharp sand and 2 parts peat moss. Feed every 2 weeks from April to September with mild liquid fertilizer.

Erica

Erica, or heath, used to be a very fashionable blooming house plant around Christmas. It has been replaced by Poinsettia in many cases. Nevertheless, there are a number of African species which are excellent for use in a living room or on a balcony. They are usually thrown away when they have ceased flowering, but it is perfectly possible to keep them throughout the year. The upper photograph shows *Erica gracilis*, a variety that will flower outdoors from late September for at least two months until a severe frost puts an end to it. It is also very satisfactory in a cool room.

Erica hyemalis, shown in the lower photograph, flowers from February on. The blossoms are white, salmon pink or rose-red. This plant is only suitable for indoors.

Erica willmorei, found at nurseries in spring, produces very large, tubular flowers of a magnificent cherry-red. In summer we occasionally find the lilac-flowering *Erica ventricosa.*

All the species mentioned must be given the coolest possible position in order to last. It is therefore advisable to put them in a corridor or an entrance hall, provided it is well-lit and frost free. In frost-free weather some species may do well outdoors, especially *Erica gracilis.*

If you want to keep the plants for a second season, they should be cut back a little after flowering. In May they should be planted, pot and all, in a half-shady spot in the garden. Do not forget to give sufficient water. If possible use rainwater because heath dislikes lime and tapwater is quite hard in many regions. Ordinary potting mix contains far too much chalk for these plants.

Propagation is from tip cuttings in July through August but they are not easy to grow into flowering plants.

 Well-lit to sunny location, especially in summer.

Cold: 40° to 50°F (3° to 10°C) at night. Keep cool in winter 40° to 45°F (6° to 8°C).

Water moderately with soft water, pH 4 to 4.5.

Moderate humidity.

Acid, humus soil.

Espostoa

Peruvian Old Man

This is one of the so-called 'Old Man' cacti, plants entirely covered in fine hairs as a protection against the sun. Although it looks similar to *Cephalocerous,* page 42, it can be distinguished by its sharp central spines. In its native Peru the *Espostoa lantana* shown here may grow to a height of 12 feet (4m) and the trunk will sometimes branch like a candelabra. In its native habitat pale pink flowers, 2-1/4 inches (6cm) appear at night, but indoors the plant will not flower. In the winter it requires a considerably higher temperature than other cacti and it can therefore be grown in the living room. Indoors it may grow to 3 feet (1m) in height. It is advisable to spray occasionally.

The specimen illustrated has been grafted. Forms with purplish or almost black bodies such as *Espostoa melanostele* are also available.

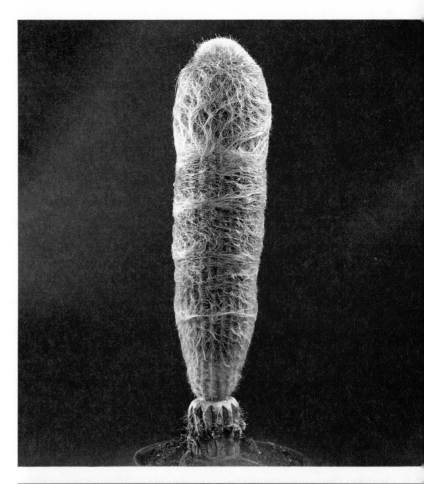

- Always in a sunny position.
- Warm: 60° to 70°F (16° to 20°C) at night. In winter the temperature should not drop below 60°F (15°C).
- In the flowering season water fairly freely. Keep dry in winter.
- Moderate to low humidity.
- Cactus mixture or chalky potting mix.

Euonymus

Spindle Tree
Winter Creeper

This plant is related to the garden shrub of the same name but the indoor species rarely produces fruit. It can reach 3 feet (1m) or it can be pruned to any size desired. This should be done in spring. It thrives only in a cool position, particularly in winter, but too high humidity can cause mildew. Wash the leaves monthly. Watch for aphids, leaf miners, mealybugs, mites, red spiders and scale. Repot in March, but do not overpot. It likes being slightly potbound. The photograph shows three variegated forms of *Euonymus japonicus,* from left to right: 'Medio-Pictus,' 'Albo-Marginatus,' and 'Microphyllus Variegatus.' Propagation is from young shoots in fall.

- Tolerates both sun and half-shade. Needs good air circulation.
- Cold: 35° to 50°F (3° to 10°C) at night. Must be kept cool in winter. Will stand up to slight night frost.
- Water regularly, a little more in early summer than during the rest of the year. Allow soil to dry between waterings. Needs good drainage.
- Moderate humidity. Spray frequently.
- Mix 1 part sand with 3 parts standard potting mix. Feed monthly from April to September with mild liquid fertilizer.

Euphorbia

Crown of Thorns

This native of Madagascar is the first *Euphorbia* to become known as a house plant. Its common name, Crown of Thorns, comes from a legend that says it once had white flowers which turned red when its thorny stems were used to make the crown of thorns Jesus wore.

It is extremely hardy and, with reasonable care, it can spread enormously and will produce beautiful red flowers each winter. Sometimes the leaves suddenly drop; when this happens, give the plant a month's rest with very little water and do not increase moisture until new leaves appear. It can be propagated from cuttings. Allow the milky juice to dry before inserting cuttings in sandy soil. **WARNING: This milky juice is poisonous and can irritate skin and eyes.**

Euphorbia milii—Crown of Thorns

☼ Prefers full sun.

🌡 Warm: 60° to 70°F (16° to 20°C) at night. Tolerates normal room temperatures even in winter.

💧 Water regularly, but sparingly, especially in winter. Needs good drainage.

⛆ Sensitive to humidity; ideal for a dry living room.

🪴 Mix 1 part peat moss, 1 part perlite and 2 parts standard potting mix. Feed weekly from March to October with mild liquid fertilizer.

Euphorbia

Poinsettia

Poinsettia's large colorful bracts are leaves, not flowers. White and pink forms are available up to 48 inches (120cm) tall. Prolong the bloom by keeping the plant at a constant temperature with plenty of light. After flowering, stop fertilizing and move to a cool, shady spot. In May, trim stems and put plant in a shady spot outdoors. In fall repot in a clay pot and bring indoors. Resume fertilizing. Limit light to ten hours a day or it will not flower. A sudden leaf-drop indicates too much water or too great a change in temperature. Watch for aphids, mealybugs, red spiders and scale. Propagate from cuttings in summer. **WARNING: The white, sticky sap is poisonous and can irritate the skin.**

Euphorbia pulcherrima—Poinsettia

☼ Half day of sun. Avoid drafts.

🌡 Moderate: 50° to 60°F (10° to 16°C) to warm: 60° to 70°F (16° to 20°C) at night. During flowering keep a little cooler.

💧 In the flowering season water fairly freely using tepid water; afterward water sparingly. Needs good drainage.

⛆ Moderate humidity; spray from time to time.

🪴 Mix 1 part vermiculite, 1 part sphagnum moss and 2 parts standard potting mix. Feed weekly from September to March with mild liquid fertilizer.

Euphorbia

Succulent Species

The *Euphorbia* genus is extremely versatile—just look at the *Euphorbia melformis* on the left which looks exactly like a cactus. Only its flowers indicate its relationship to the Poinsettia or Crown of Thorns which are discussed on the facing page. **NOTE: Most forms have a milky sap that can irritate skin. In some cases the sap is even poisonous.**

The *Euphorbia pseudocactus* on the right in the photograph, another succulent species, is still quite small. At a later stage it will branch. Large specimens are sometimes several feet in height and not only have great decorative value but are also very hardy in indoor cultivation. Their only requirements are little water and, if possible, a cool position in winter.

Euphorbia—Succulent Species

- Well-lit, sunny position. Some may be placed outdoors in summer.
- Warm: 60° to 70°F (16° to 20°C) at night. Keep cool in winter, like cacti.
- Water sparingly. Needs good drainage.
- Satisfied with low humidity.
- Sandy and loamy potting mixture.

Exacum

Arabian Violet

In summer this member of the Gentian family is frequently found in well-stocked nurseries. *Exacum affine* is an annual sown from December on. The seedlings are planted in groups of three in 4 inch (10cm) pots. Flowering commences in June and will usually last a long time if the plants are not kept in too warm a location. If you are prepared to spend a little more money, try buying several plants to fill an antique container or a jardinière. It is practically impossible to keep the plants after flowering, but cuttings can be taken from old plants and started in soil.

- Will tolerate good light but not direct sun.
- Warm: 60° to 70°F (16° to 20°C) at night.
- Water moderately but make sure the soil-ball does not dry out.
- Normal living room atmosphere is adequately humid.
- Mix 1 part standard potting mix, 1 part perlite and 2 parts peat moss. Fertilize every 2 weeks with mild liquid fertilizer.

Fatshedera

Tree Ivy
Botanical Wonder

In 1912 the French nursery of Lizé-Frères achieved a successful crossing of two genera: *Fatsia japonica* and *Hedera helix,* resulting in *Fatshedera lizei.* The 'Variegata' strain has cream-mottled foliage. *Fatshedera lizei* itself, illustrated here, is all green. In both the leaves are five-lobed.

This semi-climber can grow very tall but it needs support. It can reach 3 feet (1m) or more. To achieve bushy growth it is necessary to prune the tips several times. The tip cuttings will root readily either in water or in equal parts of sand and peat fiber with bottom heat. Sections of stems about 4 inches (10cm) long with leaves will also sprout. Once the cuttings have rooted, place them in groups of three in a pot. After a few years they may produce small pale green flowers in autumn.

Fatshedera is a hardy plant, rarely subject to disease. It is even resistant to mealybugs. Watch for aphids, red spiders, scale and thrips. It prefers being potbound. It is important to keep this plant in a cool position because heat will cause the lower leaves to drop. 'Variegata' accepts a slightly higher temperature. The leaves of both varieties will also drop almost inevitably if the plant is left standing in water after watering. Withered leaves should be removed. In winter keep in fairly good light but out of the sun. If the plant remains in your living room it should be sprayed regularly to avoid damage caused by dry air. The leaves should also be sponged about once a month to keep the pores of the leaves clear. Use clean room temperature water only.

To use the plant as ground cover, 12- to 16-inch (30-40cm) shoots should be bent down and anchored where they will soon root. Ivy may be grafted on *Fatshedera* to improve the strain. This applies particularly to variegated forms.

Satisfied with little light but will also thrive in a better-lit spot. Does well with artificial light.

Cold: 40° to 50°F (3° to 10°C) to moderate 50° to 60°F (10° to 16°C) at night. May spend the winter in the living room.

Water freely in summer, moderately in winter. Needs good drainage.

If left in the living room in winter provide adequate humidity. Mist frequently.

Standard potting mix. Feed every 2 weeks from March to October with mild liquid fertilizer.

Fatsia

Castor Oil Plant
Japanese Aralia

Fatsia japonica, shown here, is a tropical ever-green native to Japan. It can grow to as tall as 16 feet (5m) and may produce small creamy flowers and black berries in fall or winter. Remove buds to encourage foliage. Prune in February or pinch back to keep compact. Wash leaves monthly with clear water and remove withered leaves. The form 'Moseri' has a compact shape. Variegated forms such as 'Variegata' and 'Albomarginata' grow slowly and require a higher temperature, as much as 60°F (16°C) in winter.

Yellowing leaves indicate too warm and dry an environment. If the plant loses its lower leaves it may be air-layered. It can also be propagated from cuttings or seeds. Watch for aphids, mealybugs, red spiders, scale and thrips.

Tolerates shade; may be placed outdoors in summer. Does well in artificial light.

Cold: 35° to 50°F (3° to 10°C) at night. Variegated strains require a higher temperature than green forms. Temperature in winter 45° to 50°F (6° to 10°C).

Water freely in the growing season; less the rest of the year. Do not let soil-ball dry out. Needs good drainage.

Moderate humidity. Mist frequently.

Standard potting mix. Feed monthly from February to October with mild liquid fertilizer.

Faucaria

Tiger's Jaws

Of the more than 35 succulents belonging to this genus originating in South Africa, those in cultivation in this country include *Faucaria tigrina*, *Faucaria felina* and *Faucaria lupina*.

The keel-shaped toothed leaves grow in opposite pairs that are joined at the base. Despite their appearance the teeth are fragile and end in a hair-like tip. They rarely reach more than 3 inches (8cm) high. The golden-yellow flowers appear from the end of August on. These plants rot easily from over-watering. Mealybugs and scale are also hazards. The plants can be repotted once every three years in April, but it is generally best just to leave them alone. They may be divided at the same time. Seed may be sown in spring and cuttings taken from June to August. Let these dry for two days before planting.

A sunny spot is desirable. In summer the plant likes to be placed outdoors.

Moderate: 50° to 60°F (10° to 16°C) at night. 40°F (5°C) in winter.

Water moderately in summer. Keep completely dry during the dormant season. Needs excellent drainage.

Dry air very well tolerated. Do not spray.

Mix 1 part standard potting mix with 2 parts sharp sand. Do not feed.

Felicia

Aster
Blue Daisy

This delightful plant with its sky-blue flowers will bloom almost year-round and requires very little special care. Sizes range from 4 inches (10cm) to 3 feet (1m) depending on the variety. Pinch back straggly stems to maintain shape and improve bloom. Soil should be aerated monthly. Treat this plant as an annual. Seed is easily obtainable and should be sown from late January on in bowls under glass at a temperature of about 60°F (16°C). Between June and August cuttings can be taken from tip shoots. Plants grown by this method must be kept cool in winter and repotted in spring. Tall plants may require staking. The photograph shows *Felicia amelloides*.

- Requires a well-lit, sunny spot. Make sure it has adequent ventilation.
- Moderate: 50° to 60°F (10° to 16°C) at night.
- Water moderately. The soil-ball must be kept constantly moist. Needs good drainage.
- Moderate humidity.
- Equal parts standard potting mix and sand or perlite. Feed every 2 weeks with diluted mild liquid fertilizer.

Ferocactus

Barrel Cactus

These barrel-shaped cacti are known for their beautiful thick spines. The dish contains, from left to right, *Ferocactus viridenscens, F. horridus* and *F. latispinus*. Bright sunshine is essential to achieve fine coloring of the spines. The cacti should be grown near a south-facing window or in a greenhouse. Allow the soil to dry out between watering and use soft water or rainwater. The pot should have good drainage and not be too small. Toward the end of October it is better to stop watering and place the plant in a cool place, but not below 40°F (5°C). Resume watering in March after repotting the plants.

- In summer set outdoors in a warm spot in the sun. Keep cool in winter.
- Moderate: 50° to 60°F 10° to 16°C) at night. Temperature in winter about 45°F (8°C).
- Water normally in summer. Do not water in winter.
- Low humidity. Spray on unusually hot summer days.
- Special cactus mixture.

Ficus

The *Ficus* genus comprises over 900 species of immense variety: trees, shrubs, climbing plants, hanging plants and epiphytes. Some species are winter-hardy and others are not. Some are deciduous and others are evergreen. The species used as house plants originate in Australia, Southern Asia, especially in India and Indonesia, and in various parts of Africa. The fig tree, *Ficus carica,* is indigenous to Southern Europe and North Africa.

In spite of this great variety there are of course some botanical affinities. An example is the unusual flower and fruit development. The extremely insignificant flowers are found in spherical or pear-shaped stem sections. These later develop into fig-shaped fruits. Another common characteristic is the milky secretion. At one time the sap of some species was used in the production of rubber. Today other species are used and the *Ficus* is now of ornamental value only.

The *Ficus benjamina,* or Weeping Fig, in the upper photograph has a graceful appearance. The curving twigs and leaves make it look a little like a weeping willow. This evergreen *Ficus* grows very rapidly without requiring too much light. In the course of a few years it may reach the ceiling. Prune to control size and repot when necessary. It may respond to being moved by dropping leaves. This leaf drop can last for months, but the plant will survive. Wash leaves occasionally with tepid water. Remove withered leaves if they appear. Too much dryness may encourage red spiders.

Ficus deltoidea, shown in the lower photograph, is the only *Ficus* species which will produce fruit in the living room. The pseudo-fruits are yellowish-green, round and almost 1/2-inch (1cm) in diameter. As a rule, this plant remains fairly small. It has oval leaves that are pointed at the lower end and it branches rather freely. It requires fairly high humidity. The fact that *Ficuses* like these are so easy to care for is due mainly to their leathery foliage which reduces evaporation. A dry, warm atmosphere can be tolerated but the foliage should be sprayed or sponged to remove dust, particularly the variegated types.

Ficus benjamina—Weeping Fig

- Good light preferred but never in full sun. Move as little as possible.
- Warm: 60° to 70°F (16° to 20°C) at night. In the dormant season the temperature must not drop below 55°F (12°C).
- Water fairly freely in the growing season; the soil-ball must not be allowed to dry out. Water sparingly from October to March.
- Spray regularly.
- Standard potting mix. Feed monthly from March to October with mild liquid fertilizer.

Ficus (continued)

The well-known *Ficus elastica* 'Decora,' a product of specific seed selection, grows upward until the ceiling gets in the way or until you prune the top. The variety shown in the upper photograph is one of the finest variegated forms available. Remember that 'Decora' is sensitive to temperature variations. Too warm an environment in winter and too low a soil temperature can injure the plant. Yellow leaves can mean either too much or too little water. Older plants tend to have bare stems. Cut back to within five inches (12cm) of the soil to renew. Reduce watering until leaves appear. Air-layer the top to form a second plant.

The *Ficus lyrata,* also known as *Ficus pandurata* or the Fiddle-leaved Fig, is shown in the lower photo. It has enormous violin-shaped waxy leaves with a wavy edge. It is best used as a specimen plant, lit from all sides. It will maintain an erect shape 2 to 4 feet (60-120cm) tall. Other erect-growing species include *Ficus benghalensis*, which has large leaves which are hairy, especially on the underside and in young plants. It has aerial roots and may grow to a great height. *Ficus cyathistipula,* has pale green leaves up to 8 inches (20cm) in length and will branch freely. It prefers a temperature between 55° to 70°F (14° to 20°C).

Ficus aspera, also called *Ficus parcelli,* is a small shrub with large white and green marbled foliage. At a fairly early age it produces cherry-like red and white veined figs. Temperatures below 70°F (20°C) will injure this plant.

Ficus religiosa requires plenty of light and air. Its leaves are thin, long-stalked and up to 6 inches (15cm) in length. *Ficus retusa,* formerly called *Ficus nitida,* is a dense shrub whose branches grow erect then droop. It can reach a height of six feet (2cm) and needs pruning to retain its shape.

Ficus rubiginosa is an ideal plant for a greenhouse with a winter temperature of 50° to 55°F (10° to 12°C). It may be placed in a sheltered outdoor position in summer. Its blunt, shiny-green leathery leaves grow up to 4 inches (10cm) long. Twigs root easily.

Ficus elastica—Rubber Plant
Ficus lyrata—Fiddle-leaved Fig

 Good light preferred but never in full sun. Does well in artificial light.

Warm: 60° to 70°F (16° to 20°C) at night. During the resting period the temperature must not drop below 55°F (12°C).

Water moderately in growing season. Let soil dry between waterings but don't let the soil-ball dry out. Water sparingly from October to March.

Spray regularly. Wash foliage monthly with room-temperature water.

Standard potting mix. Feed twice a year with mild liquid fertilizer.

Ficus (continued)

A well-known recumbent or climbing form is called *Ficus pumila* or *Ficus repens,* shown in the upper photograph. It has small heart-shaped leaves. It is easily trained to climb a wall in place of ivy and within a short time may cover a considerable area. *Ficus radicans,* another creeper, has 2- to 4-inch-long (5-10cm) leaves. Roots are developed from the leaf buds. It is fabulous as a ground cover in planters. The plant in the lower photograph is the variegated form 'Variegata.'

A less-known species is *Ficus montana,* whose leaves resemble oak leaves. At one time it was occasionally referred to as *Ficus quercifolia.* It is suitable as a hanging plant.

Other photographs of *Ficus* plants may be found in the introductory chapters of this book. If they are properly cared for the chance of disease is slight, but watch for aphids, mealybugs, red spiders, scale and thrips. While the plants don't mind being potbound, they are fast-growing and naturally require a great deal of nourishment. Regular feeding may not be enough because the soil in the pot will eventually be poisoned by the minerals it retains. Timely repotting is therefore essential. Often *Ficus* are kept in tiny pots until they capsize and this is just asking for trouble.

It is advisable to water with tepid water. In winter the soil should be kept just moist. In the growing season feed every two weeks.

A standard potting mix is satisfactory. Adequate drainage is most important; water should never be allowed to collect at the bottom of the pot. A propagator is essential for raising plants from cuttings. Only a bottom temperature of 75° to 85°F (25° to 30°C) will give a reasonable chance of success. Frequently *eye* cuttings are used. Cut the stem 1/2 inch (1cm) above and below an eye. This will give you a cutting with an eye, a leaf stem and a leaf. In large-leaved species, such as *Ficus elastica,* the leaf is rolled up and held in position with a rubber band in order to minimize evaporation. Cuttings are grown in equal parts of sand and peat, thoroughly moistened and placed in a well-lit spot, but not in full sun. When the cuttings have rooted, the little plants can be potted as soon as the first leaf appears. Plants may also be grown from seed or by air-layering, a method for which *Ficus elastica* provides a textbook example. Air-layering is used chiefly to induce the plant to branch or when it has lost its lower leaves. See page 7 for directions for air-layering.

Fittonia

Mosaic Plant
Nerve Plant

These beautiful foliage plants will thrive only in high humidity. They can reach a height of 10 inches (25 cm). Kept on the windowsill in ordinary flowerpots they will tend to droop. They do better placed in a plant window or in hanging baskets. The foliage should be sprayed frequently and withered leaves should be removed. Prune or pinch back straggly trailers and buds to maintain shape and improve foliage. Watch for mealybugs, mites and scale. The photograph shows two forms of *Fittonia verschaffeltii,* 'Pearcei' in the foreground and 'Argyroneura' at the rear. Propagation is from cuttings rooted in sand in spring. They must be kept warm, even under glass. A miniature version called *Fittonia argyroneura nana* has recently been developed.

- Sensitive to direct sunlight. Will tolerate shade. Needs air circulation. Does well in artificial light.
- Warm: 60° to 70°F (16° to 20°C) at night.
- Water moderately throughout the year using tepid soft water. Do not let soil dry out completely between waterings. Needs good drainage.
- Very high humidity is essential. Mist frequently.
- African violet mix or mix 1 part standard potting mix, 1 part perlite and 2 parts peat moss. Feed monthly with a mild acid fertilizer.

Fuchsia

Lady's Eardrops

The finest *Fuchsia* plants are grown in cool shady greenhouses where they can remain throughout the winter at a low temperature. However, many species will thrive on the windowsill away from the sun, while others will do extremely well outdoors. Some may reach a height of 3 feet (1m). Success depends on finding a suitable spot. You will have to experiment. Thousands of *Fuchsia* strains are available with flowers in different color combinations and sizes, and with upright or trailing stems. The trailing types are excellent for hanging baskets. *Fuchsia* plants respond to special care but it is not entirely necessary. If they are kept cool, watered daily and fed frequently they will flower for months on end.

Commercial African violet mix may be used for planting but it must provide very good drainage. The soil mix should be kept moist but the roots should not be allowed to stand in water.

Older plants should be trimmed in March or April before new growth appears, and the soil should be replaced. The plant can be repotted at this time if it seems necessary. These plants do not like being potbound. Watch for aphids, mealybugs, mites, red spiders, scale and thrips. Yellow leaves indicate too little water. Remove older blossoms.

Fuchsia (continued)

The photograph on the previous page shows the erect-growing, small-flowered 'Dollar Princess.' On this page you see the hanging form 'La Campanella,' which has larger flowers.

Fuchsia plants are easily grown from stem cuttings but should not be kept in too warm an environment. To achieve bushy growth and better bloom, the tips should be pinched back, but pinching may also delay flowering. Special pruning can create pyramid-shaped plants. More vigorous varieties can be trained to climb.

If you want more detailed information on your plant, write The American Fuchsia Society, 738 22nd Avenue, San Francisco, CA 94121.

☀ Half-shady position in summer. In winter give plenty of light but no direct sunlight.

🌡 Moderate: 50° to 60°F (10° to 16°C) at night. 50°F (10°C) in winter.

💧 Maintain constant moisture. In winter water a little more sparingly than in summer. Needs good drainage.

💦 Maintain high humidity to avoid buds dropping. Mist frequently.

🪴 Mix 1 part peat moss and 2 parts standard potting mix. Feed monthly from March to October with diluted mild liquid fertilizer.

Gardenia
Cape Jasmine

Gardenia jasminioides is an evergreen shrub that grows from one to three feet (30 to 60cm) tall. It needs warm days, cool nights and a humid atmosphere. Hard water, lack of iron or too alkaline soil will produce yellow leaves. Use room-temperature soft water or rainwater if possible. The loss of buds or black leaf tips are usually due to changes in temperature or amounts of water. Temperatures below 60°F (16°C) will produce malformed buds. Above 65°F (18°C) will cause shedding. Prune back after flowering to maintain the plant's shape and conserve its energy. Remove faded or brown flowers as they appear. Watch for aphids, mealybugs, scale and whiteflies. In January young shoots may be rooted with bottom heat. The plants may also be grown from seed.

☀ Plenty of light but screen from direct summer sunlight. May be put outdoors in summer.

🌡 Warm: 60° to 70°F (16° to 20°C) at night. 60° to 65°F (16° to 18°C) in winter. Soil temperature must be maintained at a minimum of 65°F (18°C).

💧 Water moderately using tepid soft water. Do not allow soil to dry out completely. Needs good drainage.

💦 High humidity. Spray foliage frequently.

🪴 Acid potting mix rich in humus. Feed from March to September with a mild acid liquid fertilizer.

Gasteria

Ox Tongue

The leaves of these robust succulents are sword-shaped, fleshy and often covered in pearly warts or gray blotches. They grow to 12 inches (30cm) tall and are very easy to care for, but overwatering will cause rotting. Older plants may lose their lower leaves, but that is not a sign the plant is ill. In summer they may be put outdoors—even in the sun. In winter they should be placed in a cool spot. Red, orange or pink flowers appear at the tips of tall stems, particularly if the plants have been allowed a resting period. Repot when plant appears overcrowded. Propagation is from leaf cuttings or from offsets. The species illustrated is *Gasteria verrucosa*. A mottled green species, *Gasteria liliputana*, has its leaves arranged in a spiral.

- Place in either a sunny position or light shade. Does well in artificial light.
- Warm: 60° to 70°F (16° to 20°C) at night. Cooler in winter 45° to 55°F (6° to 12°C).
- Water very moderately especially in the cooler season. Water when soil is dry. Needs good drainage.
- Extremely well-suited to a dry atmosphere.
- Equal parts standard potting mix and sharp sand. Feed monthly from April to August with mild liquid fertilizer.

Grevillea

Silk Oak

In Australia this plant may grow into a 65 foot (20m) tree, but indoors it is usually kept about three feet (1m) tall by topping. Young specimens of *Grevillea robusta* tend to spread. Prune severely in spring to retain fullness and remove faded flowers. It is best not to combine it with other plants in a warm room. Because it is a vigorous grower it is likely to become rootbound and require periodic repotting, but do not use too large a pot. Use clay pots only. Cover the drainage hole with a good-sized rock or piece of broken pot. Too much or too little water can permanently injure this plant's roots. Watch for mealybugs, mites and red spiders. Propagation is from seed, three to five to a pot.

- Semi-shade in summer, good light in winter. Needs good air circulation.
- Moderate: 50° to 60°F (10° to 16°C) at night. Winter in a cool spot 40° to 45°F (4° to 8°C).
- Water moderately. The soil-ball must not dry out. Needs good drainage.
- Spray frequently around plant, especially in spring when the plant puts out new shoots. Do not spray directly on foliage.
- Mix 1 part sharp sand and 3 parts standard potting mix. Feed every 2 weeks from April to September with mild liquid fertilizer.

Guzmania

These attractive bromeliads are sometimes used in combination with other plants in planters or for other decorative purposes. In these circumstances it does not matter whether the growing conditions are ideal because the flowering rosettes are already dying. This process can be delayed, but not halted, by cooling the environment. The guidelines below apply chiefly to the plant's propagation from the offsets that form at the base of the rosette. These should not be removed until the mother plant has faded. The young plants grow very slowly and are not easy to raise in a living room. Clay pots are best for these plants. Watch for scale and thrips. The form shown here is *Guzmania lingulata* 'Minor.'

- ☀ A plant for a semi-shady spot. Direct sun can burn leaves. Needs good air circulation. Does well in artificial light.

- 🌡 Warm: 60° to 70°F (16° to 20°C) at night. Minimum temperature in winter should be 60°F (16°C).

- 💧 Give tepid soft water, poured into the funnel at the center of the plant in summer only. Do not soak soil. Keep drier in winter.

- 💦 Needs high humidity. Spray frequently in summer, never in winter.

- 🌿 Fertilize monthly with fish emulsion. Osmunda, fir bark or commercial orchid or bromeliad medium works well.

Gymnocalycium   Chin Cactus

These decorative little cacti are unusually colored and most species readily produce flowers as shown by the specimen in the center. They can be either grafted onto a green stem of another cactus, as shown here, or planted in a mix of equal parts potting mix and sharp sand. From left to right you see the *Gymnocalycium mihanovichii* strains 'Rosea,' 'Black Cap' and 'Optima Rubra.' A yellow mutation is also available. The plants freely produce offsets, as on the left side of the center plant. These may be removed and grafted separately. Both the base and the globular offset are cut level. They need only be pressed together and temporarily secured.

- ☀ Good light but sensitive to direct sunlight.

- 🌡 Moderate to warm: 50° to 70°F (10° to 20°C) at night. In winter not lower than 50°F (10°C).

- 💧 Water very sparingly; keep dry in winter.

- 💦 Dry living room atmosphere adequate.

- 🌿 Equal parts standard potting mix and sharp sand, or special cactus mixture.

Gynura

These plants rarely grow more than 3 feet (1m) tall. The yellow flowers have an unpleasant smell and buds should be snapped off. Maintain a compact form by pruning. Remove withered leaves. You can mist foliage to maintain humidity, but beware of staining leaves. Rinse leaves with room-temperature water to clean pores. Greenish leaves mean too little sun. Watch or mealybugs, mites, scale, slugs and snails, and whiteflies. Overwatering may cause rotting. In winter the *Gynura aurantiaca,* shown here, may become unsightly as a result of inadequate light, although it will usually survive. These plants are also apt to become rootbound. It is easy to raise new plants from cuttings each year.

 To maintain the purple sheen the plant must have plenty of light but not more than four hours of direct sunlight. Does well in artificial light.

Warm: 60° to 70°F (16° to 20°C) at night.

Water moderately but not on the leaves. Needs good drainage.

Moderate humidity.

Mix 1 part peat moss, 1 part perlite and 2 parts standard potting mix. Feed monthly with weak solution of mild liquid fertilizer.

Habranthus

This little known bulb is obtainable from mail-order firms. It is treated in approximately the same way as the familiar *Hippeastrum.* In autumn place it in well-draining pots, preferably about five to a pot. At first keep the plant fairly cool, about 50° to 60°F (10° to 16°C) and give it very little water. When the bulbs put forth shoots keep the plant a little warmer and moister. After flowering the foliage will continue to grow for a time; afterward keep the soil increasingly dry until all the leaves have faded. Keep the bulbs in the pot until fall. Then replace the soil and start the growing cycle over again. Repot only once every 2 or 3 years.

The photograph shows *Habranthus robustus.*

 Not full sun but requires plenty of light.

Moderate: 50° to 60°F (10° to 16°C) at night. After flowering allow a resting period.

Water moderately.

Moderate humidity.

Standard potting mix with additional humus.

Haemanthus

Blood Lily

The bulbs or young plants of various Blood Lily species are obtainable from mail-order firms. They are rarely found at a nursery. The plants are usually available in spring and on receipt they should be potted in nutritious soil. Water sparingly first, a little more when the shoot develops. At the end of the summer the plant should be allowed to die back by withholding water.

The species *Haemanthus albiflos* is evergreen and resembles *Clivia*. It develops a large white blossom that looks like a paint brush and is usually sold already sprouted. It should be placed in a cool location in winter, but it must be watered throughout the year. It dislikes being transplanted and consequently may lose its foliage, but new leaves will appear. It is a very hardy house plant.

Red-flowered species are more difficult to cultivate. They require bottom heat and are best grown in a greenhouse. *Haemanthus katharinae* dies back in winter. It has four to five leaves on a short stem. The flowers are red and very large, up to 9-1/2 inches (24cm) across. *Haemanthus multiflorus*, shown here, resembles *H. katharinae* but the flowers are smaller. It flowers in April but the leaves develop later. The plant must be properly cared for or it will not flower the following year.

It is not necessary to repot every year. In many cases it is sufficient to replace the top layer with fresh soil and repot in the second or third year.

New plants may be grown from offsets, but it takes several years before the young plants can flower, even in a greenhouse.

A sunny location. These plants dislike being moved.

Warm: 60° to 70°F (16° to 20°C) at night. Slightly cooler: 55° to 60°F (12° to 15°C) in winter.

Water normally. Less from mid-August on. Keep practically dry in winter to give the plant a rest.

Fairly high humidity is desirable.

Standard potting mix with additional humus.

Hamatocactus

These freely flowering cacti are relatively easy to grow and are often found in a cactus-lover's greenhouse. They can also be grown on the windowsill, provided they are given a cool spot during the winter resting period. During the winter your plant may lose color and even take on a red or purple tinge, particularly on the side facing the sun. This should not be cause for concern.

The several species available are conspicuous because of the large curved central spines. The *Hamatocactus setispinus,* shown here, is probably the best known species. It has 12 to 14 ribs and produces fragrant yellow flowers with a red throat. Even young plants may flower profusely. Plastic pots are preferred because they help to slow drying of the soil-ball. Propagation is from seed.

- ☼ Plenty of sun.
- 🌡 Moderate to warm: 50° to 70°F (10° to 20°C) at night. Cool in winter.
- 💧 Water sparingly. Keep drier in winter.
- Low humidity is desirable.
- Equal parts sharp sand and standard potting mix, or special cactus mixture.

Haworthia

Aristocrat Plant
Zebra Plant

This genus of slow-growing succulents belongs to the Lily family. Most species have thick fleshy leaves arranged in rosettes that grow to 8 inches (20cm). New plants are grown from offsets or from seed in spring or summer. The dormant season of species with transparent foliage is in summer. Plants with pearly warts on the reverse of the leaves, such as the *Haworthia reinwardtii* shown here, need a resting season in winter. Other well-known species with pearl-covered leaves are *H. attenuata, H. fasciata* or Zebra Haworthia, *H. margaritifera* and *H. papillosa.* Allow these plants to dry out between watering. Overwatering will cause rotting. Watch for mealybugs and scale.

- ☼ Very well-lit position but not direct sunlight. Does well in artificial light.
- 🌡 Warm: 60° to 70°F (16° to 20°C) at night. In the dormant season 40° to 60°F (5° to 16°C) depending on the species.
- 💧 Water moderately but don't water among the leaves. Needs good drainage. Water very sparingly in the dormant season.
- No special requirements.
- Mix 1 part standard potting mix and 2 parts sharp sand. Feed monthly from April to August with mild liquid fertilizer.

Hebe

Veronica

The *Hebe andersonii* hybrid shown here is a shrubby evergreen plant with small leathery leaves native to New Zealand. It flowers in late summer and autumn. The plant in the photograph has purple blossoms but there are white and red flowered forms as well. In many cases the flowers drop when the temperature is too high and the air too dry. After flowering the plants must be cut back. Cuttings may be rooted with moderate bottom heat. During the growing season give your plant a small feeding every two weeks. In winter keep at 45° to 50°F (6° to 10°C). This plant is often called *Veronica.*

- In summer a sheltered outdoor position; bring indoors in early fall. The plant is very sensitive to cold.
- Moderate to cool: 40° to 55°F (5° to 12°C).
- Water freely in summer, sparingly in winter.
- Moderate humidity.
- Standard potting mix or a chalky mixture rich in humus. Feed every 2 weeks during growing season with mild liquid fertilizer.

Hedera

Canary Island Ivy
English Ivy

Hedera, or ivy, requires a cool environment. Propagation is from cuttings placed in a pot and covered with clear plastic until rooted. Prune to maintain shape. Watch for mealybugs, mites, red spiders and scale. Older plants may be placed in the garden. Garden species can also be grown indoors but small-leaved decorative forms of *Hedera helix* are used more often. 'Garland,' shown on the left foreground in the photograph, and 'Glacier,' shown in the center, are good examples. The sub-species *Hedera canariensis* is not hardy. It is available in the variegated form 'Variegata,' sometimes called 'Glorie de Marengo,' shown on the right. It tolerates a slightly higher temperature.

- Satisfied with little light. Does well in artificial light.
- Cool to moderate: 40° to 55°F (4° to 12°C) at night. In winter keep in an unheated but frost-free room.
- Water moderately, the soil-ball must remain moist. In winter water sparingly. Needs good drainage.
- Spray frequently in summer. Sponge leaves often.
- Mix 1 part peat moss, 1 part perlite and 2 parts standard potting mix. Feed monthly from February to December with mild liquid fertilizer.

Hemigraphis

Waffle Plant

These tropical foliage plants require high humidity. In Malaysia they are often grown in gardens. We use them chiefly as a groundcover in greenhouses, although occasionally they keep in remarkably good condition in indoor plant combinations. *Hemigraphis alternata* shown here is usually used for this purpose. Its leaves have a beautiful silvery-purple sheen. In a heated indoor propagator young tip-shoots will easily root at any time of year. Pinch out the tips from the young plants once or twice to encourage branching.

☼ A shadow plant; never place in full sun.

🌡 Warm: 60° to 70°F (16° to 20°C) at night.

💧 Water moderately with demineralized water. Keep moist.

🔆 Requires high humidity and is therefore difficult to keep in the living room.

🪴 Standard potting mix.

Hibiscus

Chinese Rose
Rose Mallow

These freely flowering evergreen shrubs can be placed either indoors or out. They will retain their leaves down to 40°F (5°C). Compact varieties make excellent container plants while full-size varieties can be grown as 5-foot (1.5m) trees in warmer sections of the United States. Flowers are single or double in form and available in white, pink, red, yellow and orange. Individual blossoms last a short time but new flowers will bloom continuously throughout summer and autumn.

The photograph on this page shows a well-known double form of *Hibiscus rosa-sinensis.* The single red strain, which has flowers similar to those of the variegated 'Cooperi' illustrated on the facing page, is used chiefly as a foliage plant. Some people own shrubs 3 feet (1m) in diameter with innumerable flowers. These plants should be kept warm. In early spring the plants may be cut back quite drastically, put pinching and pruning during the growing season will help maintain shape and encourage blooming. Keeping the plant potbound will also control overall size. Take care that the soil does not dry out too much for this will kill the plant.

All strains tolerate full sun. The variegated forms require extra good ventilation as well.

Hibiscus (continued)

From early June on the plants may be placed outdoors but only in a very sheltered position. Bring inside when frost threatens. Poor light, irregular watering or changes in temperature can cause buds to drop. Curled leaves are a sign of too low humidity. Yellow leaves indicate lack of nitrogen. Watch for aphids, mealybugs, mites, red spiders, scale and whiteflies.

Propagation is only from cuttings with bottom heat under glass or plastic.

☀ Likes a sunny location; in summer it may be placed in a sheltered outdoor spot.

🌡 Warm: 60° to 70°F (16° to 20°C) at night. 55° to 60°F (12° to 15°C) during the dormant season in winter.

💧 Requires a regular and generous water supply but a little less in winter. Needs good drainage.

░ Occasional spraying with tepid water is advisable.

🪴 Standard potting mix. Feed monthly with mild liquid fertilizer.

Hippeastrum
Amaryllis

The *Hippeastrum*, often called *amaryllis* is usually brought into flower easily and these bulbs are very popular. Named strains, though a little more expensive produce flowers that are far more beautiful than those of bulbs sold in the supermarket by color only. In the photograph you see from left to right: 'Belinda,' also shown on the next page, 'Fire Dance' and 'President Tito.' Other fine forms are the so-called 'Picotee' strains with a contrasting margin to the petals. These named bulbs are obtainable only from specialist growers through mail order. Usually it is possible to indicate the size of the bulbs required. Extra large bulbs may produce three or four flower stems.

Prepared bulbs may be potted as early as October. The pot should not be too much larger than the diameter of the bulb. Set the bulb so that about half of it is above the soil. Cover the pot with a plastic bag and place in a warm position, even above a radiator if it is not too hot. Water sparingly until bud appears, but make sure the soil-ball does not dry out. Increase watering as the bud grows.

When the flower stem has reached 6 to 8 inches (15 to 20cm) the plant may be placed in a well-lit window to flower. The leaves will not properly

Hippeastrum (continued)

start into growth until after flowering. If you want to keep the bulb for another season the foliage should develop at a minimum temperature of 70°F (20°C). The flower stem is cut off close to the bulb. Water freely and feed once every two weeks to replenish the bulb. From September on, gradually decrease watering until the leaves have died. Keep the bulb dry in the pot and store the pot on its side in a cool place. In January carefully replace the soil-ball with fresh soil and start into growth once more. A teaspoon of bone meal added to the soil will help. Bulbs will probably need repotting after three or four blossoming seasons. Small offset bulbs can be divided and planted in their own pots. Given regular feeding they should produce blossoms in two years.

🌣   Plenty of light but screen from bright sunlight.

🌡   Moderate: 50° to 60°F (10° to 16°C) at night. Keep the bulb at 45°F (6°C) in winter.

🜄   Water regularly in the growing and flowering season. From September on cease watering. Needs good drainage.

〽   Moderate humidity.

🪴   Standard potting mix with additional humus. Feed monthly from January to September with mild liquid fertilizer.

Homalocladium

The stems of this remarkable plant, which comes from the Solomon Islands, have taken over the function of the foliage. Occasionally leaves are produced as well, but as a rule these quickly drop. Although rare, the plant is easy to grow. From late May on it may be placed outdoors.

In winter the most favorable temperature is between 45° to 60°F (8° to 16°C). Cuttings readily root with slight bottom heat. Combine a few of the young plants in one pot. Mature plants produce small flowers and pink-purple fruits.

Homaloclaium platycladum is shown here.

🌣   Very well-lit or sunny position. May be outside in summer.

🌡   Warm: 60° to 70°F (16° to 20°C) at night. Lower temperatures are tolerated.

🜄   Water moderately.

〽   Spray occasionally; the air should not be too dry.

🪴   Standard potting mix.

90

Howeia

Kentia Palm
Sentry Palm

This slow-growing, feathery palm is a native of Lord Howe Island in the South Pacific and it likes warmth. It requires a resting period in winter but this means only the feeding should cease. Beware of overwatering in undrained containers as palms are very sensitive to soggy roots. It likes being potbound and should be repotted as seldom as possible. Use deep clay pots with good drainage. Fronds should be rinsed occasionally to clean their pores. Watch for mealybugs, red spiders, scale and thrips. Propagation is from seed.

The photograph shows *Howeia forsteriana,* or Kentia Palm, which can grow 15 feet (4.5m) tall. *Howeia belmoreana,* Sentry Palm, is more compact.

- A good plant for a shady spot, but it needs room. Avoid drafts.
- Moderate: 50° to 60°F (10° to 16°C) at night. Keep moderately warm in winter 55° to 65°F (14° to 18°C).
- Water moderately throughout the year, preferably with softened water. Allow to dry out between waterings. Needs good drainage.
- Spray regularly.
- Mix 1 part standard potting mix and 2 parts peat. Feed monthly from March to November with very mild liquid fertilizer.

Hoya

Wax Plant

Hoya is called Waxplant because of the waxy texture of its flowers and leaves. *Hoya bella,* shown here, has trailers which can reach 4 feet (1.2m) and looks best in a hanging pot. They have been tied to supports here so the flowers can be seen. *Hoya* blooms from April to November. Do not remove stems that have had blooms for they will bloom again. Other parts may be pruned to shape the plant. It can be trained to climb with support. Keep potbound for best bloom. Cooler and drier conditions during winter dormancy will prevent aphids. Also watch for mealybugs, mites, nematodes and scale. Poor drainage may cause root rot. Overfeeding may cause buds to drop. Propagation is from cuttings.

Hoya Bella

- Slightly shady position. Do not turn the plant.
- Warm: minimum 60°F (16°C) at night. Minimum in winter 55°F (13°C).
- Water moderately and allow soil to go almost dry between waterings. Keep a little drier in the winter and spring. Needs good drainage.
- High humidity. Spray frequently.
- Mix 1 part peat moss, 1 part perlite and 2 parts standard potting mix. Feed monthly from February to August with mild liquid fertilizer.

Hoya (continued)

Hoya carnosa, or Large Waxplant, shown here, is an excellent house plant which may last for years. The long winding stems can reach 8 feet (2.5m) and need to be trained on bent wire. After the buds appear the plant should not be turned, even though the flowers will always grow on the side facing the window. When they open, the flower clusters are very fragrant. Do not remove the flower-stalks as a second flowering frequently follows the first. Potbound plants are more likely to bloom. Strains with variegated leaves are available. *Hoya carnosa* 'Compacta' is a smaller variety. Propagation is from cuttings in June and July. Root with bottom heat under glass. Watch for mealybugs.

Hoya Carnosa

☼ Good light, screened from brightest sunlight.

🌡 Warm: minimum 60°F (16°C) at night. Minimum 50°F (10°C) in winter.

💧 Water moderately; a little more in summer. Keep drier in the dormant season.

〰 Tolerates normal living room atmosphere but likes be sprayed frequently.

🪴 Mix 1 part peat moss, 1 part perlite and 2 parts standard potting mix. Feed monthly from February to August with mild liquid fertilizer.

Hyacinthus
Hyacinth

For winter bloom, bulbs may be potted from early October on. Plant them 3/4 inch (2cm) deep and scatter bone meal over the soil. The bulbs need darkness and the soil temperature must be below 55°F (13°C). When you feel the flower-bud, the pots may be brought into the light. They may grow to 18 inches (45cm) tall.

If your prefer to grow bulbs in water, be sure to keep them cool. Add charcoal to the water to keep it fresh. When white roots fill the glasses, bring them into a warm, bright room to force the bloom. After blooming, remove yellowed foliage and store the dry bulb in a paper bag. Plant outside in fall. A bulb that has been forced cannot be forced again.

☼ Good light but not full sun. Keep in the dark to start them into growth.

🌡 Bulbs should be rooted in a cool, frost-free place for 8 to 10 weeks. When bud appears, keep cool for 9 days. Increase to 60°F (15°C) as plants grow.

💧 Water plants in soil moderately with soft water. For bulbs in water, keep the water level just below the bottom of the bulb.

〰 Moderate humidity. Mist occasionally.

🪴 1 part sand and 2 parts standard potting mix, or in water. Feed bulbs in soil every 2 weeks with mild liquid fertilizer. Do not feed bulbs in water.

Hydrangea

The most commonly grown hydrangeas are the double-flower *hortensia* variety, shown here. They may be grown indoors or out but a cool, shady location is essential to achieve successful results. A hydrangea will not thrive in a centrally heated living room with windows on all sides. A cool hall facing east or north is much better. If the foliage droops, immediate plunging may save the plant.

In summer plenty of water and liquid fertilizer are required. The pot can be buried in the garden in a slightly shady position but be sure it is not in a draft. Water with soft water or rainwater whenever possible. Tapwater contains too much lime. Hydrangeas normally have blooms in red, pink, white or purple. Plants with blue flowers are created from pink varieties by adding aluminum sulphate or iron to make the soil acid. Put one tablespoon in the pot every two weeks for the three months after new leaves appear. Blue blossomed plants are particularly sensitive to hard water. White blossoms will not change color.

Immediately after flowering the branches should be cut back a little. Plants are usually kept about 3 feet (1m) tall. If possible, the plant should be repotted in acid soil. From the end of August on stop feeding and reduce the water supply. At the onset of frost the plant must be brought indoors but it should be placed in a very cool position to prevent the buds drooping. Transfer to a slightly warmer location should be very gradual. Branches laden with buds about to bloom may need support. Watch for aphids, mites, scale, thrips and whiteflies.

All indoor hydrangeas are forms of *Hydrangea macrophylla.* They are not entirely winter-hardy. If you plant them in the garden the buds may freeze in winter. The lower photograph shows an extra-hardy garden strain of the same species growing happily in acid soil among rhododendrons.

New plants are grown from young shoots without a flower-bud. These should be rooted in May to July with bottom heat. The cultivation of young plants should really be confined to a cold frame or an unheated greenhouse.

- Plenty of light but not direct sun, especially when flowering.
- Moderate: 50° to 60°F (10° to 16°C) at night. Temperature in winter: 40° to 45°F (4° to 8°C).
- Water freely during the flowering season. In the dormant season the soil-ball must not dry out. Use soft water. Needs good drainage.
- Moderate humidity. Mist frequently.
- Mix 1 part perlite, 2 parts peat moss and 2 parts standard potting mix. Feed weekly with mild acid fertilizer.

Hypocyrta

Candy Corn Plant
Goldfish Plant

This accommodating plant with its unusually shaped flowers deserves a place in any living room. The best known species is *Hypocyrta glabra,* shown here, which may reach 24 inches (60cm). The round orange flowers emerge from the angles between the stems. A low temperature and some sunshine in winter are essential for bud formation. Prune before new growth starts. *Hypocyrta* flowers on new shoots. It makes an excellent hanging plant and does not mind being potbound. Watch for mealybugs, mites, scale and whiteflies. Misting with cold water can spot leaves. Propagation is from cuttings, which root easily, or by division in spring. Six to eight cuttings in a pot will produce a bushy plant. *Hypocyrta nummularia* has similiar requirements.

- Likes slight shade but some sun is essential to ensure flowering. Does well in artificial light.
- Warm: 60° to 70°F (16° to 20°C) at night. In winter keep at 55°F (12°C). Avoid rapid temperature changes.
- Water moderately. Avoid excessive watering but keep soil moist. Needs good drainage.
- High humidity in the growing season. Spray often.
- Commercial African violet mix. Feed every 2 weeks from March to October with mild liquid fertilizer.

Hypoestes

Freckle Face
Pink Polka Dot Plant

Hypoestes taeniata and *Hypoestes sanguinolenta* are natives of Madagascar. Both owe their beauty to their mottled foliage. The small spike-like flowers, usually lilac, are very inconspicuous. This plant will usually stay less than 2 feet (60cm) tall, but if it spreads too much or loses its lower leaves, it should be cut back drastically. Tip-shoot cuttings can be rooted in shallow bowls. The soil should not be packed too tightly. New plants may also be grown from seed. Pinch the tips to produce a bushy plant. Rinse the foliage to clean pores. Watch for mealybugs, mites, scale, slugs or snails, and whiteflies. After flowering your plant may die back to soil level. Keep soil moist and remove dead foliage. New growth will soon appear.

- Slight shade. Likes fresh air. Does well in artificial light.
- Warm: 60° to 70°F (16° to 20°C) at night.
- Water fairly freely in the growing season using lukewarm soft water.
- High humidity, especially in summer. Spray often.
- Slightly acid soil, rich in humus. Equal parts standard potting mix and peat moss work well. Feed every 2 weeks with mild acid fertilizer.

Impatiens

The *Impatiens balsamina*, illustrated in the upper photograph, has pale green foliage and double, pink flowers. It is suitable for use on a balcony or in a garden. The lower photograph shows *Impatiens walleriana,* a fairly low-growing species best suited for pot cultiviation. Flowers range in color from deep red to white, the foliage is bright green. The decorative form 'Petersiana' has bronze-colored to red stems and leaves and red flowers.

The above are the most commonly domesticated species but the mountains of tropical eastern Africa have yielded others of the same genus. *Impatiens repens* has small, dark-green leaves on creeping stems and large yellow flowers. *Impatiens niamnia-mensis* is an erect growing species with unusual red flowers and fairly large green leaves on unbranched stems.

Propagation is simple. Cuttings will readily root in both water and sharp sand. The Latin word *impatiens* means 'unable to endure.' This refers to the fact that the seed capsules open at a touch. The seed will germinate in about ten days.

Young plants should have their tips pinched off several times to encourage branching. Premature buds should be pinced out to encourage a fuller bloom. Plants that are slightly potbound will produce more blossoms. They will rarely reach a height of more than 24 inches (60 cm).

If the leaves drop it is often due to too low a temperature. Too little light will cause the flowers to drop. Rotting stems are usually due to constant overwatering. If the plant grows too lanky, pinch it back. Use the cuttings to grow new specimens. Excessively dry air may result in attacks by white-flies. Do not spray when the plant is in flower for this will cause staining. Red spiders or aphids may appear if the plant stands in direct sun.

☼ Well-lit position but out of the sun; half-shady in autumn and spring. Does well in artificial light.

🌡 Moderate: 60° to 70°F (10° to 16°C) at night. Plants will continue to flower in a winter temperature of 55°F (13°C).

🜄 Always water freely using soft water, except during a resting period.

≋ Moderate humidity.

▼ Standard potting mix. Feed weekly with mild liquid fertilizer.

Ipomoea

Morning Glory

This attractive climber is very easily grown from seed. Soak the seed for 24 hours or make scratches on the individual seeds to aid rapid germination. Then sow at 65°F (18°C). The plant will grow rapidly and will need support early. It can reach 10 feet (3m) tall. The *Ipomoea violacea,* shown here, has soft green heart-shaped leaves and large funnel-shaped flowers that are white at the center, merging into deep blue. *Ipomoea learii* is a very suitable house plant which produces a profusion of blue flowers. It has a spreading form and likes being potbound. Individual blossoms last only a short time but new blossoms continue to appear. Sow in mid-summer for a winter bloom, in March for summer flowers. Remove dead blossoms. This plant may be pruned at any time.

☼ Requires as much sun as you can give it. Avoid drafts.

🌡 Warm: 60° to 70°F (16° to 20°C) at night.

🫖 Water freely, especially in warm and sunny periods. Use tepid water.

≋ High humidity. Mist frequently with tepid water.

🪴 Standard potting mix or a slightly chalky mixture. Feed from April to October with mild liquid fertilizer.

Iresine

Blood-Leaf

Iresine herbstii, shown here, is a shrub-like annual native to Brazil. The surface of the leaves is slightly ruffled. The decorative form 'Aureireticulata' has gold-mottled foliage and red stems. Another all-red species is *Iresine lindennii;* it has smooth, pointed leaves. To achieve a shapely plant the tips should be pruned several times. Tip cuttings root easily. *Iresine* can reach a height of 18 inches (45cm). In summer it may be placed outdoors. The red color is caused by the pigment anthocyanin. Bright light is necessary for good color. Do not let the soil-ball dry out but do not overwater. Pinch out flower buds to encourage foliage growth. Wash leaves with tepid water. Watch for mealybugs, mites, scale, slugs and snails, and whiteflies.

☼ A sunny position. Does well in artifical light.

🌡 Moderate to warm: 50° to 70°F (10° to 20°C) at night.

🫖 Give plenty of tepid water from February to October, moderate amounts during the rest of the year. The soil-ball must not dry out. Needs good drainage.

≋ Moderate humidity. Mist frequently.

🪴 Standard potting mix. Feed every 2 weeks from February to October with mild liquid fertilizer; monthly the rest of the year.

96

Ixora

The *Ixora coccinea* hybrids are the best-known of this genus. 'Bier's Glory,' shown here, has flowers from May to September. During this time it is very sensitive and may go into shock if moved. After flowering it is cut back and given a short rest. If necessary repot. *Ixora* needs slightly acid conditions. Faded flowers should be removed. Yellow or falling leaves mean the water or the location is too cool. Rolled leaves mean too much sunlight; pale leaves mean iron deficiency. Watch for aphids, mealybugs and scale. Tip cuttings can be rooted in spring in bottom heat at 80°F (25°C). Pinch out tips after the appearance of every second pair of leaves. Mature plants may grow up to 4 feet tall (120cm) and may flower three times a year.

 Slight shade. Do not move and keep out of direct sun.

Warm: 60° to 70°F (16° to 20°C) at night. Minimum temperature in winter 60°F (16°C). Bottom temperature about 65°F (19°C).

Water normally in the growing season using soft water at room temperature. In winter give a little less water.

Maintain high humidity.

Mix 1 part sand, 1 part perlite, 1 part standard potting mix and 2 parts peat moss. Feed every 2 weeks from March to September with mild liquid fertilizer.

Jacaranda

In its native Brazil the *Jacaranda* grows into a tree with graceful foliage and a profusion of lilac flowers.

Jacaranda mimosifolia, shown here, is popular as a house plant chiefly because of its feathery foliage.

Propagation is from seed at about 80°F (25°C) or from cuttings in spring or summer with young shoots.

Eventually the lower leaves will drop. When the plant has reached 20 to 24 inches (50 to 60cm) pinch out its tip to control growth from time to time.

Plenty of light and space, possibly diffused sunlight.

Warm: 60° to 70°F (16° to 20°C) at night. Minimum temperature in winter 60°F (14°C).

Use tepid soft water. Do not overwater. Keep dry in winter.

A humid atmosphere is essential.

Standard potting mix. Feed every 2 weeks from April to September with mild liquid fertilizer.

Jacobinia

Jacobina species suitable for indoor cultiviation may be divided into two groups according to appearance and treatment. *Jacobinia carnea,* as shown in the upper photo, and *Jacobinia pohliana* each have a terminal flower cluster consisting of slender, tubular pink flowers. The flowers of *Jacobinia carnea* are sticky and the leaves are soft and hairy. Cuttings are rooted from January to April with bottom heat. Mature plants are cut back after flowering in August or September, and are placed in a well ventilated, moderately heated greenhouse. The plants should be kept at 55° to 60°F (12° to 16°C) in winter. In spring they are repotted into roomy pots; the tips should be nipped out two or three times. Watch for red spiders, scale and whiteflies. Brown leaves indicate overwatering. Rolled leaves mean too low humidity.

Jacobinia carnea

Roomy spot in slight shade preferred. Needs good air circulation.

Warm: 60° to 70°F (16° to 20°C) at night. Temperature in winter 55° to 60°F (12° to 16°C) rising to 70°F (21°C) in early spring.

Maintain constant moisture, but avoid overwatering.

Fairly high humidity in summer. Not too dry in winter.

Standard potting mix. Feed every 3 weeks from March to September with mild liquid fertilizer.

Together with *Jacobinia ghiesbreghtiana* and *Jacobinia penrhosiensis, Jacobinia pauciflora,* shown in the lower photograph, belongs to the winter-flowering group of *Jacobinia.* They have leathery leaves and scattered flowers or small plumes. These species are very sensitive. Too much dryness will cause them to shed their leaves. They should be repotted in May after flowering. Propagation is from cuttings in bottom heat in January or February. Keep fairly warm until the root system has developed after repotting. Then give the plant a slightly cooler position. The tips should be pinched out once or twice to maintain shape and encourage flowering. Overwatering will cause the leaves to turn brown. Watch for red spiders, scale and whiteflies.

Jacobinia pauciflora

Requires more sun than *Jacobinia carnea.* May be placed outdoors in summer.

Cool: 55° to 65°F (12° to 18°C) at night. As low as 45° to 50°F (6° to 10°C) until the flowers appear.

Never let the soil-ball dry out, but do not overwater.

Maintain high humidity, especially in the flowering season. Spray occasionally.

Mix 1 part peat moss with 2 parts standard potting mix.

Jasminum

Jasmine
Jessamine

The abundantly flowering plant in the photograph is *Jasminum officinale*, a native of China. It is a deciduous shrub that can reach 30 feet (9m) tall. Most varieties of *Jasminum* do well under the conditions described below. They are vigorous growers and most require support. They bloom from spring to fall and rest from October to March. After flowering they should be pruned drastically. Repot if necessary. They require high humidity and plenty of light to flower. From May to September some varieties may be placed outdoors in full sun. Watch for mealybugs, scale and whiteflies. New plants may be grown by layering or from cuttings rooted in sand. *Jasminum polyanthum* blooms in January and has a pleasing fragrance.

 The best possible light in the living room but not in full sun outdoors in summer.

🌡 Moderate: 50° to 60°F (10° to 16°C) at night. Keep cool in winter, minimum about 35°F (2°C).

💧 Constant water supply, fairly generous in the growing period. Needs good drainage.

💦 High humidity. Frequent spraying is excellent.

🪴 Mix 1 part vermiculite with 2 parts standard potting mix. Feed weekly from March to October with mild liquid fertilizer.

Kalanchoe

Air Plant
Panda Plant

Kalanchoe blossfeldiana or Christmas Kalanchoe, shown here, is the best-known of the 200 species of this genus. It grows to 8 inches (20cm). Like all *Kalanchoes,* it is a short-day plant and may be brought into flower any time by limiting the light it receives to ten hours a day. There are strains with yellow, orange, red and pink flower clusters. They like plenty of light and fresh air. Too much sun turns the foliage red. Too much humidity can cause mildew. Pinch back stems to maintain shape and encourage bloom. Remove stalks when flowers fade. Watch for aphids, mealybugs, mites and scale. Propagation is from seed or cuttings.

Kalanchoe blossfeldiana—Christmas Kalanchoe
Kalanchoe tomentosa—Panda Plant (see next page)

🌞 In summer a well-lit, slightly shady spot. In winter in the best possible light.

🌡 Moderate: 50° to 60°F (10° to 16°C) at night. Minimum temperature in dormancy of 50°F (10°C).

💧 Water moderately, sparingly in winter. Allow soil to dry out between waterings. Needs good drainage.

💦 Moderate humidity.

🪴 Mix 1 part perlite with 2 parts standard potting mix. Feed every 2 weeks from May to September with mild liquid fertilizer. Feed Panda Plant 2 times a year.

Kalanchoe (continued)

Kalanchoe tomentosa or Panda Plant, shown in the right foreground of the upper photograph, is cared for in the same manner as *Kalanchoe blossfeldiana* on the previous page, except they should be fed only twice a year. The branching stems are erect growing and can reach 3 feet (1m) tall. The oblong leaves are densely covered with gray hairs. A few brown hairs at the top create a very unusual effect. This plant rarely flowers. *Kalanchoe miniata* grows to 10 inches (25cm), has bell-shaped flowers and is cared for like *Kalanchoe blossfeldinia*. *Kalanchoe pinnata*, the Air Plant, and *K. daigremontiana*, the Good-Luck Plant also need similar care.

BRYOPHYLLUM SPECIES

The genus *Kalanchoe* now also embraces *Bryophyllum* species and they have slightly different requirements. *Kalanchoe laxiflora* in the upper photograph, background left, is completely covered in blue-gray bloom. The flowers are red and grow in clusters. Little plantlets may appear along the margins of the leaves.

In the lower photograph the plantlets of *Kalanchoe daigremonitana* on the right, and *Kalanchoe tubiflora* on the left are clearly visible. In the latter species they appear at the extremities of the cylindrical gray-green mottled leaves which are slightly furrowed on the upper surface. The orange-red, bell-shaped flowers grow in flat-topped clusters and bloom from the center out. The plantlets develop leaves and roots while still attached to the mother plant and then drop.

These plants are very undemanding and easy to grow. They like being potbound, but can be repotted every other year. The dry atmosphere in centrally heated homes is tolerated. In winter they need little water. During the growing and flowering season water regularly and feed once every three weeks. The plants are propagated from the little plantlets or from runners in spring. Watch for aphids, mealybugs, mites and scale. Avoid using Malathion to treat pests. It will injure or kill your plant. Mildew is caused by too high humidity.

Kalanchoe uniflora is a creeping species with 3/4-inch-long (2cm) flowers. *Kalanchoe schizophylla*, which has elongated, deeply incised leaves, is a climber suitable for a moderate greenhouse.

Kalanchoe—Bryophyllum species

- ☼ Good light and ventilation, not in bright midday sun.
- 🌡 Warm: 60° to 70°F (16° to 20°C) at night. Keep at 50° to 55°F (10° to 12°C) in winter.
- 💧 Water thoroughly and allow soil to dry out between waterings. Needs good drainage.
- Fairly tolerant of dry living room atmosphere.
- 🪴 Standard potting mix. Feed every 3 weeks from May to September with mild liquid fertilizer.

Lachenalia

Cape Cowslip

These unusual bulbs came from South Africa and they are commonly known as Cape Cowslips. A number of colors are available. Plant groups of five or six bulbs about 1/2 inch (1cm) deep in shallow pots in August or September. *Lachenlia aloides* bulbs, shown here, flower between January and March. The most graceful form is 'Aurea.' The flower stalks are reddish-brown and grow about 12 inches (30cm) tall. They usually bear 12 to 18 pendulous, orange-yellow tubular flowers. The tips of the petals are sometimes slightly greenish. From May, when the foliage fades, to September, the bulbs are dormant and should not be watered. In October they should be repotted and placed in good light in a cool position. They should be watered very sparingly. They can be forced into blossom year after year.

Propagation can be from offsets or from seed.

- Fairly sunny spot, enjoys fresh air.
- Cold: 35° to 50°F (1° to 10°C) at night.
- Be sure to water regularly once the bulbs put out shoots. Provide good drainage.
- Moderate humidity.
- Standard potting mix. Fertilize monthly from September to May with mild liquid fertilizer.

Lampranthus

Afternoon Flower
Ice Plant

This very popular shrub-like succulent grows to about three feet (1m) and bears a profusion of radiating flowers from June to October. It does not need fertilizing, but should be repotted each spring. It needs a sunny location because the flowers only open when the sun is shining. Pinch back tips to encourage blossoming and maintain compact form. They will remain closed in inadequate light. Propagate in autumn from tip cuttings. Allow the cuttings to dry before setting them in the growing medium. They root and grow rapidly. Seed may be sown in spring at 70°F (21°C) in sandy soil. Watch for mealybugs, scale and thrips. The color range of the *Lampranthus* species originating in South Africa includes white, pink, yellow, orange and red. The photograph shows *Lampranthus blandus.*

- Throughout the year in the sunniest spot available. May be placed outdoors in summer.
- Warm: 60° to 70°F (16° to 20°C) at night. Slightly lower temperature is acceptable. In winter: 45°F (6°C) will be tolerated.
- Water very moderately, especially at lower temperatures. Needs good drainage.
- Very tolerant of dry living room air.
- Mix 1 part loam, 1 part peat moss and 3 parts sand, or use commercial cactus potting soil.

Lantana

This undemanding plant is considered a weed in its native tropics. Only *Lantana camara* hybrids, shown here, and *Lantana montevidensis,* known as Trailing or Weeping Lantana, are cultivated. Hybrids are available with yellow, pink and red flowers, but the colors fade in the course of flowering. Plenty of light and adequate nourishment are the main requirements for successful cultivation. *Lantana* needs to be pruned heavily once or twice a year to maintain a healthy growth. It can be trained as a small bush or trailing plant for a hanging basket. Repot in February if necessary. Whiteflies are attracted to this plant, but regular spraying controls them. Watch for mealybugs, red spiders and scale. Propagation is from seed in January or from cuttings in August and planted in moist sandy soil. **WARNING: All parts of this plant are poisonous.**

- ☀ A sunny spot. In summer place outdoors.
- 🌡 Cool to moderate: 40° to 60°F (5° to 15°C) at night. Rest in a cool, airy place 45°F (8°C). From March on, increase to about 55°F (12°C).
- 💧 Water moderately but regularly. Needs good drainage.
- 💦 Moderate humidity. Spray regularly.
- 🪴 Standard potting mix. Feed every 2 weeks from April to October with mild liquid fertilizer.

Laurus

Laurus nobilis originates in the Mediterranean area and its leaves are often used as a seasoning. It can reach a height of 30 feet (9m) or be kept smaller with pruning. It is not winter-hardy, although it likes a very cold location in winter. Too high a temperature in spring will cause it to grow too rapidly and make it susceptible to disease and pests. It likes being potbound and should not be repotted until its roots fill its pot. Wash foliage monthly to clean pores. Watch for aphids, mealybugs, mites and scale. Start feeding before the new growth appears in spring. Overwatering in winter will cause yellow leaves.

Cuttings may be taken in spring or fall and rooted in equal parts sand and peat at a bottom temperature of 60° to 70°F (16° to 20°C).

- ☀ A sunny location. In summer it may be placed outside from May to October, depending on the weather. Needs good air circulation.
- 🌡 Moderate: 50° to 60°F (10° to 16°C) at night. Temperature in winter 35° to 45°F (1° to 6°C).
- 💧 Water fairly freely in the growing season. Allow soil to dry out between waterings. Needs good drainage.
- 💦 Normal humidity. Spray regularly.
- 🪴 Standard potting mix. Feed weekly from April to September with mild liquid fertilizer.

Lilium
Lily

The photograph shows a number of well-known *Lilium* species and hybrids. They vary in height from 1 to 6 feet (30 to 180cm). For a spring bloom the bulbs must be potted in fall and they should not be allowed to dry out. Make sure the pot or tub is sufficiently wide and deep. A layer of pebbles at the bottom should be covered with a thin layer of sand on which the bulb is placed. The pot is then filled with the soil mix to just above the tip of the bulb. Once the bulb starts growing, usually in early March, the temperature should be gradually increased to 65°F (18°C). Overwatering or poor drainage can cause bulb rot. Orange spots on the leaves or buds indicates botrytis blight. Treat immediately by removing infected parts. Watch for aphids, mealybugs, scale and thrips.

- Half-shade or sun. Needs good air circulation.
- Cold: 35° to 50°F (3° to 10°C) at night. Lilies dislike warm roots and should never be placed over a source of heat.
- Water moderately. Keep soil moist. Must have good drainage.
- Moderate humidity. Mist frequently.
- Mix 1 part sand and 2 parts standard potting mix, plus 1 tablespoonful of bonemeal per pot.

Liriope
Lilyturf

This lily-like plant is slowly becoming more popular. The best known species is *Liriope muscari* which has bright violet flower spikes and strap-shaped leaves, as shown in the photograph. There is also a slightly smaller species, *Liriope spicata*, which puts out runners and has small, pale pink flowers. These natives of eastern Asia flower late in summer. The berries which follow keep well.

In summer *Liriope* plants may be placed out-doors. They should be watered moderately and fed every two weeks. Propagation is by division of the root system. The sections are potted in coarse soil.

- Tolerates some shade but prefers good light, especially in summer.
- Moderate: 50° to 60°F (10° to 16°C) at night. 50° to 55°F (10° to 12°C) in the dormant season.
- Keep moderately moist. Do not let the soil-ball dry out.
- Moderate humidity.
- Standard potting mix. Feed every two weeks with mild liquid fertilizer.

Lithops

As you can see in the photograph, *Lithops* is a quite remarkable looking plant. This succulent consists of two very thick leaves joined at the base. It has a deep tap root and therefore needs a fairly deep pot. although it only grows about 1 inch (3cm) high. During the dormant season, from November to April, a new pair of leaves grows from the old. The old leaves eventually shrivel up, but should not be removed. In September and October radiating flowers may appear in the groove at the top. These are usually yellow or white.

Propagation is from seed or division. The plants will flower in two to three years. Overwatering can cause root rot. Watch for mealybugs and scale.

- Keep in the best available light throughout the year. Good in artificial light.
- Moderate: 50° to 60°F (10° to 16°C) at night. In winter allow the plant to rest at 40° to 45°F (5° to 8°C).
- In the growing season water extremely sparingly. Keep dry in winter. Do not moisten foliage. Needs good drainage.
- Low humidity is preferred.
- Coarse mixture of 1 part sand and 2 parts standard potting mix, or cactus soil mix. Do not feed.

Lobivia

Cob Cactus

This genus, which originates in South America, contains more than 70 cacti, including *Lobivia densispina* shown here. Their appearance varies considerably. They are globular to cylindrical in shape and their spines may grow close together or far apart, and may be long or short. As a rule they flower freely producing large numbers of blooms varying in color from white to yellow to red. Some well-known species are *Lobivia aurea*, with yellow flowers, *L. backebergii* with red, *L. haageana* with pale yellow to red and *L. jajoiana* with red flowers with black centers. Propagation is from seed or from cuttings.

- Full sun. A south-facing windowsill is good.
- Warm: 60° to 70°F (16° to 20°C) at night. Cool in winter.
- Keep moderately moist; dry in winter.
- Low humidity.
- Cactus mixture with a little extra humus, or equal parts standard potting mix and sharp sand.

Lycaste

These tropical epiphyte orchids produce long-lasting flowers in pink, white, yellow or brown. Some species, including the *Lycaste virginalis* shown here, grow indoors with little difficulty. The fragrant *Lycaste aromatica* is a native of Mexico. It has small but profuse yellow-orange flowers in winter. *Lycaste cruenta* produces large orange or greenish-yellow flowers. Between March and May these plants should be potted and kept in a fairly cool and shady spot until September. Reduce watering until the leaves have dropped. Yellow leaves mean too much light. Dark green leaves but no bloom means too little light. Watch for aphids, mealybugs, scale, slugs and snails, and thrips. Remove withered blooms.

- Half-shady position in summer; provide more light in winter. Does well in artificial light.
- Moderate: 50° to 60°F (10° to 16°C) at night. Cooler in winter, around 45°F (7°C).
- Water regularly in the growing period with tepid soft water. Never allow the pseudo-bulbs to shrivel up. Needs good drainage.
- High humidity, but never spray directly on flowers.
- Orchid mixture, shredded bark or osmunda. Feed every 2 weeks with mild liquid fertilizer.

Mammillaria

Nipple Cactus
Old Lady Cactus

This cactus genus comprises more than 200 species, most of them natives to sunny Mexico. Most *Mammallaria* cacti require as much light and sunshine as possible throughout the year. Nevertheless there are a few pale green species containing a large amount of chlorophyll which need to be screened from bright sunlight in summer. *Mammillaria centricirrha,* shown in the center of the photograph, is a blue-green more or less spherical cactus containing a milky liquid. *Mammillaria dawsonii* on the left has beautiful spines and carmine flowers. *Mammillaria herrerae* at right is a small species with proportionally large flowers.

These plants are best watered from the bottom. With white-haired species, such as *Mammillaria hahniana* shown on the following page, it is particularly important to avoid getting the plant wet. Turning these plants occasionally will help them develop an even shape.

Propagation is from seed in April or May, at a temperature of 70°F (21°C). Some species produce offsets and these can be rooted separately. Allow them to dry for two or three days before potting them.

Mammillaria (continued)

Mammillaria cacti should be repotted every April in a nutritious mixture containing loam, sand, some leaf mold and peat. These cacti are very popular because they flower so readily and are so undemanding. In many cases the spines are also attractive.

Mammillaria magnimamma on the right in the upper photograph has very conspicuous nipples, as does *Mammillaria centricirrha.* In both species the flowers grow in a circle around the crown.

In the spherical *Mammillaria hahniana* or Old Lady cactus at left in the upper photograph, the spines are conspicuously long. Older specimens frequently grow into a more elongated shape. The flowers are deep red. *Mammillaria gracilis* var. *fragilis,* in the lower photograph on the left, remains a fragile tiny cactus through its life. It is densely covered with relatively long thorns. The cream to yellow flowers are fairly inconspicuous. *Mammillaria spinossissima,* lower photograph on the right, is very densely thorned and gives a prickly and wooly impression. This species prefers chalky soil and, like *Mammillaria rhodantha,* it must be kept out of full sun. *Mammillaria prolifera* or Sprouting Mammillaria develops clumps and has yellow flowers.

☀ Plenty of sun in summer; turn occasionally to prevent a lopsided shape. Good light in winter.

🌡 Warm: 60° to 70°F (16° to 20°C) at night. Keep at 40° to 45°F (6° to 8°C) in winter.

💧 Water regularly in summer, preferably in the morning. In winter water sparingly, but take care that the plant does not dry out.

〰 Stands up well in dry living room atmosphere.

🪴 Equal parts sharp sand and standard potting mix or commercial cactus mixture. Feed monthly in summer with mild liquid fertilizer.

Maranta

Arrowroot
Prayer Plant

This genus grows wild in the rain forests of Brazil, chiefly in open spaces. It is one of our finest foliage plants, frequently used in combination with other plants. The *Maranta* is sometimes nicknamed Prayer Plant because its leaves fold at night to conserve moisture. Depending on the species, *Maranta* can reach 3 feet (1m) tall.

Maranta leuconeura 'Kerchoveana' in the lower photograph, has purplish-brown blotches, usually arranged in five pairs on the bright green leaves. The 'Fascinator' strain, shown in the upper photograph, has foliage that is red-veined on a velvety green, mottled background. The leaves of *Maranta bicolor* have six to eight brown blotches on a dark green background and are purple on the underside.

In all species the flowers are rather inconspicuous. Because *Maranta* plants produce runners, they make useful groundcover. Straggly leaves should be pruned regularly.

These plants prefer to be potbound, but they can be repotted in April in a porous potting mix rich in humus. It is advisable to use wide, shallow bowls so that the foliage hangs over the moist soil. From May to September spray frequently. Spraying is also beneficial in winter but less water should be given. Leaves should be washed monthly, but do not use oils or shiners. Remove withered leaves when they appear.

Always use tepid water with a pH of 4 to 4.5. No excess water should be allowed to collect in the pot. At the same time be careful not to let the soil-ball dry out. From September to February allow the plant to rest. Propagation is by division in spring. From May to August cuttings may be taken. Three shoots, each with two or three leaves, should be potted together in a mixture of equal parts of sand and peat, at a temperature of 70°F (21°C). When rooted they are repotted separately. Watch for aphids, mealybugs, red spiders, scale and thrips.

- A good plant for a half-shady position, but good light is acceptable. Does well in artificial light.

- Warm: 60° to 70°F (16° to 20°C) at night. Daytime temperature in winter 65° to 70°F (18° to 20°C) with a minimum of 55° (14°C) at night.

- In the growing season water freely using tepid soft water. Water less at lower temperatures. Needs good drainage.

- Fairly high humidity is desirable. Spray frequently.

- Standard potting mix. Feed every month from February to October with a weak solution of liquid fertilizer and water.

Medinilla

Medinilla magnifica, shown here, has large leathery leaves, depressed veins and striking flowers. Its pendulous plumes consist of large pink bracts surrounding numerous little pink flowers. The total blossom may grow to 16 inches (40cm). Flowering usually occurs between February and August. In the growing season the plant should be fed every two weeks. After the dormant season, which lasts from November to the end of January, the plant may be cut back a little and repotted. Do not feed until the flower buds are visible. Propagation is by air-layering or from cuttings rooted in a mix of equal parts sand and peat with a bottom heat of 75° to 85°F (25° to 30°C). Blossoms may not appear until the third year.

- Well-lit position out of the sun.
- Warm: 60° to 70°F (16° to 20°C) at night. Keep at 60° to 65°F (15° to 17°C) in the dormant season.
- Water fairly freely in the growing period, using soft tepid water, less thereafter. Make sure plant drains well.
- Spray, including the underside of the leaves, to provide high humidity; or use the deep-plate method.
- Bromeliad or orchid mixture. Feed every 2 weeks from February to November with mild liquid fertilizer.

Microcoelum

Microcoelum weddellianum, illustrated, has gracefully curving feathery leaves which may grow to 5 feet (1.5m) in length. The narrow side-leaves are gray on the underside. The stem is surrounded by brown fibers. Brown tips on the leaves are usually due to too little water or inadequate humidity. If the plant turns yellow it means that it is standing in too cold a position. This palm must be kept indoors throughout the year but it should be cool in the winter. In the growing season feed every two weeks or so. These palms prefer a tall but not too large pot. Propagation is from seed, but is a very slow process.

- Well-lit position out of full sun.
- Warm in summer: 60° to 70°F (16° to 20°C) at night. Keep at 60° to 65°F (15° to 18°C) in winter.
- The soil-ball must never dry out. In the growing season water frequently using soft water. Needs good drainage.
- High himidity in summer.
- Standard potting mix. A slightly acid condition is fine. Feed every 2 weeks with mild liquid fertilizer during growing season.

Microlepia

This fern has a feathery, soft bright-green foliage and is a native of the tropics. The only species grown as a house plant is *Microlepia speluncae* and its special strain 'Cristata,' shown here. Its leaves broaden at the tip.

This plant likes to be potbound but, if necessary, repot in spring in a tall pot. *Microlepia* requires a richer mixture than other ferns. In the growing season water freely and give a small feeding every two weeks. In winter maintain a minimum temperature of 60°F (15°C), water less and do not feed. Propagation is from spores.

Slight or deep shade.

Moderate: 50° to 60°F (10° to 16°C) at night.

Water freely using soft water. Plunging several times a week is excellent. Needs good drainage.

High humidity. Spray often.

A mixture rich in humus, such as 3 parts leaf mold, 2 parts manure and 1 part coarse sand. Feed every 2 weeks with very mild liquid fertilizer during growing season.

Mimosa
Sensitive Plant

The photograph shows what happens when, in the daytime at a minimum temperature of 65°F (18°C), a *Mimosa pudica* is touched. The feathery pinnate leaves fold immediately. They also fold at night.

The plants are easily grown from seed in March; germination takes 12 to 15 days. Select the most vigorous of the seedlings and do not pinch out the tip until the sixth leaf has appeared. This will promote branching. In the growing season and during the flowering period which follows soon after, water freely and feed every two weeks. The plant usually flowers between June and October. *Mimosa* seldom grows taller than 18 inches (45cm). Watch for mealybugs and scale. *Mimosa* dislikes smoke.

Requires good light and ventilation. Does well in artificial light.

Warm: 60° to 70°F (16° to 20°C) at night.

Water regularly to prevent the soil-ball from drying out but avoid overwatering. Needs good drainage.

Requires fairly high humidity. Spray regularly.

Mix 1 part perlite and 3 parts standard potting mix. Feed every 2 weeks from April to September with mild liquid fertilizer.

Monstera

This genus embraces about 50 species which grow wild in Central and South America. They are hardy evergreen climbers but usually require support. In addition to their normal roots, they develop aerial roots that change into ordinary roots as soon as they touch the soil. In young plants the leaves are smooth-edged. The incisions appear at a later stage, followed by the perforations which only appear if the plant is given adequate light and nourishment. The photograph shows the *Monstera deliciosa*, which originates on the western slopes of the Mexican mountains. It can grow to more than 3 feet (1m) tall by 2 feet (60cm) wide and is recommended for large rooms. Mature plants produce an unusual blossom consisting of a creamy bract and a spike on which berries develop. The berries smell like pineapple and are edible. The 'Borgsiana' variety is slightly smaller. Among other strains in cultivation are *Monstera obliqua*, which has oblong perforations and unincised leaf-edges; *M. accuminata*, which has large, asymmetrical and deeply slashed leaves; and *M. pertusa*, a rapid climber with dense foliage.

Monstera is an undemanding plant and stands up well to temperature variations. It is most attractive placed in a well-lit, humid environment. Propagation is by air-layering or from cuttings or seed. Tip shoots are used for cuttings but it is also possible to take stem sections, preferably with a leaf and one or more aerial roots. In the case of tip cuttings, the growing point and a mature leaf are rooted with bottom heat. Stem cuttings are placed directly in soil without rooting.

Young plants should be repotted each year until they reach a 10 to 12 inch (24 to 30cm) pot. Growth usually tapers off at this size. Mature plants prefer to be potbound, but they should be repotted every two or three years. Yellowing of the leaf tips may indicate too much or too little water. Undersize leaves or leaves that fail to split are usually due to lack of light or low humidity. Leaves should be sponged off about once a month. Do not use oils or shiners. Withered leaves should be removed, but let aerial roots develop. They will eventually root in the soil. Watch for aphids, mealybugs, red spiders, scale and thrips.

Satisfied with little light. Does well in artificial light.

Warm: 60° to 70°F (16° to 20°C) at night. Keep a little cooler in winter with a minimum 50°F (10°C).

Water moderately but regularly so that the soil does not dry out entirely. Needs good drainage.

Moderate humidity. Spray frequently and sponge the foliage.

Standard potting mix. Feed every 2 weeks from March to October with mild liquid fertilizer.

Myrtus

Myrtle

Myrtus communis, shown here, is an evergreen shrub up to four feet (120cm) tall. It has leathery leaves and small round flowers with protruding stamens. Both foliage and flowers are fragrant. Flowering occurs between June and September. In fall the flowers are succeeded by blue-black or white berries, depending on the strain. Propagation from seed or from 4 inch (10cm) tip cuttings. These are dipped in rooting powder and rooted in moist sand. Repot in March, but plants should be slightly potbound for best performance. Prune to maintain shape and watch for aphids, leaf miners, mealybugs, mites or scale. Foliage should be washed monthly.

- Place outdoors in summer. Keep in a well-lit, roomy position out of the sun throughout the rest of the year. Needs good air circulation.
- Cold to moderate. 40° ro 55°F (5° to 14°C) at night. In winter: 35° to 40°F (2° to 5°C) at night, up to 50°F (10°C) during the day.
- Water sufficiently to prevent the soil-ball from drying out but avoid excess water in the pot. Needs good drainage.
- Moderate humidity.
- Mix 1 part sharp sand and 3 parts standard potting mix. Feed monthly from April to September with mild liquid fertilizer.

Narcissus

Daffodil
Jonquil

Both *Narcissus* 'Cragford,' shown here, and 'Paperwhite' with all-white flowers, do well indoors. 'Paperwhites' may be set in bowls from September until January and covered about half way with gravel. Add water to just below the bottom of the bulbs. Touching water can cause decay. Keep cool until shoots reach 3 inches (8cm). Move to a warmer position for three or four days, then to full sun. Other species root in soil in the dark at a temperature of 45° to 50°F (8° to 10°C). Soil should just reach their tips. They are brought into light when the bud has left the bulb, which takes eight to twelve weeks. Mature plants may reach 2 feet (60cm) tall. After flowering the foliage withers. Place the pots in a cool dry location. In fall, replace the soil in the pot and plant the bulbs outside. Watch for aphids, mealybugs, mites, slugs and snails, and thrips.

- Well-lit airy location.
- Cold: 35° to 50°F (3° to 10°C) at night. Flowers will last much longer in a moderately heated room.
- Water moderately but regularly.
- Moderate humidity. Mist often in dry location.
- Mix 1 part sand and 2 parts standard potting mix or plant in gravel. No fertilizing necessary.

Neoporteria

This is a genus of spherical cacti which may become somewhat cylindrical at a more advanced age but will always remain fairly small. They originate in Chili and northern Argentina. The thorns are usually very beautiful. They vary in color from white or yellow to brown or black. *Neoporteria subgibbosa*, shown here, has up to twenty ribs subdivided by notches. The flowers are pink and yellow. Other species are *Neoporteria nidus*, *N. napina*, and *N. senilis* which resembles the 'Old Man' Cactus. *Neoporteria* cacti grow slowly and are therefore often grafted.

☀ Good light in winter and as much sun as possible in summer.

🌡 Warm: 60° to 70°F (16° to 20°C) at night. Keep cool in winter at 40° to 45°F (6° to 8°C).

💧 Water regularly in summer, then gradually decrease. Keep completely dry in winter.

༄ Spray thoroughly in high temperatures.

🪴 Cactus mix.

Neoregelia

This bromeliad from Brazil develops tubular rosettes and long narrow leaves, often beautifully colored. The foliage surrounding the short flower-stalks, which do not emerge from the tube, is often brightly colored. The best known species is *Neoregelia corolinae*, shown here, which can reach 24 inches (60cm) in diameter. *Neoregelia concentrica* forms large rosettes of prickly, mottled leaves and has violet bracts.

Bromeliads are watered by filling the "vase" formed by the foliage, but do not overwater. After the bloom the main rosette will die but new rosettes appear around the base. After these produce five or six leaves they can be cut away with a sharp knife and placed in their own pots. The old rosette can then be discarded. Yellow leaves are a sign of too much sun. Watch for scale and thrips. Treat with soap and water. Pesticides will injure your plant. Too cool temperatures can cause rotting.

☀ Good light but keep out of direct sunlight.

🌡 Warm: 60° to 70°F (16° to 20°C) at night. 60° to 65°F (15° to 18°C) in winter.

💧 Water regularly. In very high temperatures water freely. Keep the vase filled with water.

༄ High humidity. Mist frequently.

🪴 Special bromeliad soil, osmunda fiber or fir bark.

Nephrolepis

Boston Fern
Sword Fern

This genus, found everywhere in the tropics and sub-tropics, comprises about 30 species of ferns. They are easily grown. Some reach an overall height of five feet (150cm), but most are smaller. *Nephrolepis cordifolia* is terrestrial growing as well as epiphytic; its creeping root-stock develops runners with tubers 3/4 to 2 inches (2 to 5cm) thick. These are used to store water. The fronds grow up to 24 inches (60cm) and resemble feathers. They are very sensitive and will turn brown if touched. In the 'Plumosa' strain the individual leaf sections look like feathers. The best known variety for indoor cultivation is *Nephrolepis exaltata,* of which numerous ornamental strains exist including *N. exaltata* 'Bostoniense' or Boston Fern. The fronds may grow up to 40 inches (1m) in length. In the photograph at the rear is the strain 'Rooseveltii Plumosa,' with crisped leaves. Also shown are 'Rooseveltii,' center, and 'Teddy Junior.' The ornamental forms are fairly similar.

Propagation is from spores, by planting runners, or by division. This is best done in spring, though runners may be detached from the mother plant in summer as well. Grow in a mixture of equal parts of sand and peat and later transfer to the mixture below. Plant in clay pots. Mature plants prefer being potbound, but can be repotted in February or March. Provide at least 1 inch (3cm) of gravel under the plant for drainage.

Living room air is often too dry for *Nephrolepis.* The stone and tray method or an evaporator may solve the problem. It is important to water adequately in the growing period. If the plant deteriorates in spite of your attention, it should be given a rest with less water and no fertilizer. Remove brown foliage. After about five weeks give a little more water, repot if necessary and try to bring the fern into growth. Decrease the water supply in winter to allow for less evaporation. Do not water directly on fronds. Watch for aphids, mealybugs, red spider and thrips. Treat with soap and water. Pesticides will kill your fern.

Will take a fair amount of light but no direct sunlight. Keep roots cool. Needs air circulation, but avoid drafts.

Moderate: 50° to 60°F (10° to 16°C) at night. Minimum temperature in winter 60°F (14°C).

Keep the soil moist throughout the year. Water fairly often in the growing season, less during cooler seasons.

Ensure high humidity. Mist often with room-temperature water.

Mix 1 part vermiculite, 2 parts standard potting mix and 2 parts peat moss. Feed twice a year with a very weak solution of liquid fertilizer.

Nerium

Oleander

Nerium oleander, shown here, is an evergreen shrub that can reach a height of 5 feet (150cm). Flowers appear in terminal clusters. There are double forms and color can be white, red or even yellow. In temperate parts of the United States, the plant can spend the winter outside. Elsewhere it must be brought indoors. In September it should be pruned heavily. In February it can be repotted, for it likes lots of space for its roots. Watch for mealybugs, scale and whiteflies. Propagation is from tip shoots which root even in water. It may take up to three years for the bloom to appear. **WARNING: All parts of this plant are extremely poisonous. Do not burn trimmings because they release poisonous fumes.**

Always the sunniest spot available. Does well in artificial light.

Warm: 60° to 70°F (16° to 20°C) at night. Will tolerate a few degrees of frost. Temperature in winter 40° to 45°F (4° to 6°C).

Water generously in summer, using tepid water. Does not mind wet feet.

Tolerates dry air.

Mix 1 part vermiculite, 1 part peat moss and 2 parts standard potting mix. Feed monthly from April to September with mild liquid fertilizer.

Nertera

Bead Plant

This little plant, a native of South America, is grown for its orange berries which appear in such large numbers from April to June that the leaves are practically invisible. They may last for several months. Its correct specific name is *Nertera grandensis*.

Propagate from seed in February or March in sandy soil or by division in August. Pot in a well-draining mixture. Feed sparingly using a nitrogen-free fertilizer to avoid excessive leaf development. Pot in half-size pots because this plant has a shallow root system and is low growing.

Requires a fair amount of light but does not tolerate full sun. Place in an airy spot.

Moderate: 50° to 60°F (10° to 16°C) at night.

Water moderately from the bottom. Keep leaves dry.

Requires high humidity. Provide by the deep-saucer method rather than spraying.

Equal parts sharp sand and standard potting mix. Feed every 2 months with mild nitrogen-free fertilizer.

Nidularium

This bromeliad genus originates in Brazil. All species develop rosettes. As a rule the central leaves of these epiphytes are vividly colored. The curving leaves of *Nidularium fulgens* widen at the base and are up to 12 inches (30cm) in length. They are prickly and have green blotches. Little violet-colored flowers grow in the angles of the red bracts. *Nidularium innocentii*, shown here, has dark olive-green leaves that are purplish-brown on the underside. Before the plant comes into flower, the central leaves are bright red. The flowers are cream-colored.

Propagation is from seed or runners, or by division of new plants that form near base. Bromeliads are watered by filling the "vase" formed by the foliage. Yellow leaves are a sign of too much sun. Too cool temperatures can cause rotting. Watch for scale and thrips. Treat with soap and water. Pesticides will injure your plant.

- ☀ Slight or semi-shade.
- 🌡 Warm: 60° to 70°F (16° to 20°C) at night. Needs a constant temperature.
- 💧 Water generously in summer. Keep the vase filled.
- 💦 High humidity. Mist frequently.
- 🪴 Osmunda fiber, fir roots or special bromeliad mix.

Notocactus

Indian Head
Silver Ball

This cactus genus embraces 15 species, natives of South America. Usually these cacti are spherical in shape, with ribs divided into knobs. Both the spines and the yellow or red flowers that grow from the crown are very fine. Flowers tend to open only at midday. These cacti are extremely easy to grow and even young plants soon flower profusely. The species photographed is *Notocactus ottonis,* or Indian Head, which has a bright green globular body and may develop offsets. The thorns are yellow to red-brown. The flowers, 1-1/2 inches (4cm) in diameter, appear from May to July. Other species are *Notocactus apricus, N. concinnus* and *N. scopa,* or Silver Ball.

- ☀ Outdoors or in a fairly sunny position indoors in summer.
- 🌡 Warm: 60° to 70°F (16° to 20°C) at night. Cooler in winter: 50°F (10°C).
- 💧 Keep moist in summer using soft water. Avoid stagnant water in the pot.
- 💦 Spray in the growing period. Otherwise keep dry.
- 🪴 Equal parts standard potting mix and sharp sand.

Odontoglossum

Tiger Orchid

The more than 200 epiphytic tropical orchids included in this genus originate in Central and South America. They grow in a damp, cool environment on the edges of mountain forests, usually at altitudes between 5,000 and 10,000 feet (1,500— 3,000m). The pseudo-bulbs vary in shape. They can be single- or double-lobed and are surrounded at the base by leaves from which the flower stalk, often fairly tall, develops.

Odontoglossum bictoniense, shown in the upper photograph, puts out a flower stalk up to 40 inches (1m) in length, bearing three to four flowers in winter. The petals are yellowish-green with dark blotches and the lip is pink. *Odontoglossum grande*, in the lower photograph, is a native of Guatemala. It has broad, oval pseudo-bulbs and a flower stalk which grows up to 16 inches (40cm). From October to December it bears four to eight yellow and brown flowers more than 6 inches (15cm) in diameter. Other species suitable for living room cultivation are *Odontoglossum insleayi* which has yellow and red flowers in winter, *O. pulchellum* which is a small plant with fragrant yellow and red flowers, and *O. schlieperianum* which produces its yellow and brown flowers from July to September. All these species like a cool location and are reasonably tolerant of a dry atmosphere. *Odontoglossum grande* is the strongest orchid for indoor cultivation. When repotting in spring it is important to put a good layer of rocks or broken pottery in the bottom of the pot to ensure adequate drainage. Watch for aphids, mealybugs, slugs and snails, and thrips. Yellow leaves indicate too much light. Too much or too little watering will produce wrinkled foliage.

Other species belonging to this genus are more suited for cultivation in a moderately cool greenhouse. They include *Odontoglossum cervantesii*, a fragrant winter-flowering form with brownish-red with white flowers, *O. cordatum* and *O. maculatum.*

 Bright light but no direct sun. May be put outdoors in summer or indoors in an airy spot.

Moderate: 50° to 60°F (10° to 16°C) at night. Minimum temperature in winter 45°F (7°C).

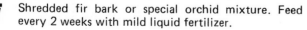 Keep moist in the growing season using soft water. Keep drier in the dormant season. Needs good drainage.

High humidity in summer. Mist often, but not directly on flowers.

Shredded fir bark or special orchid mixture. Feed every 2 weeks with mild liquid fertilizer.

Ophiopogon

Lilyturf

When not in flower, *Ophiopogon jaburan* bears great resemblance to *Lirope muscari* shown on page 103, but *Ophiopogon* produces white flowers and red berries. *Ophiopogon japonicus* has runners, curved leaves and flower spikes lower than the foliage. The form in the photograph is *Ophiopogon jaburan* 'Vittatus,' and creamy longitudinal strips on the leaves.

These plants are undemanding and are easily kept in good condition.

Propagation is by division in spring. The sections should be potted in a mixture of equal parts peat moss and standard potting mix.

- Tolerates shade.
- Moderate: 50° to 60°F (10° to 16°C) at night. Keep at 40° to 50°F (5° to 10°C) in winter. Stands up well to considerable temperature variations.
- Water generously in the growing period, moderately in winter.
- Moderate humidity.
- Standard potting mix.

Oplismenus

This plant belongs to the family of grasses. It has bare creeping or hanging stems and pointed, wavy-edged leaves. When the stems touch the soil they will readily root. Rooted cuttings are potted in a mixture of standard potting soil with some peat fiber and leaf mold added. Place a few cuttings together in one pot to make a bushy plant. In addition to the *Oplismenus hirtellus* illustrated here, there is a form called 'Variegatus' which has long longitudinally white-striped foliage, sometimes touched with pink.

- A very well-lit position in winter, slight shade in summer.
- Warm: 60° to 70°F (16° to 20°C) at night. Keep at 50° to 70°F (10° to 20°C) in winter. This means it may stay in the living room.
- Water generously in the growing period. Decrease watering from late August to February.
- Moderate humidity.
- Feed sparingly with mild liquid fertilizer. Standard potting mix.

Opuntia

Beaver Tail
Prickly Pear

This genus embraces 250 species. Originally found only in the Americas, the fruit formed an important source of nourishment for the Indians. Centuries ago the plants were brought to other parts of the world where they now grow wild. Hardier species include *Opuntia compressa,* which has creeping branches with flat oval joints from which pale yellow flowers appear, *Opuntia rhodantha,* with brownish-red joints and magnificent red flowers, and *Opuntia fragilis.* Flat-jointed *Opuntia* species, sometimes called Prickly Pears, are particularly undemanding. There are also cylindrical species, known as Chollas, as well as *Tephrocactus* species, whose joints are spherical or club-shaped. The two later require a slightly heavier soil mixture containing more clay. *Tephrocactus* species are sensitive to dampness. They grow very slowly and for that reason are sometimes grafted onto *Austro-cylinder Opuntia* forms.

Be careful when handling *Opuntia* cacti for they may give you painful pricks. Some varieties even have barbed spikes that are difficult to extract.

The *Opuntia* can be propagated from seed or from cuttings. The joints must first be allowed to dry for two to three days before being repotted. Cuttings are taken in June or July; sow in early spring at 70°F (21°C). The seeds should be soaked first.

Opuntia bergeriana, in the right foreground of the photograph, bears orange-red flowers and may grow very tall. *Opuntia delactiana* in the background on the right, has little spine development and bears orange flowers. *Opuntia microdasys,* in the foreground on the left, is relatively slow-growing. Each areole bears a tuft of golden-yellow, barbed bristle. *Opuntia scheerii,* rear left, is densely spined and may grow very tall.

- Sunny outdoor position in summer. Keep cool and in good light in winter.
- Warm: 60° to 70°F (16° to 20°C) at night. Temperature in winter 40° to 45°F (6° to 8°C).
- Moderately in the growing season, let soil dry out between waterings. From mid-August on decrease the water. Keep dry in winter. Needs good drainage.
- Maintain low humidity.
- Equal parts standard potting mix and sharp sand.

118

Oxalis

Four-Leaf Clover
Wood Sorrel

Two of the more than 800 *Oxalis* species are illustrated here. *Oxalis lasiandra,* on the left, is a native of Mexico. It has five- to nine-lobed leaves that are mottled red on the underside. These appear from small, yellowish-brown tubers. The little lilac-pink flowers grow in clusters from a single stem. *Oxalis deppei* on the right, is the lucky four-leaf clover. It has rose-red flowers in summer and autumn. The bright green leaves are crossed by a pink stripe. At night the flowers close and the leaves fold along the center vein. Tubers may be potted after January in groups about 1 inch (2cm) deep in 6-inch (15cm) pots. In fall sift through the soil and replant all the little bulbs. Large plants may be propagated by division. Remove faded flowers and watch for aphids, mealybugs, mites and scale.

- Well-lit, sunny position.
- Cool to moderate: 45° to 55°F (6° to 12°C) at night. Daytime temperature should preferably not exceed 65°F (18°C).
- Water moderately. Too much will cause the stems to grow lanky.
- Moderate humidity.
- Standard potting mix. From February to August feed once a week with diluted liquid fertilizer.

Pachyphytum

Moonstones
Silver Bract

This is a genus of succulents originating in Mexico. *Pachyphytum oviferum,* shown on the left, has bell-shaped flowers which are deep red. *Pachyphytum hookeri,* right, has red and yellow bell-shaped flowers. The leaves of these plants break off at the slightest touch and older plants tend to look straggly. They may also need support to grow upright. Watch for mealybugs and scale, but insecticides can damage the leaves of these plants. It is best not to spray them with anything but plain water. These plants also rot easily and need good drainage. Crossing *Papchyphytum* and *Echeveria* resulted in *Pachyveria,* shown in the center which is described on page 121. Propagation is from seed or from leaf or tip cuttings. These should be allowed to dry before planting.

- Airy, sunny spot in summer. In winter it should have plenty of light. Does well in artificial light.
- Moderate: 50° to 60°F (10° to 16°C) at night. Keep at 45° to 50°F (6° to 10°C) in winter.
- Keep fairly dry throughout the year.
- Stands up very well to dry living room air.
- Mix 1 part standard potting mix and 2 parts sharp sand. Feed monthly from April to August with mild liquid fertilizer.

119

Pachypodium

The 20 species belonging to this genus are natives of South Africa, Angola and Madagascar where they live in deserts and dry plains. They have thick, often tuberous, fleshy stems. True trunk-forming species are often thorny with leaves growing in rosettes at the top, as shown in the photograph of *Pachypodium lameri.* The flowers are very striking and occur in shades of yellow, pink or red. **WARNING: The sap of these plants is extremely poisonous.**

Propagation is from seed, which germinates in sandy soil at a high temperature.

- A well-lit, sunny spot throughout the year.
- Warm: 60° to 70°F (16° to 20°C) at night. In winter the temperature should be 55° to 60°F (14° to 16°C).
- Water moderately in winter, which is the main growing season. Keep fairly dry in summer. Needs good drainage.
- Low to moderate humidity.
- Coarse loamy mixture in deep pots.

Pachystachys

The *Pachystachys lutea,* shown here, is widely marketed today. It originates in the region between Mexico and Brazil. The plant resembles the *Aphelandra,* but has softer, plain green leaves. The flowers are 6 inches (15cm) long and are covered in a number of lemon-yellow bracts which last for several weeks. The white flowers soon drop. In spring the plant should be cut back a little and repotted. The pot should have good drainage.

Pachystachys is easily grown from cuttings. Shoots or stem cuttings may be rooted from mid-January until the end of July. The young plants should have the tips pinched out occasionally to produce a bushy shape.

- Good light, possibly diffused sunlight but avoid bright sun.
- Warm: 60° to 70°F (16° to 20°C) at night. 50° to 60°F (10° to 15°C) in winter.
- Water generously in the growing period and plunge from time to time. Be very sparing with water in the dormant season. Needs good drainage.
- Likes fairly high humidity. Less at lower temperatures.
- Equal parts peat and sand. Feed regularly with mild liquid fertilizer.

Pachyveria

This hybrid genus is the result of crossing *Echeveria* and *Pachyphytum.* The photograph shows *Pachyveria scheideckeri,* with spatulate blue-green foliage and blossoms consisting of bracts which drop and orange flowers. In summer these succulents may be put outdoors in a sunny position. In winter they must be kept cool and dry.

Propagation is from tip-cuttings, leaf-cuttings or side-shoots, which must be allowed to dry before being set in a mixture of peat moss and sand, or in sand alone.

- ☼ May be placed in a sunny outdoor position in summer. Requires plenty of light in winter.
- 🌡 Moderate: 50° to 60°F (10° to 16°C) at night. Keep cool in winter.
- 💧 Water moderately in summer. Keep practically dry in the dormant season.
- Dry to moderately humid air.
- Mix 1 part standard potting mix and 2 parts sand. Feed monthly from April to September with mild liquid fertilizer.

Pandanus

Screw-Pine
Tourist Pineapple

This genus comprises more than 600 species of tropical evergreen shrubs and trees. The *Pandanus veitchii,* illustrated, is a native of Polynesia. The strap-shaped green leaves are very prickly and have longitudinal cream-colored stripes. This species is the one most often grown indoors because it stands up well to dry air. Mature specimens may reach 10 feet (3m) tall and develop offsets at the base. These may be removed to grow new plants. Treat the cut surface with charcoal powder and root the cuttings with bottom heat of 75° to 85°F (25° to 30°C). Sponge foliage monthly with water. Do not use shiners or oils. Watch for aphids, mealybugs, red spiders, scale and thrips.

- ☼ Good light, no direct sunlight. Does well in artificial light.
- 🌡 Warm: 60° to 70°F (16° to 20°C) at night. Minimum temperature in winter 65°F (24°C).
- 💧 Water generously in the growing season, using slightly demineralized tepid water but let soil dry between waterings. Water less from October to March.
- Likes a humid atmosphere. Mist frequently.
- Standard potting mix. Feed every two months with mild liquid fertilizer.

Paphiopedilum

Lady's Slipper

The representatives of this genus of orchids, which embraces over 50 species, are immediately recognizable by the slipper-shaped lip. Most of these terrestrial-growing plants originate in Asia. They have an underground rootstock without pseudo-bulbs and their roots are fleshy. The leaves develop from the base and are leathery. They may be plain green, mottled or marbled. As a rule the flower stalk bears only one flower which lasts a long time. The upper sepal is called the *flag;* the two side sepals remain small. The side petals are often elongated and of the same color as the lip. Plain-leafed forms usually flower in winter, mottled or marbled forms usually in summer.

Green-leaved species are repotted after blooming around February, others in June. It is best to keep these plants crowded, so use small pots. Instead of repotting it is sometimes sufficient to replace the upper layer of soil. Provide good drainage and be careful that the roots do not rot from overwatering. In September place in slightly better light. Most *Paphiopedilum* species form flower-buds in October but dry air is harmful to this process. In November maintain the temperature at about 55°F (14°C) and decrease the water supply a little. In December water twice a week but maintain a humid atmosphere; a living room is usually too dry. The following are some of the green-leaved species suitable for a moderately heated greenhouse. *Paphiopedilum fairieanum* has white flowers striped with green and purple. *P. hirsutissimum* is very hairy with flowers of green, purple and brown. The colors merge into one another. *P. insigne,* a well-known orchid, has greenish-white with reddish-brown flowers which must be grown in a very cool environment. *P. villosum,* produces white-green-brown flowers between December and April. There are numerous hybrids. *P. nitens* shown here is the result of crossing *P. insigne* and *P. villosum.*

Some light but no direct sun.

60°F (15°C) at night. 75° to 85°F (25° to 30°C) during the day. In winter 60° to 65°F (15° to 18°C). at night and 65° to 70°F (18° to 20°C) during the day. Species with multi-colored foliage prefer slightly warmer temperatures.

Water regularly, using soft water. There is no real dormant season but give a little less water in winter.

Likes humidity.

Orchid mixture or shredded fir bark. Feed every 2 weeks with mild liquid fertilizer.

Parodia

This genus of spherical cacti comprises about 40 different species. They are very popular because they flower profusely, have beautiful spines and present few problems in cultivation. Most species are slow-growing and only reach a height of about 3 inches (8cm). They should be watered carefully for the root-neck is very sensitive to water. Propagation is from seed.

Parodia aureispina, shown here, is a native of northern Argentina. This cactus is densely spined with barbed central thorns. The flowers are golden-yellow. *P. chrysacanthion* has yellow spines and yellow flowers. *P. nivosa* has white spines and red flowers.

- Very sunny in summer. Cool and in good light in winter. Seedlings must be protected against bright sunlight.
- Warm: 60° to 70°F (16° to 20°C) at night. Keep at 45° to 55°F (8° to 12°C) in winter.
- Water very sparingly. Keep dry in winter. Needs good drainage.
- Low humidity.
- Cactus mixture or leaf mold mixed with coarse sand.

Passiflora   Passionflower

The passion flower owes its name to the unusual shape of its blossom, which has been seen as a symbol of the Passion of Christ. The *Passiflora violacea,* shown here, is not quite so well-known as *P. caerulea,* which is often grown on walls. Another species suitable for indoor cultivation is *P. racemosa,* which has orange flower clusters and threefold leaves. Do not worry if the leaves turn yellow and drop, provided some foliage remains. *Passifloras* are vigorous vines and can become untidy. They rest from October to January. Prune fairly heavily in January to encourage branching. They should be repotted periodically and given support. Crowded roots will restrict growth and reduce vigor. Repotting can be done anytime between spring and the end of summer. Watch for mealybugs, red spiders and scale.

- Will flower only in a warm and sunny spot.
- Moderate: 50° to 60°F (10° to 16°C) at night. Keep cool, 40° to 50°F (5° to 10°C), in winter. May be put outdoors.
- Water regularly in the growing and flowering seasons. Decrease in autumn. Do not let soil dry out.
- Moderate humidity. Mist occasionally.
- Standard potting mix. Feed weekly from April to October with mild liquid fertilizer.

Pavonia

The 170 species of this genus occur in many countries but only the *Pavonia multiflora,* shown here, has become common as a house plant. This winter-flowering plant is a native of Brazil and grows in the form of a shrub, usually single-stemmed with evergreen foliage. The flowers are erect terminal stalks. The leaves of the reddish-purple sheath are linear in shape, curling at the tip. The purple outer envelope never opens. The stamens appear before flowering. Propagation is from tip-cuttings in a mixture of peat fiber and sand with bottom heat, 80°F (30°C).

Prefers a half-shady position.

Warm: 60° to 70°F (16° to 20°C) at night. Keep at 55° to 65°F (12° to 18°C) in winter. Place in a warmer spot when the plant starts into growth.

Plenty of water in the flowering period. Water sparingly in the dormant season.

Fairly humid. Spray occasionally.

Standard potting mix. Feed every two weeks with mild liquid fertilizer.

Pelargonium
Geranium

There are about 250 *Pelargonium* species. *Pelargonium grandiflorum,* at the left, is a true house plant. Called the French Geranium, it flowers from April to September. Overfeeding may produce much foliage, but few blossoms. Overwatering will cause leaves to yellow. Standing water in the pot can cause rotting. Keep slightly potbound to encourage bloom. Pinch out growing tips to increase fullness. After flowering, prune to encourage compact and sturdy growth. Propagate in August from stem cuttings 4 inches (10cm) long taken from below the leaf joint. Remove the lower leaf and root in standard potting mix. Watch for aphids, mealybugs, mites, sow bugs and whiteflies.

Pelargonium grandiflorum

Very good light but screen against too bright midday sun. Does well in artificial light.

Moderate: 50° to 60°F (10° to 16°C) at night. Keep cool in winter at 50° to 60°F (10° to 16°C).

From March to August water freely using demineralized water. Allow soil to dry out between waterings.

Normal humidity. Mist occasionally. Likes fresh air.

Standard potting mix. Feed every 2 weeks from April to September with mild liquid fertilizer.

Pelargonium (continued)

The widest color range is found among the *Pelargonium zonale* hybrids shown on the left in the photograph. When bruised, the leaves have a distinctive scent. These plants flower from April to October. *Pelargonium peltatum* hybrids, on the right, have shiny ivy-like foliage and a creeping form. They are excellent in hanging baskets or trained as climbers. Prune heavily at the end of summer to avoid straggly look. From among the scented geraniums, *Pelargonium radens* is shown at right in lower photo, page 124. Feathery leaves are lemon- or rose-scented. Flowers are white, red or pink. It is grown from cuttings taken in spring. Further information about your plant can be obtained from The International Geranium Society, 1413 Shoreline Road, Santa Barbara, CA 93105.

Pelargonium zonale and *Pelargonium peltatum*

- Outdoors in summer. *P. zonale* may be placed in full sun. *P. peltatum* prefers half-shade.

- Moderate: 50° to 60°F (10° to 16°C) at night. Keep cool in winter 43° to 46°F (6° to 8°C).

- Water freely in growing season, sparingly in winter.

- Normal humidity. Likes fresh air.

- Standard potting mix. No feeding necessary.

Pellaea
Button Fern
Cliff Brake Fern

This genus occupies a special place among ferns, for *Pellaea* has leathery leaves and stands up well in dry living room air. The species illustrated is *Pellaea rotundifolia,* or Button Fern. It has fairly low-growing spreading form and looks good in a hanging basket. *Pellaea viridis* has elongated triangular leaves.

Propagation is from spores or by division, which is much easier. Pot in a fern mixture or in standard potting mix. Ferns like being potbound, but can be repotted in February or March. Plants that are ailing can be cut back to 2 inches (5cm) from the soil and repotted. Foilage should be washed monthly with water, and withered fronds should be removed. Watch for aphids, mealybugs, red spiders and thrips. Pesticides will injure your plant, use soap and water.

- Satisfied with little light. Never place in full sun.

- Moderate: 50° to 60°F (10° to 16°C) at night. Can stay in a heated room in winter 50°F (10°C) minimum.

- Maintain constant moisture. Don't let dry out, but don't let pot sit in water. Needs good drainage.

- Stands up in dry living room air. Spray frequently.

- Mix 1 part vermiculite, 1 part limestone and 2 parts standard potting mix. Feed every two weeks with very weak solution of mild liquid fertilizer.

Pellionia

Trailing Watermelon Begonia

Pellionia is an herb species that has a trailing form and does well in a hanging basket. The color of the leaves of *Pellionia repens,* shown here, depends on the amount of sun the plant receives, but they are usually pale green with dark brown margins. The growing stems stand erect initially but later become hanging. *Pellionia pulchra* has the same form but its foliage is much darker and pale green blotches appear only along the veins. The underside of the leaves is purple.

Pot in well-draining bowls. Do not overwater. *Pellionia* rots easily. Prune to prevent straggly growth. Repot as needed. Rinse foliage with tepid water to clean pores. Cuttings are rooted with bottom heat in spring. Watch for mealybugs, mites, slugs and snails, scale and whiteflies.

- ☀ Well-lit to moderately shady position. Does well in artificial light. Avoid drafts.
- 🌡 Warm: 60° to 70°F (16° to 20°C) at night. Keep at a minimum of 50° to 55°F (10° to 12°C) in winter.
- 💧 In the growing period water freely using soft water. Water sparingly in winter. Needs good drainage.
- 💦 Fairly high humidity. Mist frequently.
- 🪴 Standard potting mix. Feed every 2 weeks from February to October with mild liquid fertilizer.

Peperomia

Radiator Plant

Nearly all the species of this genus are tropical or sub-tropical herbs originating in Central and South America. They grow as epiphytes on tree trunks or branches or on the ground in the rain forest. About one thousand species are known, most of them with very decorative foliage. Many species and strains are suitable for use indoors, especially in bottle gardens. Few reach more than 1 inch (3cm) tall.

These plants are so-called leaf- and stem-succulents. Like tree succulents, they are able to store a reserve water supply in their leaves and stems, although in *Peperomia* the leaves are not so obviously thickened. In practice this means that you must be very careful with watering. As long as the foliage does not shrivel up the plant will not dry out. Too much water is likely to cause rot. Exposure to direct sun will discolor leaves.

The photograph on this page shows the well-known *Peperomia caperata* on the left. It has strongly crimped dark green leaves that are pale. green on the underside. The leaf stalks and flower stalks are rose-red, the spikes are white. The leaves of *P. verticillata,* on the right, grow in fours around the stem.

Peperomia (continued)

Peperomia argyreia, in the foreground of the upper photo, has shield-shaped fleshy leaves with silvery markings between the veins. The flower stalks and leaf stalks are red. The leaves of *P. arifolia* are similar in shape but the stalks and leaf stalks are dark green. *P. blanda* has reddish-brown erect growing stems and is covered with short hairs. The leaves grow in fours and are red on the underside. *P. glabella* has trailing stems and can therefore be used as a hanging plant. *P. incana* has thick fleshy leaves which are white with a felt-like texture on both surfaces. *P. maculosa* has reddish-brown mottled leaf stalks and dark green leaves with a white center vein. The leaves of *P. obtusifolia,* shown in the center of the lower photograph, are short-stalked, densely growing, thick and fleshy. The plant has firm bare stems and terminal spikes. 'Longenii,' in the lower photograph, foreground, and 'Variegata,' upper photograph, rear, are variegated strains and require more light than their all-green counterparts. *P. resediflora,* now called *P. fraseri,* is a species with small stalks of fragrant white flowers. A creeping species is *P. rotundifolia,* which has circular marbled leaves and slender runners. *P. serpens* has limp, bare, slightly winding stems bearing widely scattered pointed green leaves. The variegated form 'Variegata' is shown in the background of the lower photograph.

Propagation is from leaf- or tip-cuttings or from shoots, preferably in spring. Cuttings should be allowed to dry first. They are rooted with bottom heat in a sandy mixture. Initially they should be kept under glass or plastic but care must be taken that the fleshy parts do not rot. Mature plants prefer shallow clay pots and do not mind being potbound.

Erect growing species may have the tips pinched out to encourage bushy growth. Foliage should be washed frequently with tepid water to clean pores. Watch for mealybugs, mites, slugs and snails, and whiteflies.

- ☼ Well-lit place, out of direct sunlight. Does well in artificial light.

- 🌡 Warm: 60° to 70°F (16° to 20°C) at night. Variegated forms are kept at 65° to 70°F (18° to 20°C) in winter, all green plants at 60°F (15°C).

- 💧 Water moderately using tepid soft water. Water very sparingly in winter. Allow soil to become dry to touch between waterings. Needs good drainage.

- 〰 Very humid in summer, less so in winter. Mist frequently.

- ▼ Equal parts peat moss, perlite and standard potting mix. Feed monthly from February to October with mild liquid fertilizer. Feed half strength from November through January.

Pereskia

Leaf Cactus

This genus comprises 20 shrubby cacti, of which *Pereski aculeata* is illustrated. This is a climbing shrub with elliptical pointed leaves mottled in shades of yellow. The branches are thorny with the thorns growing singly or in twos or threes. They help the young shoots to support themselves. Pinkish-white flowers appear in October, but they have a very unpleasant smell. Placed against a sunny wall, these plants can grow very large, sometimes reaching 30 feet (9m) in height, but they will require support.

Propagation is in spring from seed sown in bottom heat of 70°F (21°C). In summer young shoots may be rooted in equal parts of peat and sand. When the leaves have dropped the plant is pruned and left to rest.

☀ Slightly shady position with a little sun in the afternoon and evening.

🌡 Warm: 60° to 70°F (16° to 20°C) at night. In winter a minimum temperature of 50°F (10°C).

💧 Water generously in the growing season, very little after the foliage has dropped. Needs good drainage.

☷ Moderate humidity.

▽ Cactus soil mix.

Persea

Avocado

This plant is rarely obtainable from a nursery but can be easily grown from the seed of an avocado, planted point up. It may also be rooted in water. Insert three toothpicks halfway up the seed and place it so the toothpicks rest on the edge of a glass. The seed should be suspended so the rounded end just touches the water. When roots form, plant the seed. After the first few leaves appear, pinch back the growing tip to increase fullness and encourage branching.

Persea americana, shown here may be propagated from cuttings taken in spring and rooted with bottom heat. Mature indoor plants have elliptical leaves. Unfortunately they do not bear fruit.

☀ Good light, a little sun will do no harm.

🌡 Moderate to warm: 55° to 70°F (12° to 20°C) at night. Temperature in winter 50° to 55°F (10° to 12°C).

💧 Keep the soil-ball constantly moist.

☷ Moderate humidity. Spray the foliage occasionally.

▽ Standard potting mix.

Philodendron

The *Philodendron* genus comprises 275 species. Some reach 7 feet (2m). There blossoms are shaped like an Arum Lily, as shown in the upper photograph of *Philodendron karstenianum,* but they are unlikely to flower in a living room. Some, often called *vining,* are vigorous climbers, with or without aerial roots. They are usually tender and require support. Others are shrubs, with or without a stem and are referred to as *arborescent.* These tend to be hardy and become large, sturdy, almost tree-like plants requiring much space. Frequently, the leaf-shape of young plants differs from that of mature specimens. Climbing species may be propagated by air-layering or from tip-cuttings rooted with bottom heat. Pinch out tips of cuttings before setting them under glass. A stem section with 2 or 3 nodes may also be used as a cutting. Aerial roots can be pushed into soil or cut off. Shrubby species can be propagated from seed or by division. If you intend to divide a plant, the growing point should be removed. After about a year the side-shoots should be sufficiently developed and the plant should be divided so that part of the parent stem remains attached to each shoot. Keep at 75°F (24°C) until the sections have rooted. Mature plants like being potbound and repotting is necessary every other year.

Philodendron imbe has a green or purple stem with 10 to 14 inch (25 to 35cm) leafstalks, bearing large, arrow-shaped leaves. The variegated form 'Variegatum' is shown in the lower photograph.

Philodendron bipinnatifidum is an erect-growing species with densely leaved stems and heart-shaped foliage. *P. laciniatum,* shown in the photo on the next page is a climber with divided and lobed leaves. *P. hastatum* has leaves shaped like arrowheads. *P. elegans* is an undemanding climber with deeply incised foliage. *P. selloum* is slow-growing with saddle-shaped leaves. *P. squamiferum* has long red leafstalks covered in scaly hairs.

The following are the best-known climbing or creeping species with undivided leaves. *Philodendron elongatum* has elongated large leaves. *P. erubescens* has leaves that are initially dark brown and later turn green and shiny. Its flowers have a red sheath and an ivory-white spike. *P. melanochrysum* has dark olive, almost velvety leaves. It is difficult to maintain and requires a moss post or damp wall for its aerial roots to grip. *P. panduriforme,* or Fiddle-Leaf Philodendron, has 10-inch (25cm) leaves that resemble a violin and *P. scandens,* has fairly small, heart-shaped leaves. *P. cordatum* also has heart-shaped leaves and is one of the most common species.

Philodendron martianum has a short stalk and

Philodendron (continued)

elongated leaves. Apart from *P. scandens,* which is very easy to grow, all species are sensitive to location and care. Always provide adequate warmth. Philodendrons with glossy foliage should have the leaves cleaned occasionally with a damp sponge, but do not use oils. Watch for aphids, mealybugs, red spiders, scale and thrips. Remove withered leaves and aerial roots. Brown spots on leaves or yellowing usually indicate overwatering. Too little light will cause small leaves or stragglyness. An abrupt change in environment will cause some species to drop their leaves. **WARNING: All varieties are poisonous if eaten. Contact with some varieties has been known to cause skin rashes.**

- Never put in full sun. A fair amount of shade can be tolerated. Does well in artificial light. Avoid drafts.
- Warm: 60° to 70°F (16° to 20°C) at night. In winter a minimum of 55°F (14°C) is required for green-leaved forms and 65°F (18°C) for variegated and velvet-leaved forms.
- In summer give plenty of tepid water. Soil should not dry out between waterings. Needs good drainage.
- Fairly high humidity is desirable. Spray often.
- Standard potting mix. Feed monthly from February to October with mild liquid fertilizer.

Phlebodium
Hare's Foot Fern

This fern was formerly marketed under the name *Polypodium* and originates in South America. *Phlebodium aureum* is illustrated. *Phlebodium aureum undulatum* has larger fronds, up to 20 inches (50cm) in length. Plant on gravel in clay pots. The roots, which eventually fill the entire pot, are light brown and scaly. They are said to resemble rabbit's feet which leads to the common name. The plant may grow to 6 feet (2m). Growing tips can be cut and rooted. Propagation is also by division or from seed. Wash fronds monthly with water and remove withered leaves. Watch for aphids, mealybugs, red spiders and thrips. Treat with soap and water. Pesticides will injure your plant. If plant looks bad, cut back to 2 inches (5cm) from soil and repot.

- Shady location. Needs good air circulation, but avoid drafts. Does well in artificial light.
- Warm: 60° to 70°F (16° to 20°C) at night. 65° to 70°F (18° to 22°C) in winter.
- Keep the soil moist using soft, room-temperature water but not too wet. Needs good drainage.
- High humidity is essential. Mist often.
- Mix 1 part vermiculite, 2 parts peat moss and 2 parts standard potting mix. Feed monthly with very weak solution of mild liquid fertilizer.

Phoenix

Date Palm

As its name indicates, the *Phoenix canariensis*, shown here, is from the Canary Islands. It is hardier than the true Date Palm, *Phoenix dactylifera*. Both species are grown from pits, but they grow slowly. A five-year-old palm may be only 5 feet (1-1/2m) tall. Repotting is required annually for the first few years because of the large masses of roots. Brown leaf-tips are generally caused by hard water, over-watering in winter or a dry soil-ball, which occurs when the root system has filled the pot. Yellow spots are due to insufficient light. Leaves should be wiped with a wet sponge to clean pores. Watch for mealybugs, red spiders, scale and thrips.

- Slight shade outdoors in summer, otherwise a warm room with good light. Does well in artificial light. Needs good air circulation but avoid drafts.
- Moderate: 50° to 60°F (10° to 16°C) at night. Keep frost-free in winter, preferably at 40°F (4°C). Warm temperatures are needed to stimulate growth.
- In summer give plenty of tepid demineralized water. Water sparingly in winter. Needs good drainage.
- High humidity. Mist frequently in hot weather.
- Mix 1 part peat moss, 1 part vermiculite and 2 parts standard potting mix. Feed monthly from March to November with very weak solution of liquid fertilizer.

Phyllitis

Hart's Tongue Fern

This fern is indigenous to Europe and North America. It is an evergreen winter-hardy plant with undivided, shiny leathery leaves. Some varieties have very crinkly foliage, others have divided leaves. The spores appear in bands parallel to the lateral veins.

The best known species is *Phyllisis scolopendrium*, of which the garden form 'Undulata' is illustrated. This is a strain with wavy-edged foliage. Propagation is by seed, by division or from lower stem cuttings rooted with bottom heat.

- Satisfied with very little light; may be grown indoors or out.
- Cold: 35° to 50°F (3° to 10°C) at night. Cool but frost free in winter.
- Water regularly. Keep the soil moist during spring and summer. Give a little less water in fall and winter.
- Fresh to humid air.
- Standard potting mix.

Pilea

Aluminum Plant, Artillery Plant
Baby's Tears, Creeping Charlie

Representatives of the more than 400 evergreen and hardy species of this genus may be found in tropical regions all over the world.

The best known *Pilea* species comes from Vietnam. This is *Pilea cadierei* or Aluminum Plant, which has green leaves with silvery blotches between the veins. It grows 12 to 15 inches (30 to 38cm). The insignificant white flowers appear in the angle between the stalk and the leaf in spring and summer.

Pilea depressa or Baby's Tears is a good ground cover for terrariums. It has small, round apple green leaves and a creeping form.

Pilea involucrata, shown in the upper photograph, has oval deeply wrinkled green and dark brown leaves and plumes of white flowers. *P. microphylla*, the Artillery Plant with its tiny opposite-growing leaves, makes useful groundcover. This moss-like plant originates in South America; the little flowers grow in clumps and spreads its pollen in little explosive puffs. *P. nummularifolia* or Creeping Charlie has small circular leaves on creeping or trailing stems. It makes a handsome hanging plant.

Pilea spruceana has hairy, wrinkled foliage; between the wrinkles the surface is quilted. The upper surface is bronze-green, the underside is purple. The beautiful 'Norfolk' strain shown in the lower photograph, has silvery stripes between the veins.

The plants are propagated from stem cuttings rooted in water or in a mixture of equal parts peat and sand, under glass and with bottom heat. The best time to take cuttings is in May. Plants that have lost foliage should be cut back in March or April. Otherwise, prune to reduce the stragglyness. *Pilea* does not like being potbound. Repot in mix described below. Ensure good drainage by putting pieces of broken pottery in the bottom of the pot. Rinse foliage occasionally to clean pores. Watch for mealybugs, scale, slugs and snails.

 A well-lit location but out of direct bright sunlight. Too much shade makes these plants spindly. Does well in artificial light.

Warm or moderate: 50° to 70°F (10° to 20°C) at night. 50° to 65°F (10° to 18°C) in winter.

In the growing period keep moderately moist; in winter give a little less water. Needs good drainage.

 Moderate humidity. Mist occasionally.

Mix 1 part perlite, 1 part peat moss and 2 parts standard potting mix. Feed monthly from February to September after flowering stops with mild liquid fertilizer.

Piper

Pepper

There are about 700 pepper species, the best-known being *Piper nigrum*, which provides us with black peppercorns. It may be used as a hanging or climbing house plant. The leaves are leathery, dark green, about 4 inches (10cm) in length, oval and sharply pointed. The plant can reach a height of 6 feet (2m). Keep cooler in winter. *Piper betle,* illustrated here, is used in the tropics for the manufacture of betel. This plant may also be grown indoors. The finest foliage, with very delicate white and pink markings on a deep green background, is produced by *Piper ornatum.* It requires such high humidity it is best grown in a greenhouse. Leaves of all varieties should be washed occasionally to clean pores. Watch for red spiders. Repot as needed. Propagation is from cuttings.

- May be grown in a well-lit location, but will take shade. Does not tolerate full sun.
- Warm: 60° to 70°F (16° to 20°C) at night. Keep a little cooler in winter; about 55°F 14°C).
- Maintain constant moisture but never too wet. Needs good drainage.
- Normal humidity. Mist frequently.
- Standard potting mix. Feed every 2 weeks with mild liquid fertilizer.

Pisonia

The plant in the photograph is often taken for a *Ficus* but its name is *Pisonia brunoniana* or *Heimerliodendron brunonianum.* It requires approximately the same treatment as a *Ficus*; that is, to be kept in a warm room throughout the year. It does however require a fair amount of light because the variegated form contains little chlorophyll. Although there is an all-green, more resistant form of *Pisonia brunoniana,* it is the variegated strain, 'Variegata,' which is usually seen. It does not tolerate excessively dry air.

Propagation is from cuttings which root at 70°F (22°C).

- Requires fairly good light but must be protected from full sun.
- Warm: 60° to 70°F (16° to 20°C) at night. Keep fairly warm in winter 65° to 70°F (18° to 20°C).
- The soil must be kept constantly but moderately moist.
- Fairly high humidity.
- Standard potting mix.

Pittosporum

A *Pittosporum* may grow into a large shrub. Its leathery foliage makes it appear suitable for a warm room but this is deceptive. In winter it should have a cool environment and in summer it should be outdoors. The species seen most often is *Pittosporum tobira*, which has spoon-shaped leaves and grows about 3 feet (1m) tall. There is also a variegated form 'Variegata,' shown in the photograph. Fragrant white flowers appear from May on. Prune in late winter to maintain shape. Wash leaves occasionally to clean pores. Watch for aphids, leaf miners, mealybugs, mites and scale. Remove dead foliage. Propagate from seed or cuttings of young wood in moist vermiculite. Do not use too large a pot when repotting. Mature plants like being potbound.

☀ Outdoors in summer. Stands up to sunlight. Needs plenty of light throughout the year.

🌡 Cold: 35° to 50°F (3° to 10°C) at night. In winter keep cool 40° to 45°F (4° to 8°C).

💧 Water moderately. Water freely in sunny conditions. Needs good drainage.

〰 Normal humidity. Likes fresh air. Spray occasionally.

▼ Mix 1 part sand and 3 parts standard potting mix. Feed monthly from April to September with mild liquid fertilizer.

Platycerium   Staghorn Fern

Platycerium, commonly called Staghorn Fern, is a reliable and decorative plant which has proved to be extremely resistant to the dry atmosphere of a living room. This is chiefly due to the visible layer of wax which covers the foliage. If this layer is removed, the plant will rapidly dry out.

The Staghorn is best grown against a slab of bark or wood hanging against a wall. A basket can look even better but in either case you must take precautions to avoid damage from dripping water. The plant should be set in organic matter such as peat moss which is kept damp all the time. Give it lots of space to spread. Some species can reach seven feet (2m) wide.

Make a habit of taking down the plant every week and plunging the base, but not the fronds, into a large basin, so that the moss and roots can soak up plenty of water. Use room-temperature water and dissolve some fertilizer in it. Ferns like plenty of nourishment. Watch for aphids, mealybugs, red spiders and thrips. Treat with soap and water. Pesticides will injure the plant.

The best known and strongest species is *Platycerium bifurcatum*, also called *Platycerium alcicorne*. This plant is shown in both photographs. You will see that the fern develops two kinds of

Platycerium (continued)

foliage. The large antler-shaped leaves are fertile and in maturity bear black spores on their undersides. The sterile inner leaves are initially green and conceal the center of the plant. They subsequently turn brown and start to rot. They help anchor the plant and feed the roots but it is nevertheless advisable to use a fertilizer.

 Light to semi-shade, never in full sun. Can be placed outdoors on a shaded patio in summer. Needs air circulation but avoid drafts.

Warm: 50° to 60°F (10° to 15°C) at night. Keep fairly warm in winter also, 60°F (15°C).

Keep the soil-ball constantly moist. Can be a little drier in winter.

Moderate humidity is sufficient. Mist frequently with room-temperature water.

Special fern mixture composed of sphagnum, fern roots and leaf mold. Feed monthly with half-strength solution of mild liquid fertilizer.

Plectranthus
Swedish Ivy

There are people who insist that *Plectranthus,* usually the species *Plectranthus fruitcosus,* the largest plant in the photograph, will relieve rheumatism and keep moths away. While this has not been proved, the plant is fast-growing and easy to care for. It grows to 2 feet (60cm) and occasionally it puts out small blue flowers, showing that it is related to the *Coleus.* The small plant is called *Plectranthus oertendahlii.* This species requires higher humidity. It does well in a hanging basket and is very easy to propagate from cuttings. It is advisable to do this every year, rather than repotting older plants. Prune to maintain shape and encourage flowering. Watch for mealybugs and whiteflies.

Good light but not in bright sunlight. Does well in artificial light.

Moderate: 50° to 60°F (10° to 16°C) at night. Temperature in winter between 55° to 65°F (12° to 18°C).

Water regularly and plentifully. After flowering keep a little drier. Needs good drainage.

Fairly resistant to dry living room air. Mist frequently.

Mix 1 part peat moss and 2 parts standard potting mix. Feed monthly from April to September with mild liquid fertilizer.

Plumbago

Leadwort

Although this profusely flowering climber looks fairly delicate, it may be placed outdoors from the end of May on. At first it will not react very enthusiastically but as soon as the sun gains power, flowerbuds will start to form and in summer numerous magnificent sky-blue flowers will open. It will send out branches 3 feet (1m) long. Heavy pruning after completion of flowering makes the plant easier to care for in the dormant season and will not harm the plant. Originally its name was *Plumbago capensis,* but it is now called *Plumbago auriculata.*

Propagation is from cuttings in autumn. They root at 70° to 75°F (20° to 25°C).

- ☀ In summer a sunny spot outdoors. In the dormant season a well-lit location indoors.
- 🌡 Moderate: 50° to 60°F (10° to 16°C) at night. A little warmer is acceptable. 40° to 45°F (5° to 8°C) in the dormant season.
- 💧 Freely in the growing and flowering season. In winter just enough to prevent drying out.
- ⸬ Moderate humidity.
- ⚱ Standard potting mix.

Polyscias

These fine but rather difficult foliage plants are related to the *Aralia* family, which is obvious from the junction between leafstalks and stem. The long stalks bear grouped leaves which are very decorative in the case of the species illustrated. The photograph on this page shows *Polyscias balfouriana*, a species with three unusual shell-shaped leaves on each stalk. The color is a beautiful green with white margins. In the variety 'Peacockii' the veins are white.

Polyscias filicifolia has 9 to 13 small, pale green leaves on each stalk. Sometimes each leaf is subdivided or serrated. Various strains of this species exist. *P. fruticosa,* 'Elegans,' is commonly known as Ming Aralia or Parsley Panax.

The beautiful foliage plant illustrated on this page is *Polyscias guilfoylei.* Each leaf stalk bears five to seven white-edged little leaves, all beautifully incised. The photograph shows a cutting but mature plants may grow to at least 40 inches (1m) and will have thousands of leaves. All the species mentioned are ideal for a greenhouse or a flower window. In the living room the foliage will usually dry out, though I have seen a specimen of *Polyscias balfouriana* growing in an office. Propagation is from 4 inch (10cm) cuttings rooted in spring

Polyscias (continued)

with bottom heat under glass.

Mature plants of some species can reach 20 feet (6m) tall. Cut growing tip to control height. Wash leaves monthly with room-temperature water to clean pores. Do not use oils. Remove withered leaves. Watch for aphids, mealybugs, red spiders, scale and thrips. These plants prefer being pot-bound.

 Bright position, but not direct sun. Does well in artificial light. Avoid drafts.

Warm: 60° to 70°F (16° to 20°C) at night. Minimum temperature in winter 60°F (16°C).

Do not allow soil to dry out. Needs good drainage.

High humidity. Spray frequently.

Standard potting mix. Feed every 2 weeks from March to October with mild liquid fertilizer.

Polystichum

Holly Fern
Shield Fern

The best known indoor specie of this genus is *Polystichum tsus-simense*, shown here. It is a native of Japan and has fronds up to 8 inches (20cm) in length. *Polystichum* is hardier than most other ferns because the foliage is leathery and transpiration is reduced. It is best combined with other plants in a container and its roots should be kept cool. Use clay pots. Ferns like being pot-bound, but their roots adhere to the sides of pots. Be careful not to injure roots when repotting. Watch for aphids, mealybugs, red spiders and thrips. Treat with soap and water. Pesticides will injure your plant. Propagate by division in March or by spores found on undersides of fronds.

Light to half-shady position. Needs air circulation but avoid drafts.

Warm: 60° to 70°F (16° to 20°C) at night. In winter keep about 50°F (10°C).

In summer give plenty of soft water, less in winter. Do not allow soil to dry out completely. Needs good drainage.

High humidity. Mist often with room-temperature water.

Mix 1 part vermiculite, 2 parts peat moss and 2 parts standard potting mix. Feed monthly with very weak solution of mild liquid fertilizer.

Primula

Primrose

Primulas or Primroses are delightful indoor plants, true harbingers of spring. For prolonged enjoyment *Primulas* should not be placed in too warm an environment. In a heated room they should be put close to the window where it is usually a little cooler. They will grow to 2 feet (60cm) tall. Pay attention to water; primulas are thirsty plants. They like having cool roots. A pot containing *Primula vulgaris* should be put in a saucer kept constantly filled with water.

Another way to prolong their flowering season is to give regular doses of fertilizer solution. If the foliage turns yellow, it means either the plants are too dry or that you have given so much fertilizer that the mineral concentration in the soil has become excessive. The latter may also be due to hard water. Mineral poisoning may be cured by immediate repotting. Overfeeding can also burn this plant's roots.

The plants do not like being potbound. Pot in small pots. Pot small plants that appear next to parent separately. Remove stems that have ceased flowering. Watch for aphids, mealybugs, mites, slugs and whiteflies.

The upper photograph shows *Primula malacoides,* in which the flowers grow around the stem at several levels. This is probably the most beautiful of the indoor species. Flowers are pink or white. The foliage and the stems are covered in a white dust. As a rule this plant is grown as an annual but you may try to bring it through the winter by putting it in the garden. Do not expect too much.

Primula obconica, in the lower photograph, has flowers growing in spherical clusters and large, hairy leaves. **Some hairs secrete a substance called *primine* which can cause skin irritation and sometimes even a rash.** There are strains on the market in which this substance is lacking but unfortunately this fact is never mentioned on the label. The flowers are red, rose-red, blue and white. These plants tolerate a warmer location than *P. malacoides* species and they can spend the winter in the garden or in a cold frame. Repot after flowering.

In Switzerland new strains are being cultivated in red, blue, bright yellow, golden-orange, etc. These novelties make hardier pot-plants than *Primula vulgaris.* They are called *Primula polyantha* 'Niederlenz.'

Primula vulgaris with its bright colors—its former name, now obsolete, was *Primula acaulis*—is actually a garden species. It is available from nurseries from February on. It is very intolerant to high temperatures.

The adjoining photograph shows two examples of *Primula praenitens,* better known as *Primula*

Primula (continued)

sinensis. It occurs in numerous colors and is occasionally available in full flower in October. Reasonably resistant to dry living room air, it also requires slightly less water than *P. polyantha.*

All species can be grown from seed, in a cool location. **WARNING: Contact with these plants will cause a skin rash in some people.**

 Bright light but not direct sun; outside in summer. Does well in artificial light.

Fairly cool: 40° to 50°F (5° to 10°C) at night. In winter keep at 55°F (12°C).

Keep very moist using tepid water. Give even more water in the flowering period. Avoid wetting foliage. Needs good drainage.

Moderate humidity. Mist daily, but not directly on blossoms.

Mix equal parts peat, sand and standard potting mix. Feed every 2 weeks with mild liquid fertilizer.

Pseuderanthemum

This is a typical foliage plant with very dark leaves, known also as *Eranthemum.* The species illustrated is *Pseuderanthemum atropurpureum.* The wine-red leaves are frequently spotted with olive-green. In addition to brown-leaved species there are also green, golden-veined forms.

This is a suitable plant for a greenhouse or flower window. In the living room the air is too dry. Older plants soon become unsightly and it is therefore advisable to take cuttings regularly which will root at a bottom heat of 75°F (25°C). The young plants must be cultivated in the greenhouse. Overwatering will cause the leaves to drop.

 Slight shade is best.

Warm: 60° to 70°F (16° to 20°C) at night. In winter 60° to 65°F (16° to 18°C).

In the growing period the soil-ball should be kept moist with soft water. In winter keep a little drier.

High humidity. Spray often.

Standard potting mix. Feed monthly from April to February with mild liquid fertilizer.

Pseudomammillaria

In many books this plant is found under the name *Dolichothele.* However the species illustrated has differently shaped flowers and its official name is *Pseudomammillaria camptotricha.*

This cactus grows readily in any kind of soil and puts out a large number of shoots. The long spines of the individual globes intertwine, creating an extremely entangled mass. The brown and green colors go well together. In summer place the plant in very good light. In winter it must be kept cool and dry or it will die.

- As much light and sun as possible.
- Warm: 60° to 65°F (16° to 20°C) at night. In winter a temperature of 45° to 55°F (6° to 12°C).
- In the growing period it should not be too dry. Water from the bottom. Water very sparingly in winter. Needs good drainage.
- Low humidity.
- Standard potting mix or a special cactus mixture.

Pteris

Brake Fern
Victoria Fern

The *Pteris* genus comprises some of the best-known and most popular fern species. They possess scaly rhizomes and feathery fronds. There are about 300 species with widely varying, unusually shaped foliage. They are generally green although some strains have white-striped leaves. Spores grow along the margins of the leaves, except at the tip. Propagation is from ripe spores which germinate in damp peat at 75°F (25°C). The plants are then cultivated in a moderate temperature. Propagation by division is also possible.

Pteris cretica is the species best known as a house plant. It grows to about 18 inches (45cm) tall and the foliage is usually pale green and slightly leathery. The photograph shows the strain 'Albolineata' on the left, with a creamy stripe down the leaves. Other forms grown on a large scale are 'Major,' 'Wimsettii,' and 'Wilsonii' at the right in the photo.

Plant these ferns in clay or porcelain pots which help keep roots cool. These plants like being pot-bound. It is best to repot in February or March. Roots stick to sides of pots so be careful not to injure them. Wash fronds monthly to clean pores and remove withered fronds. Watch for aphids, mealybugs, red spiders and thrips. Treat with soap and water. Pesticides will injure your plants.

Pteris (continued)

Two white variegated strains of *Pteris ensiformis* are in cultivation: 'Victoriae' which is shown in the photo at the right, and 'Evergemiensis.'

Pteris multifida resembles *Pteris cretica*, but has very narrow leaves. *Pteris quadriaurita* or Silver Fern, has double- or triple-pinnate fronds with sessile side leaves, sometimes silver-striped. *Pteris tremula* is another well-known house plant, sometimes called Trembling Brake.

☀ Always a half-shady position.

🌡 Moderate: 50° to 60°F (10° to 16°C) at night. Variegated strains should be kept at 50° to 55°F (10° to 12°C) in winter; green-leaved forms at 60° to 65°F (16° to 18°C).

💧 In the growing season water freely using soft tepid water. Give less in winter but do not keep too dry.

 Maintain high humidity. Mist frequently with room-temperature water.

🪴 Mix 1 part peat moss, 1 part standard potting mix and 2 parts sharp sand. Feed monthly with very weak solution of mild liquid fertilizer.

Punica
Pomegranate

The *Punica* or Pomegranate is a deciduous, throny shrub which has been in cultivation since time immemorial. It originated in North Africa, from where it spread to Persia and India. The flowers have an orange-red corolla and the edge of the petals is flesh-colored. Flowering occurs from June to September. The fruits of *Punica granatum,* shown here, will drop with the foliage at the first sign of frost.

New plants may be grown from seed in March or from cuttings rooted with bottom heat.

☀ In summer a sunny outdoor spot is preferred but it can remain indoors.

🌡 Moderate: 50° to 60°F (10° to 16°C) at night. Keep at 40° to 45°F (4° to 6°C) in winter until new growth appears.

💧 In the growing period keep moderately moist. Water sparingly from August on. Needs good drainage.

 Likes fresh, moderately humid air.

🪴 Standard potting mix. Feed every 3 months with mild liquid fertilizer.

Rebutia

Crown Cactus

These small spherical cacti are undemanding and flower easily, even when very young. The flowers appear at the base of the globes and are often very large in proportion to the body of the plant. Propagation is by division or from seed, which should be covered with a little sand. From April to June give cactus fertilizer. In summer provide adequate fresh air. During winter the longer the period of coolness and drought, the more flowers will be produced the following spring.

The plant illustrated is *Rebutia miniscula*, which can have as many as 20 flowers at one time. Other well-known species are: *Rebutia chrysacantha*, with red flowers and golden-yellow spines; *R. marsoneri, R. senilis* and *R. xanthocarpa.*

☀ Fairly sunny position in summer. Good light in the dormant season.

🌡 Moderate to warm: 55° to 65°F (13° to 18°C) at night. Keep cool 40° to 45°F (6° to 8°C) in winter.

💧 Water fairly freely in summer after buds appear, then gradually decrease. Keep dry in winter. Needs good drainage.

🌫 Stands up well to dry living room air.

🪴 Special cactus mixture. Feed monthly from April to June with cactus fertilizer.

Rechsteineria

Brazilian Edelweiss

The soft-haired *Rechsteineria cardinalis*, shown here, is a native of Brazil. The tubular red flowers grow horizontally. Brazilian edelweiss, *Rechsteineria leucotricha*, has gray, wooly leaves and pink tubular flowers. Propagation is from seed, leaf cuttings or shoots with a section of tuber attached. Fully grown plants should be fed every two weeks from May to September. In winter the tubers are kept at a minimum temperature of 55°F (12°C). In February they are planted in damp peat or fresh soil with their tops just emerging and brought into growth at 70°F (20°C).

☀ Good light but no direct summer sun.

🌡 Warm: 60° to 70°F (16° to 20°C) at night. Tubers should be kept at 55° to 60°F (12° to 15°C) in winter. Bring into growth at about 70°F (20°C).

💧 In the flowering period water regularly, using soft water, but do not let roots dry out. Then gradually decrease until the foliage dies back. Needs good drainage.

🌫 High humidity.

🪴 African violet potting mix. Keep the tubers dry in the pot in winter. Feed every 2 weeks from May to September with mild liquid fertilizer.

Rhaphidophora

This plant is sometimes confused with *Scindapus* but the plant illustrated is *Rhaphidophora aurea*. It is a vigorous climber which attaches itself by its aerial roots. The 'Marble Queen' strain contains very little chlorophyll and is consequently very slow-growing. Good light helps bring out colors on leaves.

Sponge the leaves monthly with water. Do not use oil or shiners. Old leaves tend to drop and withered leaves should be removed. Prune back to reestablish plant.

Propagation is from severed runners or stem-sections with one or two leaf buds and aerial roots. Root in water.

- Likes light, but no direct sun. Variegated forms require more light than green species. Does well in artifical light.
- Warm: 60° to 70°F (16° to 20°C) at night. In winter the temperature must not drop below 60°F (16°C).
- Water regularly. Allow soil to dry out between waterings. Needs good drainage.
- Resistant to dry living room air. Mist frequently.
- Mix 1 part peat moss, 1 part sand and 3 parts standard potting mix. Feed every 2 weeks from October to February with mild liquid fertilizer.

Rhipsalidopsis
Easter Cactus

Rhipsalidopsis gaertneri, shown here, is a branching cactus with curving stems. The lower joints are triangular or hexagonal. The upper younger sections are flat. Segments are easily broken. If they become tinged with purple, the plant may be getting too much sun. The flowers are scarlet with slightly out-curving pointed petals and appear in late spring or early summer. The somewhat rarer species *Rhipsalidopsis rosea* has fragrant pink flowers.

Propagation is from seed or from tip-cuttings which should be allowed to dry out first. When the first buds appear, increase the water supply. Do not move or turn plant, as this increases the risk of the buds dropping.

- Light shade.
- Warm: 60° to 70°F (16° to 20°C) at night. From September on keep in a cool spot 40° to 50°F (5° to 10°C) until the buds begin to form.
- Keep the soil-ball moist but allow it to become fairly dry before flowering.
- Moderate humidity.
- Standard potting mix.

Rhoeo

Boat Lily
Moses-in-the-Cradle

Rhoeo has elongated leaves growing in funnel-shaped rosettes. The upper surface is green or has pale longitudinal stripes, as in *Rhoeo spathacea* shown in the photograph. The underside is purple. The small white flowers, surrounded by boat-shaped bracts, appear in the angle between the stems and lower leaves.

Rinse leaves with room-temperature water to clean pores. Rolled leaves indicate too low humidity. Water carefully in winter because surface shoots are subject to rot. Watch for mealybugs and mites.

Propagation is from seed, cuttings, or from shoots which will root readily in sandy soil. After rooting they should be potted in a coarse mixture rich in humus. Cuttings may be taken anytime except winter.

 Half-shady position. The variegated form requires a little more light but no direct sunlight. Does well in artificial light.

Moderate: 50° to 60°F (10° to 16°C) at night. In winter a minimum of 50°F (10°C).

In summer water freely with soft tepid water. Keep drier after flowering. Needs good drainage.

High humidity. Mist frequently.

Equal parts peat, sand and standard potting mix. Feed weekly from March to August with liquid fertilzer.

Rhoicissus

Grape Ivy

This genus comprises 12 evergreen, climbing species. The best known is *Rhoicissus capensis,* shown here. It has undivided leaves covered in brown hairs in the early stages. This plant needs a cool position, for instance in a hall. It is a good choice for a hanging basket.

Repot every year in April. From May to September feed once very two weeks. Occasionally sponge the leaves. Occasional pruning will help the plant to stay compact.

Propagation is from shoots rooted at 60° to 65°F (16° to 18°C) in a mixture of peat and sand. Stem sections with at least two nodes may also be used.

See also *Cissus.*

 Half- to deep-shade.

Cool to moderate: 45° to 55°F (8° to 14°C) at night. 45° to 50°F (6° to 10°C) in winter.

Water moderately, even less in the cooler winter season.

Not very tolerant of dry air. Spray occasionally.

Mix equal parts sand and standard potting mix. Feed ever 2 weeks from May to September with mild liquid fertilizer.

Rochea

Of the species originating in South Africa, the *Rochea coccinea,* illustrated here, is the one to be recommended most. This succulent shrub-like plant has been used as a house plant for quite some time. It stands out because of its scarlet flower clusters which appear in June. The erect-growing stems are densely covered with pairs of leaves growing on opposite sides.

Propagation is from cuttings in March, the cut surface must be allowed to dry out, or from seed which will germinate in about two weeks. Seedlings are potted in loamy, sandy soil in fairly small pots.

☼ In summer it may be put outdoors. Protect from bright sunlight. Needs good light in the dormant season.

🌡 Cold to moderate: 40° to 55°F (5° to 12°C) at night. Allow a dormant season at 40° to 45°F (4° to 8°C).

💧 In summer water adequately. Keep drier during the rest of the year.

≈ Enjoys fresh, slightly humid air.

🪴 Standard potting mix.

Rosa   Rose

While usually considered an outdoor plant in the United States, there are a number of varieties which make very successful house plants. The 'Happy' strain, illustrated here, is one of the miniature roses that flower profusely from March to October. They do not grow beyond 8 to 12 inches (20 to 30cm) tall. Faded blooms must be removed immediately, since rose-hips, if allowed to develop, take too much of the plant's strength. You can prune heavily after flowering. Wash leaves occasionally with tepid water in the morning so leaves have time to dry before night. The 'Happy' rose is semi-double, as is 'Doc,' which has slightly large flowers. 'Sleepy' is a double-pink rose.

☼ Light, sunny location.

🌡 Moderate: 50° to 60°F (10° to 16°C) at night. During the dormant season keep at 45° to 50°F (6° to 8°C). From February on gradually bring into a slightly warmer environment.

💧 In the growing and flowering seasons water fairly frequently. In winter keep only just moist.

≈ Requires humidity, especially in spring.

🪴 Standard potting mix. Feed monthly with special rose food.

Saintpaulia

African Violet

The African Violet is the most popular house plant in the United States. It originates in East Africa and is a low-growing herbaceous plant 3 to 6 inches (7 to 15cm) tall. Its leaves are hairy and cluster in groups called *crowns.* The flowers grow in clusters and appear almost any time of the year. Numerous strains have been developed in addition to the original violet-blue species. They vary in the color of the flowers and the shape and color of the foliage. Apart from *Saintpaulia ionantha*, shown in the photographs, *Saintpaulia confusa,* which has oblong leaves, is commonly grown.

The plants may be grown from seed sown in late January with bottom heat of 70°F (20°C). Crowns can also be rooted, as can cuttings from vigorous leaves. Young plants are potted in wide bowls. Soil should slope away from the crown. Water from top and let drain into saucer under pot. Do not allow water to sit in saucer more than two hours. If a white stain appears on the surface of the soil, water heavily to flush the soil or repot. The stain is minerals from your fertilizer. After flowering give the plant a short rest. New buds soon appear.

African Violets bloom best when they are crowded but, when necessary, should be repotted in a shallow, wide pot or bowl. The leaves should hang above the soil but not touch the edge of the pot where salts collect that can injure the plant.

A poor bloom is usually caused by too little light or humidity, or incorrect temperature. Too many crowns will draw energy away from blooming, They should be divided and replanted. Brittle leaves mean too much dryness. Leaves should be dusted occasionally with an artist's brush to clean pores. Cold water can cause botrytis blight and spots on foliage. Crown rot comes from soggy soil. Watch for aphids, mealybugs, mites and red spiders. Curled leaves indicate cyclamen mites; the plant should be discarded.

For further information write Saintpaulia International, Box 10604, Knoxville, TN 37919 or The African Violet Society of America, Inc., Box 1326, Knoxville, TN 37901.

☼ In summer a slightly shady position; in winter good light. Will stand some sun. Does well in artificial light.

🌡 Moderate to warm: 55° to 65°F (13° to 18°C) at night. 60° to 65°F (15° to 18°C) during the resting period.

💧 In the growing and flowering seasons water with tepid soft water. Needs good drainage.

〰 Needs high humidity but spraying may spot leaves.

🪴 African Violet mix or equal parts peat moss, perlite and standard potting mix. Feed every two to four weeks with commercial African Violet fertilizer.

Sansevieria

This plant has been very popular since about 1930. This is partially due to the fact that its somewhat succulent nature makes it resistant to temporary neglect. Its tolerance of dry air is another advantage. Almost the only ways to kill a *Sanservieria* are overwatering or putting it in too cold a location.

Most species originate in tropical regions of South Africa where *Sanservieria cylindrica* is still being used as raw material in the production of fibers. In the background on the right, you see *Sansevieria trifasciata*, which has dull-green erect lancet-shaped leaves, cross-banded in paler green. To the left is the very well-known form 'Laurentii' which has leaves with a golden yellow margin. 'Hahnii' on the left foreground, is low-growing and forms funnel-shaped rosettes. 'Golden Hahnii' on the right, has yellow bands along the margins. There is also a 'Silver Hahnii' with white banding. All these small *trifasciata* forms are slightly more tender than their larger counterparts. They must not be kept too moist, require a resting period in winter and their position must be neither too well lit or too dark.

Sansevieria longiflora is not very well known. It has striking blossoms and beautifully marbled, dark green foliage. At the back of the pot in the left foreground you see *Sansevieria senegambica*, which has green leaves, sometimes faintly striped along the edges.

The plants are best propagated by division. They may also be grown from leaf cuttings by cutting 3 inch (7cm) long pieces and setting them in moist sand, bottom-side down. Cuttings taken from variegated forms will revert to green, because the green parts of the leaf take root. Plants that are too tall can be pruned by cutting growing ends. These can also be rooted in moist sand. Leaves should be washed monthly with room-temperature water. Do not use oils. Remove withered leaves. Brown edges mean too cool a temperature. This plant likes being potbound, but can be repotted in spring.

- No special requirements but bright sunlight will affect the foliage markings. Does well in artificial light.

- Warm: 60° to 70°F (16° to 20°C) at night. Minimum temperature in winter 55°F (13°C).

- Water moderately. In winter keep fairly dry, but do not allow soil to dry out completely. Needs good drainage.

- Stands up well to dry air. Mist occasionally.

- Standard potting mix. Feed weekly from February to October with mild liquid fertilizer.

Saxifraga

Mother-Of-Thousands
Strawberry Begonia

Saxifraga stolonifera is a perenial, native to Asia and grows to about 12 inches (30cm). The foliage is dull green with white veins and red on the underside. In the 'Tricolor' strain, shown here, the leaves have an irregular white and red mottling. In spring and summer it produces 8 to 16 inch (20 to 40cm) plumes of small white or pink flowers. This strain grows slowly, flowers less profusely and requires a higher temperature than the main species. Faded blossoms should be removed and the leaves should be dusted with a soft brush to clean pores. Faded leaves mean too much fertilizer. Watch for mealybugs, scale and whiteflies. Propagation is by rooting the plantlets which appear on the runners.

- Requires plenty of light but no direct sun.
- Moderate: 50° to 60°F (10° to 16°C) at night. In the dormant season maintain a temperature of 50° to 55°F (10° to 12°C).
- The soil-ball must be kept moist. Beware of overwatering, especially in winter. Needs good drainage.
- Moderate humidity.
- Mix 1 part peat moss, 1 part perlite and 2 parts standard potting mix. Feed monthly from March to October with mild liquid fertilizer.

Schefflera

Umbrella Tree

Although now classified as *Brassaia*, this plant is still widely known as *Schefflera*. In its native Australia it is an evergreen tree, growing to 130 feet (40m). As a houseplant, it is pruned to maintain a compact growth and fullness. *Schefflera digitata*, shown here, requires a slightly higher temperature than *Schefflera actinophylla* with its thicker leaves. A new dwarf variety, *S. aboricola* has recently been introduced.

In summer give your plant a well-lit and airy location out of the sun and especially out of any draft. Wash leaves with room-temperature water. Excessive wetness or dryness will cause the leaves to drop. Watch for aphids, mealybugs, red spiders, scale and thrips. Propagation is from seed.

- Plenty of light and space throughout the year although it will tolerate a fair amount of shade.
- Moderate: 50° to 60°F (10° to 16°C) at night. Temperature in winter 55° to 60°F (12° to 16°C). May be placed outside in summer.
- Water moderately. Keep fairly dry in the dormant season. Needs good drainage.
- Moderate humidity. Mist occasionally.
- Standard potting mix. Feed every 6 months with mild liquid fertilizer.

Scindapsus

Devil's Ivy
Pothos

Scindapsus pictus, shown here, originates in Southeast Asia. It is a climber with thick dark green leaves with blue-green and cream spots. Depending on the species, *Scindapsus* can reach 15 feet (5m) with support. The 'Argyraeus' strain has smaller leaves with clearer white markings and a silvery margin. It is more sensitive than the main species and likes to be kept warmer. Propagate from cuttings rooted in water.

Leaves should be washed monthly with water, not oil. Remove any withered leaves. Older leaves will drop and you may have to prune the plant to reestablish it. High humidity is important, but avoid soggy soil. These plants are relatively easy to maintain. See also under *Rhapsidophora.*

☀ A well-lit location out of the sun. Tolerates shade. Does well in artifical light.

🌡 Warm: 60° to 70°F (16° to 20°C) at night. Requires a fairly high temperature in winter, too.

💧 Water moderately throughout the year using tepid water. Allow soil to dry out between waterings. Needs good drainage.

❄ Requires high humidity. Mist frequently.

🪴 Mix 1 part perlite, 1 part peat moss and 3 parts standard potting mix. Feed monthly from February to October with mild liquid fertilizer.

Scirpus

Club Rush

This graceful, grass-like little plant grows to 10 to 12 inches (25 to 30cm). Its bright green, needle-fine leaves initially grow erect and later curve down, so that the plant may be used in a hanging basket or pot. In summer little spikes of white flowers are developed at the extremities of the blades. They look like bits of fluff.

To keep *Scirpus cernuus,* shown here, in good condition, the soil must be kept constantly wet. The simplest way to do this is by placing the pot in a saucer of water. Repot when necessary. Propagation is by division in late spring or early summer.

☀ Half-shady position.

🌡 Moderate to warm: 55° to 65°F (13° to 18°C) at night throughout the year.

💧 Water very generously. There must always be water in the saucer.

❄ High humidity.

🪴 Pot in standard potting mix in pots with saucer attached.

Sedum

Burro's Tail
Stonecrop

This genus embraces 600 species of succulents from all over the world, including winter-hardy plants from colder regions. Most species have a low spreading form and are especially suited to a hanging basket. Trailers may reach as much as 3 feet (1m) long, but they grow very slowly.

Sedum dendroideum, shown at the right rear, develops an irregularly branching little trunk with fairly thick, circular or spoon-shaped waxy leaves and a stalk bearing star-shaped yellow flowers. It is a native to Mexico, as is *Sedum humisfusum,* a low-growing plant with yellow flowers, on the left foreground. *Sedum rubrotinctum,* foreground right, is a common red succulent which grows to only 8 inches (20cm). The cylindrical leaves and slender stalks, break off easily and root themselves. The stalks tend to lay down at first but later grow erect. The flowers are yellow.

In the background on the left is *Sedum sieboldii,* a native of Japan which produces pink flower clusters in autumn. The leaves always grow in threes at intervals of more than 1/4 inch (1cm). This is a winter-hardy species which fades in the autumn. There is also a variegated strain called 'Mediovariegatum.' Grow in very sandy soil.

Sedum bellum is a creamy-white, winter-flowering hanging plant. *Sedum pachyphyllum* is erect-growing. Its circular leaves are tipped with red. Another form not illustrated is *Sedum morganianum* or Donkey Tail. It has drooping stems bearing cylindrical pointed leaves, perfectly aligned, that give a braided effect. Stems can grow to 3 or 4 feet (1m) long, hanging in a pot, but leaves are easily knocked off. It likes filtered light and lots of water. *Sedum stahlii,* commonly called Coral Beads, has bead-shaped leaves on erect-growing stems.

Sedum can be propagated from stem or leaf cuttings, or seed. The cut surface must dry before they are inserted in a mixture of sand and peat.

Excessive watering causes rotting. Watch for mealybugs and scale. Dried foliage should be trimmed off.

☼ A well-lit sunny spot. In summer it may be placed in a sheltered outdoor position. Does well in artificial light.

🌡 Moderate: 50° to 60°F (10° to 16°C) at night. Keep cool in winter at 45° to 50°F (7° to 10°C) in good light.

🝙 Water moderately in summer. Keep fairly dry in winter. Needs good drainage.

Reasonably resistant to dry air.

▼ Mix equal parts sharp sand and standard potting mix. Feed monthly from April to July with mild liquid fertilizer.

Selaginella

Moss Fern
Spike Moss

There are 700 different *Selaginella* species. Most of these originate in tropical rain forests but there are a number of low-growing species from more temperate regions which can be grown in a cooler environment with a daytime temperature of 40° to 70°F (5° to 20°C). One of these is *Selaginella apoda*. The minimum temperature for the taller growing species, including *Selaginella martensii*, shown here, is 55°F (12°C). It can reach 12 inches (30cm) when young, but creeps when older.

Propagation is by division or from tip-cuttings about 2 inches (5cm) long rooted in bottom heat. The cuttings should be sprayed occasionally. Fertilizer should be greatly diluted. Mature plants prefer shallow pots and should be repotted annually. Pinch tips to promote branching.

- Very tolerant of shade. Does well in artificial light.
- Moderate to warm: 50° to 70°F (10° to 20°C) depending on the species.
- Water moderately using room-temperature soft water. Do not allow to dry out.
- High humidity. Mist often.
- Mix 1 part peat moss, 1 part vermiculite and 2 parts standard potting mix. Feed monthly from February to October with mild liquid fertilizer.

Selenicereus

Night Cactus

This cactus has blue-green limp and trailing stems, about 3/4 to 1-1/4 inches (2-3cm) thick. The shoots sometimes grow to 5 feet (1.5m) and it is advisable to train the plant against a trellis. The pale green stems become purple with age. Spines are yellow but become gray as plant grows older. As the popular name indicates, *Selenicereus grandiflorus* flowers at night during summer. Toward 3 p.m. the buds begin to swell and by 10 p.m. the flower is fully open. By about midnight it has closed again and the following morning an insignificant, limp relic is all that remains of the wonderful spectacle.

Propagation is from cuttings or from seed.

- In summer, a well-lit position out of direct sunlight. Plenty of light in winter.
- Moderate to warm: 55° to 65°F (14° to 18°C) at night. Keep at 50° to 70°F (10° to 20°C) in winter.
- In summer keep fairly moist. Spray until it flowers. In winter water sparingly.
- Enjoys fresh air.
- Cactus mixture.

Sempervivum

Hen and Chickens
Houseleek

This is an undemanding little succulent, easily grown from seed or from detached rosettes. Blooming rosettes die after setting seeds.

The photograph shows *Sempervivum tectorum calcareum* 'Nigricans,' with brown-tipped green foliage, at the left rear. In *Sempervivum arachnoideum,* foreground on the left, the rosettes appear to be covered in cobweb. This is one of the best-known species. In the center background you see *Sempervivum thompsonii.* In the background, right, is *Sempervivum tectorum,* commonly known as Hen and Chickens. In front of it is a strain of this species called 'Emerald.'

☀ Sunny, well-lit spot, indoors or outdoors.

🌡 Cold: 40° to 50°F (3° to 10°C) at night. All *Sempervivum* species are winter-hardy.

💧 Water sparingly throughout the year. Very resistant to drought. Needs good drainage.

💦 Low humidity adequate.

🪴 Mix equal parts sharp sand and standard potting mix.

Senecio

Cineraria
German Ivy

Senecio is related to the Daisy and includes some succulent varieties. The plant in the adjoining photograph used to be sold under the name *Cineraria,* but its correct name is *Senecio cruentus.* The photograph shows one of its numerous hybrids. It is an annual native of the Canary Islands with velvety flowers that range in color from red to blue or white. Flowering may be prolonged by placing the plant in a cool location and giving it only tepid water. Water from below to avoid crown or leaf root. Attacks by whiteflies are usually the result of drafts or of too warm a position. Watch for aphids, too. Propagation is by seed, but requires a cool greenhouse. Propagation should be left to the expert.

☀ A half-shady position. Avoid drafts.

🌡 Cold: 35° to 50°F (3° to 10°C) at night. Daytime temperature must not be too high either.

💧 Water moderately to freely. Keep soil moist. Needs good drainage.

💦 Enjoys fresh, slightly humid air. Spray occasionally.

🪴 Mix 1 part perlite and 3 parts standard potting mix. Feed every 2 weeks from March to November with mild liquid fertilizer.

Senecio (Succulent Species)   String-Of-Beads

The *Senecio* succulent species do not resemble the *Senecio cruentus* described on the facing page. Their leaves are fleshy and contain a great deal of sap which keeps the plants alive in times of drought. It is extremely easy to kill these plants by overwatering and it is advisable to use pots with holes in the bottom filled halfway with rocks or broken pottery.

All species like plenty of light and a cool position in winter. Sometimes they produce flowers but these are of minor importance. On the other hand the foliage can be extremely interesting. Consider the *Senecio herreianus,* in the upper photograph, with its spherical little leaves, like threaded peas. A very similar form is *Senecio rowleyanus. Senecio citriformis* or String of Beads has lemon-shaped leaves. *Senecio haworthii* has more pointed leaves. These last three species used to be called *Kleinia.*

There are also species with thick cylindrical stems such as the vigorous *Senecio articulatus.* Its joined stems and unusually incised leaves make it look like a plant from a horror film. Other species resemble *Echeveria* or *Crassula. Senecio stapeliiformis* has stems resembling those of the Carrion Flower, *Stapelia,* shown on page 159.

German Ivy, *Senecio mikaniodes,* has thin but fleshy foliage remarkably similar to ivy. It is a very vigorous hanging plant. Its variegated counterpart is called *Senecio macroglossus* 'Variegatus,' shown in the lower photograph. Do not keep it too dark.

All species are propagated from cuttings which will present no problem. Fleshy cuttings must first dry out before placing in water or moist sand to root. Repot mature plants annually in February. Pinch back to maintain and improve shape. Lower leaves may drop in plants that are climbing or twining, but that is no cause for concern.

- The best-lit position available, but not full sun.
- In winter a maximum of 55°F (12°C) at night. In summer moderate 50° to 60°F (10° to 16°C) at night.
- During the dormant season in summer water very sparingly. Give a little more in the growing season. Needs good drainage.
- Moderate humidity. Spray occasionally.
- Standard potting mix. Feed monthly from March to November with mild liquid fertilizer.

Setcreasea

Purple Heart

The photograph shows *Setcreasea purpurea,* a purple plant that grows to about 16 inches (40cm) after which the stems curve, so that it may be used as a hanging plant. The leaves are attached directly to the stem and are slightly hairy. The outer envelope of the flowers is pink. Mature plants should be pruned in early spring to encourage growth. New plants are grown from young ground shoots or cuttings. They root fairly easily in water or moist vermiculite. Older plants are repotted as needed. Overwatering can cause rotting, do not allow the soil to dry out completely. Pale foliage is a sign of overfeeding. Wash the foliage occasionally with room-temperature water to clean pores. Watch for mealybugs, mites, scale, slugs and snails, and whiteflies.

- A well-lit or sunny position. Does well in artificial light.
- Moderate to warm: 55° to 65°F (13° to 18°C) at night. In winter the temperature may drop to freezing.
- Keep the soil-ball moderately moist. Do not drip water on foliage. Needs good drainage.
- Moderate humidity. Mist frequently.
- Mix 1 part perlite, 1 part peat moss and 2 parts standard potting mix. Feed every 2 weeks from February to October with mild liquid fertilizer. Feed every 4 weeks from October to February.

Siderasis

This plant is related to the *Setcreasea* described above, as well as to the *Tradescantia. Siderasis fuscata,* shown here, a native of Brazil, is the sole species available. The upper surface of the leaves is green with a central white stripe and reddish-brown hairs. The underside is red. Mature leaves are usually 8 inches (20cm) long and 3 inches (3cm) wide. The color of the flowers varies from blue to red.

These plants are increased by division of mature plants.

- Will stand some light.
- Warm: 60° to 70°F (16° to 20°C) at night. A little cooler in winter.
- Water regularly, keeping the soil moist.
- Fairly high humidity.
- Standard potting mix. Feed every 2 to 3 weeks from April to August with a weak solution of mild liquid fertilizer.

154

Sinningia
Gloxinia

This plant grows from tubers up to 1-1/4 inches (3cm) in diameter. The hairy leaves grow to 10 inches (25cm). Flowers appear in late summer. The original species from Brazil has violet flowers, but hybrids have many shades. The form shown is a pink *Sinningia speciosa. S. pusilla* is a miniature variety. Propagation is from leaf cuttings or runners. Damp soil and cold water are fatal to these plants. During the six to twelve weeks after flowering, move the plant to a darker, cooler site and withhold water. Leaves will yellow and dry out. Give enough water so tubers do not shrivel. When tubers sprout, place each in a 6-inch (15cm) pot. Cover with 3/4 inch (2cm) layer of soil. Poor drainage causes crown or leaf rot. Too little humidity causes brown leaves. Mist around, but not directly on this plant. Watch for aphids and mites.

 Well-lit position, out of direct sun. Avoid drafts.

Warm: 60° to 70°F (16° to 20°C) at night. Keep the tubers dry at 45°F (6°C) in winter. Bring them into growth at 65°F (18°C). Avoid sudden changes.

Keep soil barely moist with lukewarm water.

High humidity. Mist occasionally.

Commercial African Violet mix. Feed every 2 to 4 weeks during growing season with a mild acid fertilizer.

Skimmia

This is a slow-growing evergreen shrub indigenous in cool but frost-free regions. The *Skimmia japonica,* in the adjoining photograph, comes from Japan and rarely grows more than 3 feet (1m) tall. It flowers in May. The flowers are creamy-white and are followed by long lasting red berries.

Skimmia is unusual in that there are separate male, *S. fragrans*, and female, *S. oblata,* plants. To obtain berries you will need both species. Outdoors insects will look after the pollination but indoors you will have to pollinate with a brush.

 A half-shady position indoors. May be placed outdoors in summer.

Cold to moderate: 40° to 55°F (5° to 12°C) at night. It is not winter-hardy.

Water moderately using water that feels hot to your hand. Make sure the soil-ball does not dry out. Needs good drainage.

Moderate humidity.

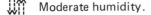 Slightly acid soil mixture.

Smithiantha

Temple Bells

This genus is well worth growing both for the multicolored leaves and the yellow, red or pink flowers. Many fine hybrids are available, such as the one shown here. Most grow to 1 to 2 feet (30 to 60cm) tall. When dormancy begins in October withhold water and let the *rhizomes*, or scaled roots, dry. Remove the leaves after they wither and store the rhizomes in a cool dark place. In March they are brought into growth. Place in a 6-inch (15cm) pot and cover with a 3/4-inch layer of soil. Delay feeding until the shoots are 4 inches (10cm) long. Stems and leaves break easily, so be careful when handling these plants. Remove faded blossoms. Poor drainage will cause crown or leaf rot. Too little humidity will cause leaves to roll. Too cold water will cause brown spots on leaves. Watch for aphids, mites, red spiders and thrips.

☼ Well-lit position with a little diffused sunlight. No direct sun. Does well in artificial light. Avoid drafts.

🌡 Warm: 60° to 70°F (16° to 20°C) at night. Keep the rootstock at 50° to 55°F (10° to 12°C) in winter.

💧 Water moderately using tepid water. Needs good drainage.

≋ High humidity. Do not let foliage get wet.

🪴 African Violet potting mix. Feed weekly from April to October with mild acid fertilizer.

Solanum

Jerusalem Cherry

The photograph shows *Solanum pseudocapsicum* as it is found at the nursery in autumn or winter. Large plants can reach 3 feet (1m) tall. Small white flowers appear in May or June. In each flower cluster only one flower is fertile. Artificial pollination increases the chance that it will bear fruits which look like small tomatoes. These keep longer in a cool location. When the leaves drop, prune and give the plant a rest. In March it will start into growth once more. Prune to control growth. Tall plants may require support. They can be trained as an espalier. Too much heat or shade will cause leaves or fruit to drop. Watch for aphids, scale or whiteflies. **WARNING: Poisonous if eaten.**

☼ A sunny position. May stand outside in summer but must be brought indoors before frost.

🌡 Cold to moderate: 45° to 50°F (7° to 11°C) at night. 45° to 50°F (8° to 10°C) in autumn. *Solanum* is very sensitive to frost.

💧 Water freely in the flowering period, less afterwards. Never let the plant dry out entirely. Needs good drainage.

≋ Above normal humidity. Spray occasionally.

🪴 Standard potting mix. Feed every 6 weeks with mild liquid fertilizer.

Soleirolia

Baby's Tears
Helxine

Soleirolia soleirolii is a low-growing creeping plant indigenous to Corsica and Sardinia. It is sometimes called *Helxine*. The little plants with their recumbent, thread-like stalks form large green mats that will spread and fall over the edge of its pot or planter. The green leaves are asymmetrical, heart- or kidney-shaped. The flowers, too, are tiny. They are greenish in color and grow in the angles between the stems and leaves.

Propagation by division is very simple. The plant grows very rapidly and in a short time you will have one to give away as a present. Pruning encourages growth.

Diffused sunlight or semi-shade. May be put outside in summer.

Moderate: 50° to 60°F (10° to 16°C) at night. Possibly a little cooler in winter.

Water freely in the growing period; keep moist in winter but don't let it stand in water.

Moderate to high humidity.

Standard potting mix.

Sonerila

This genus includes about 175 species of tropical flowering plants, of which only *Sonerila margaritacea*, shown here, is popular for use indoors. This very decorative plant, a native of Java, is very suitable for inclusion in bottle gardens or terrariums. The leaves are about 4 inches (10cm) long and the flowers are 1/2 inch (1cm) in diameter. It is a shrubby little plant with hanging red stalks bearing leaves that are shiny green on their upper surface. Silvery spots are arranged in lines between the lateral veins. The underside is paler in color, with purple veins. The flowers are bright pink. Take tip-cuttings in spring and root them with bottom heat of 85°F (30°C). Plant in shallow pots.

Semi-shade.

Warm: 60° to 70°F (16° to 20°C) at night. Keep at 65°F (18°C) in winter.

Water freely in the growing period. Do not allow plant to dry out in winter.

Maintain fairly high humidity.

Mix equal parts sharp sand and standard potting mix.

Sparmannia

House Lime

This relative of the Lime Tree may grow up to 10 feet (3m) tall in the living room, but may be held in check by pruning. It produces flowers, but no fruit. The *Sparmannia africana,* shown here, may be pruned after flowering. It is best to prune at the end of the resting period, which takes place in May. The 9-inch (23cm), heart-shaped leaves are pale green and have a texture like felt. The white flowers appear in clusters and have numerous stamens. Propagation is from flower shoots in spring. Provide adequate bottom heat.

- Well-lit, sunny and airy position. Do not place too close to other plants.
- Moderate: 50° to 60°F (10° to 16°C) at night. During the dormant season, from October to December, 45° to 50°F (6° to 10°C).
- Water freely in the growing season, a little less in winter. Do not let plant dry out.
- Reasonably tolerant of dry air.
- Standard potting mix. Feed monthly with mild liquid fertilizer.

Spathiphyllum

Flame Plant
Peace Lily

This evergreen perennial prefers a shady, warm and humid environment. It will bloom readily indoors if you provide adequate humidity. The blossom of *Spathiphyllum wallisii,* shown here will reach about 9 inches (23cm). This plant requires a large pot, but it should be kept potbound. Repot, if necessary, in February or March. Put a layer of gravel or broken pieces of pottery in the bottom of the pot. Roots may appear above the surface of the soil. They should be covered with a layer of sphagnum moss which is kept damp or repotted. Soil should never dry out. Watch for mealybugs, red spiders, scale and whiteflies. Do not let insecticide get on flowers. Roots are tender and can be burned by fertilizer. Too much sun will scorch leaves. The plant is easily propagated by division or from seed.

- Some light but not direct sun. Will not do well under artificial light.
- Warm: 60° to 70°F (16° to 20°C) at night. Minimum temperature in winter 55° to 60°F (14° to 16°C).
- Water regularly and fairly freely in the growing period. Water a little less in winter. Needs good drainage.
- High humidity.
- Mix equal parts fir bark and standard potting mix. Feed every two weeks from February to August with a weak solution of mild liquid fertilizer.

Stapelia

The photograph shows *Stapelia variegata,* which flowers from August to October. These flowers have a most disagreeable smell which give this plant its common name, Carrion Plant.

Stapelia species are fairly easily grown succulents and spineless stems that resemble cacti. Some species reach 12 inches (30cm) in diameter. It is important that they are kept cool in winter and are watered just enough to prevent them from shriveling up. Excess watering will cause the stems to decay. Watch for mealybugs.

Propagation is reasonably easy. Stem cuttings are set in sand after the cut surfaces have been left to dry. Plant in well-draining pots.

- A sunny spot in summer. Best possible light in winter.
- Moderate to warm: 55° to 65°F (13° to 18°C) at night. Keep cool in winter.
- Keep fairly dry, especially in the dormant season. Needs good drainage.
- Very tolerant of dry air.
- Standard potting mix.

Stenandrium

Of the 30 sepecies belonging to this genus, only one is cultivated, namely *Stenandrium lindenii.* This low-growing, shrubby little plant comes from Peru. Its stalks are usually less than 6 inches (15cm) long and the leaves are blistered and oval in shape. The surface is dark green with yellow veining; the underside is reddish in color. The flower spikes produce small yellow flowers. This is an excellent groundcover for plant containers or in shallow bowls.

A constant temperature of 65° to 70°F (20° to 22°C) is essential to keep the plant in fine and healthy condition. Shoots are rooted in a bottom heat of 85°F (30°C).

- Light shade.
- Warm: 60° to 70°F (16° to 20°C) at night. Keep the daytime temperature at about 70°F (20°C) throughout the year.
- Keep constantly moist.
- High humidity required. Spray often.
- Standard potting mix combined with some leaf mold.

Stenotaphrum

Buffalo Grass
St. Augustine Grass

In tropical and temperate regions this grass species is occasionally used for lawns. Wild species usually occur along the coastline. The form used as a house plant is *Stenotaphrum secundatum,* especially the 'Variegatum' strain illustrated here. It has creamy longitudinal stripes on the ribbon-shaped leaves that can reach 12 inches (30cm) long. Roots grow from joints in the stem and young plants are developed which may be potted separately. *Stenotaphrum* can also be propagated from stem cuttings. Several plants should be combined in a pot to achieve bushy growth. Overwatering can cause rotting. Watch for mealybugs, mites, scale and whiteflies. Rinse foliage occasionally to clear pores.

- A sunny location. Does well in artificial light.
- Moderate to warm: 55° to 65°F (13° to 18°C) at night. A little cooler in winter.
- Water moderately.
- Moderate humidity. Likes fresh air. Mist frequently.
- Mix 1 part perlite and 3 parts standard potting mix. Feed monthly with mild liquid fertilizer.

Stephanotis

Madagascar Jasmine

Of the five species of this genus only *Stephanotis floribunda,* the Madagascar Jasmine, is cultivated. A deliciously scented flowering specimen can be a real ornament in your home. The flowers are frequently used in bridal sprays.

In a warm or moderate greenhouse with a minimum temperature in winter of 55°F (12°C) *Stephanotis* may be trained over a large area of the glass. As a shrub it can reach 12 feet (3-1/2m) tall. In the flowering season it is a beautiful sight.

In warmer parts of the United States *Stephanotis* can be planted outdoors, but only in filtered sun. Keep the roots in full shade. It should bloom in June and continue through the summer. Indoors, the flowering season lasts from May to October and the dormant season from October to January.

In the living room *Stephanotis* is best trained on a trellis or on bent wire. The foliage should be sprayed from time to time to maintain adequate humidity. *Stephanotis* is a vigorous grower and will require pruning or repotting. The best time to repot is April, Young plants should be repotted annually, older plants every two or three years.

Too high a temperature in winter can lead to attacks by scale or mealybug. Check plants constantly, spray once a month with a solution of soap and water.

Stephanotis (continued)

Propagation is from cuttings throughout the year. They are taken from the previous year's wood and rooted at a temperature of 75° to 85°F (25° to 30°C). They will root in four to six weeks. Seed is developed fairly freely. It can be sown in warm conditions, but this method is rarely used because plants grown this way flower much later and much less profusely than those propagated from cuttings.

☀ A well-lit, airy location but out of direct sun.

🌡 Warm: 60° to 70°F (16° to 20°C) at night. Minimum temperature in winter 54°F (12°C).

💧 In summer water frequently. In winter give less water and allow some drying out.

≋ Moderate humidity. Spray occasionally.

🪴 Standard potting mix. Feed monthly from March to September with mild liquid fertilizer.

Strelitzia
Bird of Paradise

The shape of the flowers of *Strelitzia reginae* give it its common name, Bird of Paradise. Its leaves grow about 18 inches (33cm) tall and its flowers appear on long stems throughout the year. Plants may reach 5 feet (1.5m) in height. Crowded plants bloom more profusely but they can be repotted in spring or summer. Take care not to damage the fleshy roots. In warmer parts of the United States *Strelitzia reginae* is grown in the ground outdoors. In most places plants can be placed outdoors in summer. Propagation is from seed. The plants will take four to five years to flower. Dead leaves and flowers should be removed. Watch for mealybugs and scale.

☀ Keep in a well-lit, sunny spot. In summer screen against very bright sun.

🌡 Moderate: 55° to 65°F (12° to 18°C) at night. Provide fresh air in summer as soon as the temperature rises above 70°F (21°C). In winter 50°F (10°C).

💧 Water freely in spring and summer. Keep drier in winter. Needs good drainage.

≋ Moderate humidity. Spray frequently.

🪴 Somewhat loamy potting mixture. Apply fertilizer frequently. Mix 1 part perlite, 1 part standard potting mix and 2 parts peat moss.

Streptocarpus

Cape Primrose

Streptocarpus is an evergreen perennial grown for the large number of magnificent flowers it may produce over a long period of time. I say *may,* for the flowering depends on correct treatment. This native of South Africa is related to the African Violet, *Saintpaulia,* and is grown under similar conditions. *Streptocarpus saxorum* has small leaves and lavender trumpet-shaped flowers. The *Wiesmoor hybrids* grow 6 to 8 inches (15 to 20cm) tall and bloom for at least 2 months. *Nymph hybrids* are larger and last longer. They are all tough plants. These plants enjoy humid air and should never be placed above a source of heat. They are best grown in wide shallow dishes. The air should be lightly misted as often as possible, but never to the extent that the foliage retains drops of water. They will not tolerate the bright noonday sun. An east-facing window is ideal.

Mature plants should be cut back after flowering. The plant will remain dormant for up to 3 months. Watch for red spiders, thrips and whiteflies. Poor drainage can cause root rot.

Streptocarpus is usually at its best in its second year when it may produce many hundreds of flowers, usually in fall and winter. These vary in color from white to pink and red to reddish-purple and purple. There is also a pure blue form.

In the flowering season *Streptocarpus* must be fed regularly. The seed capsules are coiled and can be sown from February to midsummer. Temperature should not drop below 65°F (18°C) during sprouting. The plant is easily propagated in an indoor propagator. Cut a leaf lengthwise along the vein and insert both sections, cut edge down, in a mixture of sand and peat. In a little while numerous plantlets will develop along the cut, which may subsequently be potted separately. They are best kept under glass or plastic at first and then gradually accustomed to drier air. Plants can also be propagated by dividing large clumps into individual pots. This should be done in spring.

Streptocarpus hybrids are shown in the photographs.

☀ Plenty of light but no direct sun.

🌡 Cold to moderate: 45° to 55°F (6° to 13°C) at night. Minimum daytime temperature in winter of 50°F (10°C).

💧 Water freely in the growing period, a little less in winter, depending on the temperature. Keep moist. Needs good drainage.

∭ Moderate humidity. Do no spray the foliage.

🪴 African Violet mix. Feed monthly with mild liquid fertilizer.

Stromanthe

The *Stromanthe* genus belongs to the family of *Marantaceae*, along with *Calathea* and *Maranta*. There are 13 different species, all originating in tropical regions of South America. *Stromanthe amabilis* shown in the photograph, has gray-green foliage with dark green markings that can reach 12 inches (30cm) long. In *Stromanthe sanguinea* the upper surface of the leaves is dark green with a paler central vein and the underside is brownish-purple. Its leaves can reach 20 inches (50cm) long. In all species the blossoms rise above the foliage. The plants can be propagated by division or from offshoots.

☀ Filtered sunlight is acceptable. Direct sun will injure this plant.

🌡 Warm: 60° to 70°F (16° to 20°C) at night. Minimum temperature in winter 50°F (15°C).

💧 In the growing season water freely. Water slightly less in the dormant period. Always use tepid soft water.

💦 Fairly high humidity.

🪴 Standard potting mix.

Syngonium   Goosefoot Plant

Syngonium has a number of characteristics which distinguish it from other Arum Lily plants such as *Philodendron* or *Monstera*. All *Syngonium* species have a milky sap and the shape of the leaves varies greatly with the stages of development.

In *Syngonium vellozianum*, shown here, the leaves are initially arrow-shaped. They then become three-lobed and later five-lobed. The leaf stalks are fairly long and the bracts are pale yellow. In many cases two small ear-shaped appendages develop underneath the lower lobes. *Syngonium podophyllum*, or Arrowhead Plant, may even have eleven-lobed leaves.

Syngonium is easy to grow and can be trained to climb, hang or grow upright, as long as support is provided for its aerial roots. It will reach 3 feet (1m) in height and width. It can be rooted in water and live there without problems. Prune to maintain desired size. Sponge foliage monthly with room-temperature water. Do not use oils. This plant is pest-resistant, but watch for aphids, mealybugs, red spiders, scale and thrips.

Syngonium (continued)

The adjoining photograph shows a yellow-green marbled strain of *Syngonium podophyllum.* Mature plants may produce greenish, flower spikes from April to August. Roots develop from the nodes.

Syngonium will tolerate almost any light situation. Shade will make it produce smaller, darker leaves. Bright light will produce larger brighter green leaves. In variegated varieties the pattern will be stronger, but too much darkness will cause them to revert to green.

Propagation is by cuttings. Take a section of stem with an eye and root under glass in bottom heat. Air-layering also presents few problems.

Shady but not too dark. Does well in artificial light.

Warm: 60° to 70°F (16° to 20°C) at night. Minimum temperature in winter 60°F (16°C).

Water regularly, using tepid water a little less in winter. Needs good drainage.

Fairly high humidity preferred. Mist frequently.

Mix 1 part sharp sand, 1 part peat moss and 2 parts standard potting mix. Feed every two weeks with mild liquid fertilizer.

Tetrastigma
Chestnut Vine

This fast growing evergreen climber has composite leaves, shiny green on the upper surface, brown-haired underneath. Its young tendrils seem almost to reach out for new places to grasp for support and it will easily cover a 6-foot (2m) trellis. Old tendrils hang limply like strings. It belongs to the Vine family and originates in Vietnam. The species illustrated is *Tetrastigma voinierianum,* the only one which is cultivated.

These plants have the peculiar habit of resting for several months for no apparent reason. When this happens, reduce the amount of water until growth begins again.

The plant may be propagated throughout the year from cuttings with an eye and a leaf. They should be rooted under glass at a temperature of 70°F (25°C). It is important not to bury the eye when the cutting is rooted. The leaves are covered with a hairy down and should not be washed.

Tolerates a reasonable amount of shade.

Moderate: 50° to 60°F (10° to 16°C) at night. In winter allow a dormant season at 50°F (10°C).

In summer give plenty of soft water, a little less during the resting period.

Moderate humidity.

Standard potting mix.

Thunbergia

Black-eyed Susan Vine
Clockvine

This plant is a perennial, but is usually treated as an annual when grown indoors. *Thunbergia alata*, shown here, is a native of South Africa. It can be trained as a vine or kept in a hanging basket. The flowers are 1 to 2 inches (2 to 5cm) in diameter, and the plant can spread to 3 feet (1m) long.

Thunbergia is raised from seed in a mixture of sand and peat. If you want a winter bloom, plant in March or April. Seeds should be germinated at a temperature of 60° to 65°F (16° to 18°C). Small cuttings can also be planted in a mixture of sand and peat. Do not ever let the soil dry out completely. Watch for mealybugs, red spiders and scale.

- Can be grown in the garden as well as indoors. Needs sunny position.
- Moderate to warm: 55° to 65°F (13° to 18°C) at night. Keep at 45° to 50°F (8° to 10°C) in winter.
- Water freely in the growing period, less in winter.
- Moderate humidity. Mist frequently.
- Standard potting mix. Feed every two weeks with a mild liquid fertilizer.

Tillandsia

To date, more than 500 species of this terrestrial and ephiphytic growing bromeliad are known. Most of them are natives of Central and South America where they thrive in all sorts of habitats.

The species illustrated is *Tillandsia cyanea* which grows to 30 inches (75cm) and has a blossom consisting of pink bracts and violet flowers. A very similar but differently colored species is *Tillandsia lindenii* in which the bracts are pink, green and lilac, and the flowers purplish. *Tillandsia usneoides*, Spanish Moss, loses its roots when still in the seedling stage. It is silver-gray and survives without a pot or even soil. Simply hang it over a tree branch or piece of wire in a greenhouse. It does require high humidity, however. Watch for scale and thrips.

- Well-lit position with filtered sunlight. No direct sun.
- Warm: 60° to 70°F (16° to 20°C) at night. Minimum temperature in winter 55°F (13°C).
- Water moderately throughout the year but especially in winter. Keep vase full, but let potting mix dry out between waterings.
- High humidity required. Mist heavily often.
- Orchid potting mixture containing fern roots or osmunda fiber.

Tolmiea

Mother-of-Thousands
Piggyback Plant

Tolmiea menziesii, shown here, is a native of the coastal mountains of California, Western Canada and Alaska. It has long-stalked, heart-shaped, hairy leaves growing in rosettes up to 2 feet (60cm) high and is excellent for a hanging basket. Offsets are developed on the leaves. These grow into plantlets and root as soon as the old leaf drops. The flowers appear in 10-inch (25cm) stalks and range in color from green to brown.

Propagation is by division or by potting the plantlets in moist sharp sand. Always provide good drainage by putting rocks or pieces of broken pots in the bottom of the pot. Rinse foliage monthly with room-temperature water to clean pores. Repot whenever plant looks crowded. Watch for mealybugs, mites and whiteflies.

☼ Put in a well-lit, preferably sunny spot. Does well in artificial light.

🌡 Moderate: 50° to 60°F (10° to 16°C) at night. Minimum temperature in winter 40°F (5°C).

💧 Water regularly in the growing period from March to October, sparingly in the dormant season. Needs good drainage.

💦 Moderate humidity. Mist frequently.

🪴 Mix 1 part perlite, 1 part peat moss and 2 parts standard potting mix. Feed monthly from March to September with mild liquid fertilizer.

Torenia

Wishbone Flower

This genus comprises 50 species, of which *Torenia fournieri*, shown here, is by far the best known. It grows about 12 inches (30cm) tall. The flowers, which appear in great profusion from July to September, grow in terminal stalks. The outer envelope is pale violet, the three lower leaves are blotched with deep purple, and the throat has yellow markings. A strain called 'Alba' has a white envelope with purple blotches. 'Grandiflora' has exceptionally large flowers.

Propagation is from seed in March. Seeds should be covered with a thin layer of sifted potting soil and germinated under glass in a temperature of about 65°F (18°C).

☼ Appreciates both sun and semi-shade. In summer it may be placed in a sheltered outdoor position.

🌡 Moderate: 50° to 60°F (10° to 16°C) at night.

💧 Water moderately but make sure the soil-ball does not dry out.

💦 Moderate humidity.

🪴 Standard potting mix.

Tradescantia

Inch Plant
Wandering Jew

Most of the 60 species of this genus of vining perennials originated in South America. They can grow to 3 feet (1m) long. The photograph shows *Tradescantia albiflora* at the rear. Its fast-growing creeping stems make it suitable for use as ground-cover or as a hanging plant. This species has green leaves; in the strain 'Albovittata' they are cream-striped, and 'Tricolor' has foliage striped in pink, white and green. As indicated by the species name, *albiflora*, these forms have white flowers.

Tradescantia blossfeldiana, shown in the fore-ground, is a creeping plant which continues to grow in winter. The upper surface of the leaves is green and bare. The underside is purple and hairy. The pink flowers of this native of Argentina have a white center. The flowering season lasts from March to July. The form 'Variegata' has cream-striped foliage.

Tradescantia crassula has erect-growing stems with shiny foliage, mainly at the base of the plant. It produces terminal-growing white flowers.

Tradescantia fluminensis, or Wandering Jew, is very similar to *Tradescantia albiflora* but is dis-tinguished by its leaves which are blue-green with violet on the underside. There is also a striped form, 'Variegata.'

Tradescandia multiflora, or Tahitian Bridal Veil, has purplish-green foliage and produces delicate white flowers. It will not take direct sun.

When the plants deteriorate, prune heavily. New specimens are easily grown from cuttings. Tip-cuttings root readily either in water or in a sandy soil mixture at a temperature of 60°F (16°C). Re-pot in April, if needed. Prune to control size. The variegated forms need a little more light than the all-green plants. Overwatering will cause rotting. Wash leaves monthly to clean pores. Watch for mealybugs, mites, scale, slugs and snails, and whiteflies. Overfeeding can make the colors of the leaves fade.

If you have a heated greenhouse you will find that all Tradescantia forms make effective groundcover.

Accepts full light but will thrive even in shade. Does well in artificial light.

Moderate: 50° to 60°F (10° to 16°C) at night. Mini-mum temperature in winter 40°F (5°C).

Keep the soil-ball moist. In winter the soil may dry out between waterings.

Fairly high humidity desirable. Mist frequently.

Standard potting mix. Feed every 2 weeks from March to October with mild liquid fertilizer. Cut feeding in half during dormant period.

Tulipa

Tulip

Tulips are available in a wide variety of colors, shapes and sizes. For early flowering, pot the bulbs in September. For later flowering, wait until October. Set the bulbs in groups of 6 to 9 and cover half their height with soil mix. Dampen soil and or put the pots in a dark spot indoors at a maximum temperature of 55°F (12°C). Make sure the soil does not dry out and provide protection from frost. When you can feel that the flower bud has emerged, usually after 8 to 12 weeks, the pots may be brought into the light. Place them in the coolest possible location for 3 or 4 days and spray occasionally. Then move them to a sunny spot. Watch for aphids, mealybugs, mites, slugs and snails, and thrips. After flowering let foliage wither and save bulbs for planting outside in fall.

Semi to light shade.

Moderate to warm: 55° to 65°F (12° to 17°C) at night. Daytime temperature about 70°F (20°C). Cool temperatures will make bloom last longer.

Water regularly.

Moderate humidity.

Mixture of standard potting mix and sharp sand, with a 1-1/4 to 1-1/2 inch (3 to 4cm) layer of rocks at the bottom of the pot. Do not feed.

Vallota

This beautiful bulbous plant is exceptionally well suited for indoor cultivation. In summer the *Vallota speciosa,* illustrated here, produces fine orange-red flowers with a diameter of about 3 inches (8cm).

In spring the bulbs are potted with the neck of the bulb exposed. The first leaves will appear in a short time, followed by the flower stalk. Faded flowers should be removed and the flower cut off when it has turned yellow. Propagation is from offsets which may flower in the third year. It will flower more profusely when potbound.

Always place in good light but out of direct sun.

Moderate: 50° to 60°F (10° to 16°C) in winter.

Sparingly in spring, increasing gradually; freely in summer. Reduce water when foliage dies.

Moderate humidity.

Standard potting mix. Feed monthly with mild acid fertilizer.

Vriesea

This bromeliad genus includes both epiphytes or terrestrial-growing species. Most were discovered in Mexico, the Caribbean and the northern part of South America. As a rule, their evergreen leaves are shiny with a smooth edge. The funnel-shaped rosettes may serve as water reservoirs. Sometimes a complete biological balance is achieved in this micro-climate, as it might in a pond. Plants grow as large as 3 feet (1m) tall.

The upper photograph shows *Vriesea peolmannii,* a cross between *Vriesea gloriosa* and *Vriesea vangeertii.* It has shiny green foliage and a brownish-red flower spike. In the lower photograph you see the well-known species *Vriesea splendens*, which has curved green leaves with brown cross-banding, and a long, flat, bright red spike from which yellow flowers appear. The pale yellow-green leaf-rosette of *Vriesea fenestralis* has dark green, longitudinal stripes. The leaf tips and the bracts of the blossoms are reddish-brown. The flowers are yellow and appear at night. This is exceptional. Usually yellow-flowering *Vriesea* plants bloom in the daytime and white forms bloom at night. *Vriesea hieroglyphica* originates in Brazil and is very popular because of the interesting deep-purple markings that resemble hieroglyphs. The leaf rosette may grow to as much as 3 feet (1m) tall. Flowering occurs in spring. The bracts are red with yellow margins and the flowers are yellow.

There is no need to repot *Vriesea.* Plantlets can be split off. Too much sun will cause yellowing of the leaves. Watch for scale and thrips, but do not use insecticides. Rotting is caused by coolness.

Vriesea plants may be grown from seed but it may take 10 to 15 years before they flower. It is simpler to pot the newly formed and rooted offset rosettes. These may be removed from the mother plant when they have reached 4 to 6 inches (10 to 15cm). Pot them separately and keep them in a heated greenhouse. They may flower in two to three years.

- Requires bright light, but no direct sun.
- Warm: 60° to 70°F (16° to 20°C) at night. A few degrees cooler in winter.
- Keep funnel full of soft water. Allow soil to dry slightly between waterings.
- Average humidity. Spray frequently.
- Commercial bromeliad or orchid mix. Add a drop or 2 of mild liquid fertilizer to the water in the vase monthly.

Washingtonia

The photograph shows *Washingtonia filifera* which may be given an even cooler position than *Washingtonia robusta*. Both species are native of California and their fronds can be 2 feet (60cm) wide or more. They may be grown from fresh seed, which must first be soaked for two days in a temperature of 85°F (30°C). They are sown in a sandy mixture under glass at a bottom temperature of 75° to 85°F (20° to 30°C). Germination may take anywhere from two weeks to as much as three years. The seedlings must be treated with care.

- Good light preferred but not direct sun. Some shade is tolerated.
- Moderate: 50° to 60°F (10° to 16°C) at night. Minimum temperature in winter 40°F (4°C).
- Water regularly. Plunge occasionally.
- Palms like a fairly humid atmosphere. Spray often.
- Standard potting mix.

Yucca
Spanish Bayonet

Despite its extremely sharp pointed leaves, the *Yucca* has become a popular house plant. In the wild some species reach a height of 40 feet (13m). is very difficult to keep a *Yucca* in good condition and, kept indoors, it will only last a few years. It will thrive only if given a very well-lit, sunny position, preferably outdoors in summer. It should be kept fairly cool in winter.

The best known species, *Yucca aloifolia*, is shown in both photographs in the correct indoor and outdoor locations. The stiff sharply pointed leaves grow in rosettes. *Yucca gloriosa* does well indoors. *Yucca elephantipes,* commonly known as the Spineless Yucca, grows to 6 feet (2m) with leaves 4 feet (120cm) long.

Species with blunt leaves have arrived on the market in the last few years but only time will tell how satisfactory they prove to be.

An attack by pests indicates incorrect growing conditions. Repot in the spring of every second year. Good drainage is required to prevent drowning.

Yucca (continued)

The best soil mixture consists of sand and ordinary potting mix. Make sure that heavy plants do not overbalance. The most expensive plant displays consist of several trunks combined in a container to form an attractive group.

 In summer a warm sunny spot outdoors. In winter a well-lit position indoors.

Moderate: 50° to 60°F (10° to 16°C) at night. In winter it must be kept cool at 45°F (6°C).

Water regularly in summer. Needs good drainage.

Stands up well to dry living room atmosphere.

Mix 1 part sand and 2 parts standard potting mix.

Zantedeschia

Aram Lily
Calla Lily

Zantedeschia aethiopica, shown here, is a native of South Africa that grows to 3 feet (1m) tall. It is the species best suited for indoor cultivation and flowers from March to June. After flowering put it in good light until August and cease watering. Leaves will yellow and should be removed. Remove the plant from the pot, shake old soil off the roots and separate the individual plantlets. Repot with fresh soil when you want to begin the growth cycle again. For summer bloom, pot in April. For a winter bloom, pot in September or October. In the growing and flowering seasons water plentifully using soft water. Watch for aphids, mealybugs, mites, scale and thrips. Propagation can also be by division of the rootstock.

Well-lit sunny position on the balcony in the garden. Bring indoors in late September.

Moderate: 50° to 60°F (10° to 16°C) at night. Keep at 45° to 50°F (8° to 10°C) in winter.

Give plenty of soft water in summer. Needs good drainage.

Requires a fairly humid atmosphere indoors.

Mix 1 part sphagnum moss with 3 parts standard potting mix. Feed monthly with mild liquid fertilizer.

ebrina
Wandering Jew

This native of Central America is related to the better known *Tradescantia* but is not as hardy. They share the common name Wandering Jew. The best known species is *Zebrina pendula*. The 'Quadricolor' strain is shown here. Color depends largely on the light available. It grows to 3 feet (1m) and does well in hanging baskets. Pinch back to maintain their shape. Prune severely in spring to reestablish plant and repot if necessary. Overwatering causes rotting. Overfeeding causes loss of color in leaves. Too little humidity will cause leaves to roll. Rinse foliage monthly with room-temperature water to clean pores. Propagation is from cuttings rooted in water. Watch for mealybugs, mites, scale, slugs and snails, and whiteflies.

- Light to half-shade. Variegated forms need more light than green ones. Does well in artificial light.

- Warm: 60° to 70°F (16° to 20°C) at night. In winter preferably not below 55°F (12°C).

- Water regularly with lime-free water. In winter keep slightly less moist. Needs good drainage.

- Fairly high humidity.

- Mix 1 part perlite, 1 part peat moss and 2 parts standard potting mix. Feed every 2 weeks from February to October with mild liquid fertilizer. Feed half as much from October to February.

Zygocactus
Crab-Claw Cactus
Thanksgiving Cactus

The Christmas Cactus should not be confused with the Easter Cactus which is *Rhipsalidopis* or *Schlumbergera*. Its tubular flowers consist of outer envelopes that are usually violet but sometimes red. It can reach 2 feet (60cm) in length. After flowering the plant should rest. Withhold water but do not let the joints shrivel up. In early June it is advisable to put in a shady spot in the garden but beware of slugs or snails. Feed until the beginning of August. Bring indoors at the end of September and keep fairly dry until the flower buds appear. Raising the temperature will speed flowering; lowering will slow it. Treat this cactus very gently. It dislikes being moved and will drop its buds. Keep potbound. Propagation is from cuttings. The forms in cultivation are mainly hybrids.

- Slight diffused sunlight will do no harm. A half-shady position is preferable.

- Moderate: 50° to 60°F (10° to 16°C) at night. After September keep dry and cool until the flower buds appear.

- Water regularly, except in the dormant season.

- High humidity. Spray frequently.

- Mix 1 part sharp sand, 1 part peat moss and 2 parts standard potting mix. Feed monthly with mild liquid fertilizer.

Index

Both common and Latin names have been included for all plants discussed in this book. Latin names are in *italics*. **Bold** numbers indicate that plant's photograph.

8.914938977554

YOU CAN GROW BEAUTIFUL HOUSE PLANTS!

Here is the professional advice you need to grow lush, healthy house plants. World-respected authority Rob Herwig shares his proven secrets for success. The *House Plant Handbook* section shows you how to properly select and care for any indoor plant. *House Plants from A to Z* offers specific, foolproof directions for the care, feeding and propagation of over 600 different varieties. A complete index allows you to look up plants by either their common or Latin name. Or, you can find your plant by referring to over 350 close-up color photographs. In this one beautiful book is everything you need to select and maintain a thriving indoor garden!

Rob Herwig

One of the most widely read writers on gardening in the world, Rob Herwig has written more than 40 books which have sold more than 4 million copies throughout the world. His *128 House Plants You Can Grow* and *128 More House Plants You Can Grow* led the New York Times' bestseller list for months.

$7.95 US
$9.95 Canada

ISBN 0-89586-026-0
BIPAD 68103